KU-266-793

CM07006823

Educator's
Professional
Growth Plan

Second Edition

WITHDRAWN

LEARNING AND INFORMATION
SERVICES
UNIVERSITY OF CUMBRIA

To Greg, who has taught me how to follow my bliss.

The Educator's Professional Growth Plan

Second Edition

A Process *for* Developing Staff *and* Improving Instruction

Jodi Peine

CORWIN PRESS
A SAGE Publications Company
Thousand Oaks, CA 91320

Copyright © 2008 by Corwin Press

All rights reserved. When forms and sample documents are included, their use is authorized only by educators, local school sites, and/or noncommercial or nonprofit entities that have purchased the book. Except for that usage, no part of this book may be reproduced or utilized in any form or by any means, electronic or mechanical, including photocopying, recording, or by any information storage and retrieval system, without permission in writing from the publisher.

For information:

Corwin Press
A Sage Publications Company
2455 Teller Road
Thousand Oaks, California 91320
www.corwinpress.com

SAGE Publications India Pvt. Ltd.
B 1/I 1 Mohan Cooperative Industrial Area
Mathura Road, New Delhi 110 044
India

Sage Publications Ltd.
1 Oliver's Yard
55 City Road
London EC1Y 1SP
United Kingdom

SAGE Publications Asia-Pacific Pte. Ltd.
33 Pekin Street #02-01
Far East Square
Singapore 048763

Printed in the United States of America

Library of Congress Cataloging-in-Publication Data

Peine, Jodi.
The educator's professional growth plan: A process for developing staff and improving instruction/Jodi Peine. —2nd ed.
    p. cm.
Rev. ed. of: The professional growth plan. 2001.
Includes bibliographical references and index.
ISBN-13: 978-1-4129-4931-6 (cloth)
ISBN-13: 978-1-4129-4932-3 (pbk.)
    1. School administrators —Inservice training. 2. Educational leadership. I. Peine, Jodi. Professional growth plan. II. Title.

LB1738.5.M43 2008
370.113 —dc22   2007002112

This book is printed on acid-free paper.

07   08   09   10   11   10 9 8 7 6 5 4 3 2 1

Acquisitions Editor:	Cathy Hernandez
Editorial Assistant:	Megan Bedell
Production Editor:	Sarah K. Quesenberry
Copy Editor:	Gretchen Treadwell
Typesetter:	C&M Digitals (P) Ltd.
Proofreader:	Theresa Kay
Indexer:	Wendy Allex
Cover Designer:	Rose Storey
Graphic Designer:	Monique Hahn

Contents

Preface

. . . I would try to see that each employee, department, administrative unit, and school faculty would be required to submit a growth and improvement plan. . . . Such a procedure could not be, and should not be, installed without a great deal of support and training. It needs to be modeled from the top. . . . And the goals of the exercise should be kept clearly in mind: to maintain a focus on results; to encourage innovation and continuous improvement; and to promote growth and development in all parts of the system.

—Schlechty, 1990, p. 148

Much has changed in education since the first edition of this book was published six years ago. Even more change has occurred in the ten years since this Professional Growth Plan Process was first developed and implemented. (One need only think about education before No Child Left Behind.) Yet, given all the change, one constant remains: Student achievement ties directly to the knowledge, skills, attitudes, and beliefs of those delivering the instruction. With this in mind, one understands why relevant and useful professional learning has never been more important (Fullan, 2006). The field of education is fortunate to have a solid research base, as well as Professional Development Standards established by the National Staff Development Council, to inform and direct those who facilitate professional learning. The Professional Growth Plan Process described in this book supports those standards and research. It also supports the empowerment of educators as they take control of and assume responsibility for their professional growth. As a staff development tool, the process promotes job-embedded learning tied to professional performance standards, best practices research, and student performance data. In addition, it promotes the development of a strong professional learning community by building strong collaborative relationships with colleagues and the school leader. As a process, its structure and components promote the professional learning that improves student achievement as it improves and informs practice. By design, much of the learning occurs in the context of the educator's practice. The process is not a quick or easy fix as it requires the planning and time necessary for deep learning and change to occur (Fullan, 2005).

The purpose of this book is to support the individual(s) responsible for initiating and implementing the Professional Growth Plan Process—a district or building administrator (most commonly the building principal), staff developer, department chair, or teacher. The book refers to this plan administrator as the school leader. It also refers to educators as participants to include those not in traditional instructional positions.

The Professional Growth Plan takes school leaders step-by-step through the Professional Growth Plan Process from its introduction in the district or school through its development, implementation, evaluation, and completion.

Chapter 1 defines the Professional Growth Plan and the Professional Growth Plan Process. Chapter 2 addresses operational matters and offers tips on introducing the process to participants. Chapter 3 introduces phase one of the process, explaining how to target professional learning. Chapter 4 explains plan design, the second phase of the growth plan process. Chapter 5 discusses phase three, plan implementation and monitoring. Chapter 6 brings the process to a close describing phase four, plan completion and evaluation. Chapter 7 describes how the growth plan process continues. Each chapter also explains the roles and responsibilities of participants and school leaders in the process and discusses common problems associated with the growth plan process and their solutions. Resources A and B provide blackline masters for use in each step of the growth plan process. The blackline masters support two audiences, the school leader and the participants.

The procedures and practices that make up the Professional Growth Plan Process in this book are grounded in research and have been used at the elementary, middle, and high school levels. The process has been developed and refined in consultation with administrators, teachers, and specialists who used the process and were held accountable for their own professional growth resulting from the process. A comprehensive discussion of the research for, and development of, the process appears in the introduction.

Additional experience with the process, new strategies and directions in school improvement efforts, and the simple passing of time necessitate a second edition. Current research and terminology, contemporary topics for growth plan development, and updated participant samples are included in this edition. Advances in technology now make data and information management so much easier for both the school leader and participant. Technology has also dramatically expanded the access participants have to quality learning experiences. New also to this edition are expanded discussions of how the growth plan can support school improvement and individual professional growth, issues that impact sustainability of the process, and how the process evolves through third and fourth generation growth plans. Of all the updates, the revision of the process for targeting professional growth represents the most significant and important. With the addition of a formal student data analysis step, the needs-assessment process now provides participants with a more clear understanding of the "practice to performance link." The first step remains the same as participants examine what they do and why they do it, comparing their practice to professional performance standards and best practices research. However, the next step has become a formalized and essential step of the needs-assessment component. Participants examine student performance data looking for causal relationships between the discrepancies and deficiencies they identified in their practice and their student performance data analysis. For the participant and school leader, this improved process powerfully connects professional learning, student achievement, and classroom practice.

Acknowledgments

To acknowledge all those who have contributed to this book would take pages. Those who contributed the research base are represented in the reference list. I must, however, recognize a few individuals for their significant contributions to the development of the Professional Growth Plan Process.

Dr. Kay Burke who, through her book, consultation, encouragement, and friendship, provided the critical early direction for development of this growth plan format and, ultimately, the growth plan process. Dr. Brock Butts, now retired superintendent of schools, Tremont Community Unit District 702, whose vision and leadership guided his administrative team in the development of a supervision model and professional development model that would actually improve instruction and promote continuous learning within the individual and the learning community. Tremont Community Unit District 702 Board of Education, who trusted its administrative team and gave us the latitude and freedom to experiment and to work through obstacles and problems. They believed in us and supported us even when we could not articulate to them just how we were going to accomplish what we said we would! And, finally, the staff members of Tremont Elementary School must be recognized for their professionalism and commitment to professional growth in service to their students. They represent the best of the profession.

PUBLISHER'S ACKNOWLEDGMENTS

Corwin Press gratefully acknowledges the contributions of the following reviewers:

Linda G. Brown
Principal
Parkview Arts and Science Magnet High School
Little Rock, AR

Larry Kelly
Clinical Assistant Professor of Teaching, Learning, and Culture
Texas A&M University
College Station, TX

Gwendolyn Long-Wimes
Retired Principal
Farren Elementary School
Chicago, IL

Gabriela Mafi
Executive Director
Rossier School of Education,
University of Southern California
Los Angeles, CA

Anne Smith
Education Research Analyst
Office of Special Education Programs,
U.S. Department of Education
Washington, D.C.

Bonnie Watson
Writing Specialist
Owensboro 5–6 Center
Owensboro, KY

About the Author

 **Jodi Peine** is recently retired after 33 years in education. The last 13 years of her career were spent as a principal and Director of Curriculum and Instruction at Community Unit School District 702 in Tremont, Illinois.

Jodi is also an adjunct college instructor and has presented at national and regional educational conferences on such topics as staff development, the professional growth plan, school leadership, supervision and curriculum, and the arts in education. She currently serves as an independent consultant to school districts.

Introduction

It is hard to see how teaching can become a more vigorous learning profession unless teachers together take (and be allowed to take) more control over their own learning agenda.

—Fullan and Hargreaves, 1998, p. 84

EVOLUTION OF THE PROFESSIONAL GROWTH PLAN PROCESS

Improved student achievement is the ultimate goal of all professional development efforts. In that respect, the Professional Growth Plan Process presented here is no different from other professional development models. Its purpose is continual improvement of educators' skills, knowledge, attitudes, and behaviors, with the resulting increase in professional competence enabling educators to identify and implement activities that improve student achievement. The Professional Growth Plan Process was originally developed as a component of a differentiated supervision model for a K–12 school district in central Illinois. The model was developed in response to the ongoing frustration of the district's board of education and its administrative team (a superintendent and school principals) with two processes most schools use: teacher evaluation and staff development. Neither process was effective. Neither process produced the results for which it was designed.

QUESTIONING TEACHER EVALUATION AND PROFESSIONAL DEVELOPMENT

Initially, teacher evaluation caused the greatest concern. The evaluation process, as in many schools, was a rating system based on a few classroom observations conducted by the building principal. If one goal of evaluation was to improve student achievement by improving teacher performance, it was a goal far from realized. The reality, also as in many schools, was that the evaluation process produced no lasting change in instructional practice (Bereens, 2000). The pre-/postobservation discussions between teacher and administrator lacked truly substantive dialogues that promoted professional growth. The rating criteria were poorly defined and did not address comprehensively the complexity of teaching. Teacher evaluation offered competent teachers little benefit and was little more than a time-consuming obligation for the administrator.

Another problem for building administrators was the task of evaluating staff members who were not in traditional instructional roles. Staff members such as speech pathologists, reading specialists, and counselors just did not fit the evaluation tool.

In addition to the challenges in the evaluation system, the second major frustration was tied to the district's professional development efforts. For years the school district had made significant investments of both time and money in staff development initiatives. Instructional staff attended numerous workshops and conferences. The district brought in consultants to provide staff development programs. However, this significant investment of time and money produced little, if any, change in the daily practices of instructional staff. Those new practices, if implemented, were often dropped for lack of continuing support or interest. No enduring systemic change resulted from the numerous professional development initiatives.

From this context, the administrative team formed a study group whose goal was to find out the latest information on teacher evaluation and staff development. Then, from that knowledge base the team would develop a new plan. As Figure 0.1 outlines, the study expanded quickly to consideration of related areas, including change theory, learning theory, organizational development, systems thinking, and brain research. All became part of the Professional Growth Plan Process.

The Professional Growth Plan surfaced early in the discussions as the tool the team wanted to use to promote professional growth. But it was only after continuing investigation and discussion that the team fully realized how the topics represented in Figure 0.1 could and should influence the plan and process design. The knowledge base of the team and the Professional Growth Plan Process developed concurrently. The actual growth plan design and growth plan process evolved slowly and sporadically, changing as new information and new understandings developed among the team members.

Figure 0.1   Research Supporting the Professional Growth Plan Process

REDEFINING SCHOOL IMPROVEMENT

Very early in the discuss-and-design process, the need to reexamine and perhaps redefine the district's concept of school improvement became apparent. It was brutally obvious that few, if any, meaningful changes in instructional practices had resulted from any of the school improvement efforts instituted over the years. As the study group sought evidence for direct ties between school improvement efforts and improved student achievement, the difficulty of linking the two areas also became apparent. Closer examination revealed that most school improvement efforts addressed structural changes or surface level schoolwide staff development initiatives. Of course, implementing an eight block schedule in a high school does not necessarily improve student achievement. If teachers do not adapt their instructional strategies to accommodate the longer periods, and instead insist on using a traditional lecture format for the eighty-minute classes, student achievement may, in fact, drop or discipline referrals may increase as an unintended consequence of the structural change. Cooperative learning is sighted as a practice that can contribute to improved student achievement. However, training an elementary staff in cooperative learning strategies over a few workshop days rarely provides the depth and breadth of training necessary to enable staff to use the process effectively to positively impact student achievement. Efforts rarely addressed the individual needs of the practitioner.

ESTABLISHING NEW PRIORITIES

In light of its newly acquired and growing knowledge base, the administrative study team established new priorities for school improvement efforts. The team concluded that for school improvement efforts to truly improve student achievement, school/district improvement efforts should focus on improving the individual professional practices of those responsible for student achievement. Fullan and Hargreaves (1998) support this conclusion. With this recognition of the importance of ongoing individual professional growth to school improvement efforts also came the recognition of the importance of a vibrant, strong, and growing professional learning community fueled by that very same individual professional growth. Both realizations helped the administrative team define and visualize the "how to" of continuous school improvement. (See Figure 0.2.)

EMPOWERING TEACHERS

Two other factors significantly impacted the process design. The first was the realization that for teachers to acquire the knowledge, skills, attitudes, and beliefs necessary to improve their practice, they needed to assume primary responsibility and accountability for their own professional learning and growth. For decades teacher empowerment has been promoted as a tool of school improvement. Teachers have been empowered with control over budgets, curriculum development, textbook selection, building design, scheduling, and, supposedly, they have even been given control over professional development. In reality, their control over professional development has usually been as part of a committee to pick activities for workshop days. Teachers have been empowered in many ways, except the one way that could most greatly impact their own professional growth and performance, the way that translates most directly into improved student achievement (Guskey, 2000).

Figure 0.2 The Professional Growth Plan Process Promotes Continuous School Improvement

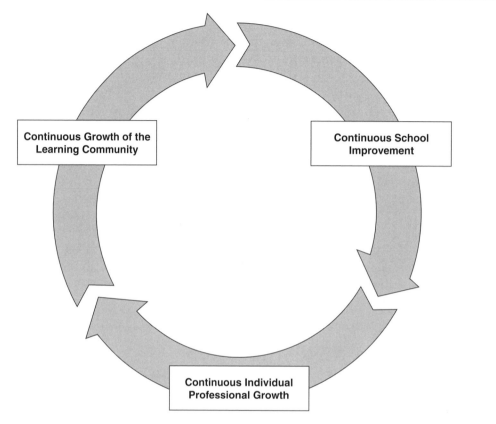

Historically, administrators have dictated what they thought teachers needed, whether or not it was what they actually needed. Because the training was appropriate for some teachers and inappropriate for others, rarely were teachers fully engaged in the training. Rarely have teachers been able to identify what they need to learn, define how they will learn it, and how they will be held accountable for the application of the learning. Truly empowering teachers for the purpose of improved student achievement is to give them responsibility and accountability for their professional growth. Once they assume this responsibility, accountability for professional growth transfers from the administrator to the teacher. This accountability factor ensures ongoing application of professional growth. With the Professional Growth Plan Process, educators assume responsibility and accountability for their own learning and professional growth.

RECOGNIZING TEACHERS AS LEARNERS

A final consideration in process design was teacher as learner. Administrative discussions began with descriptions of what student learning should look like, but attention soon shifted to the teacher as learner. What now seems obvious was then a great revelation to the administrative team. The conditions and characteristics of learning desired for students are the same as those that promote learning in teachers (Brandt, 1998). As Figure 0.3 outlines, the Professional Growth Plan Process models

Figure 0.3   A Model of Learning Conditions

A Model of Learning Conditions

The Professional Growth Plan Process models and reinforces what educators want for their students.

- Learners assume responsibility and accountability for their learning.
- The needs of the learner are identified and addressed.
- All learners receive acceptance for their current learning level and encouragement to develop to their potential.
- Learners document growth through a collection of artifacts representing their effort and learning.
- The structure of instruction accommodates each learner's style of learning.
- Learning occurs in an environment that facilitates and supports learning while also encouraging risk taking.

---

for the practitioners learning as their students should experience it. With these priorities established, the Professional Growth Plan Process continued to evolve.

As a result of redefining and reprioritizing school improvement efforts, it was obvious a new supervision model was needed. So the school district developed a differentiated supervision model. The differentiated supervision model creates a four-strand system for supervising, evaluating, and providing professional development services for instructional staff. Each strand design addresses the diverse supervision and professional development needs represented within a typical instructional staff. Anchoring each strand are the district's professional performance standards. The four strands are the developmental strand for new staff, the collaborative strand for those who demonstrate proficiency in meeting professional standards, the assistance strand for staff who need intensive support and guidance, and the remediation strand, which determines a staff member's continued employability.

The establishment of four supervision strands made it quickly apparent that the majority of the instructional staff was competent and capable and needed little, if any, direct supervision. Their greatest need was to increase their knowledge and skill base within their daily practice. So the Professional Growth Plan Process became a primary component of the collaborative strand to promote and support continuous learning while also becoming the tool for staff development in the district.

THE PROFESSIONAL GROWTH PLAN: DESIGNING A TOOL FOR STAFF DEVELOPMENT

Knowing what we wanted and making it work were two very different things. The concept at that time, though vaguely defined, seemed like a very good idea. But we knew all too well that many staff development models seem like good ideas yet fail to produce their intended results. Two questions came to dominate our conversations. First, from an administrative perspective, could growth plans be effectively yet efficiently managed for an entire staff? Second, could a growth plan be structured to provide enough direction to promote the targeted professional growth yet accommodate the unique abilities and needs of individual educators/learners?

To answer these two critical questions we needed to try, at least on an experimental basis, to use professional growth plans. And so we began.

Before teachers could develop a growth plan, we needed a growth plan format to follow. We examined the few models that were available, then decided to use the format found in Dr. Kay Burke's book, *Designing Professional Portfolios for Change* (1997). To determine whether and how that format might work for us, I decided to use it to develop a professional growth plan of my own. Doing so forced me to think through each component of the growth plan as well as start to define what the overall process might look like. Working through the format, I realized very quickly that most teaching staffs would, at least initially, need significant support to design even the most basic of plans. This concept of self-directed learning was new and different to most staff development experiences. The principal or school leader would need to play a critical role, particularly in the first generation of plans.

As I struggled to define my own growth plan and tried to apply the established format to my defined area of need, I started making what were to become numerous adaptations and modifications to the format. With each step in the format, implementation and management issues surfaced. As I addressed those issues with my district colleagues, a process of procedures and practices that was to become the Professional Growth Plan Process began to evolve.

In December 1997, I finalized my own professional growth plan (see Figure 0.4). With mine in place, and with a very superficial and quite naïve understanding of what was to happen, the administrative team began implementation of a poorly defined growth plan process with volunteers from the district instructional staff.

Those first volunteers were wonderful as they trusted, tried, persevered, and were very patient as we worked through details and procedures, establishing policies to address problems and issues as they arose. Through all the confusion and false starts, they continued to learn and grow professionally and became early strong advocates of the process. Teacher attitudes about staff development began to change dramatically as professional learning became relevant and useful to their particular practice. They experienced improved student achievement through the changes they initiated in their practice. Most important to the administrative team was that the initial two critical questions were answered in a strong affirmative. They are, again,

1. From an administrative perspective, can growth plans be effectively yet efficiently managed for an entire staff?

2. Can a growth plan be structured to provide enough direction to promote the targeted professional growth yet accommodate the unique abilities and needs of individual educators/learners?

A HOW-TO GUIDE TO IMPLEMENTING THE GROWTH PLAN PROCESS

Today, unlike when this book was first published, growth plans or professional development plans are used in many schools and districts as part of their staff development models and/or part of differentiated supervision models. The formats and procedures that accompany these growth plans vary significantly. In some situations educators are totally responsible for the design and implementation of their plan. Sometimes the plans are more compliance than learning. The Professional Growth Plan this book describes formalizes the growth process, first, by providing a clearly defined focus for learning, then by promoting the actual growth through its directed and monitored implementation. The sequence of steps and procedures ensure the successful design, implementation, and completion of the Professional Growth Plan.

Figure 0.4   The First Professional Growth Plan

Professional Growth Plan

Jodi McCormick

Time frame for plan: 3 years

TOPIC SELECTED: Differentiated Supervision/Staff Development

RATIONALE FOR SELECTING TOPIC:

While lots of money has been invested in staff development programs, little change is evidenced in classroom instructional practices and, more importantly, student achievement/performance. And while the purpose of most evaluations is to improve instruction, there is no evidence that teacher performance and, ultimately, student performance are improved through the present system of evaluation. Neither process as it exists today, staff development or teacher evaluation, is effective in improving student achievement.

ESSENTIAL QUESTION:

Can a systemic change in the teacher evaluation/supervision process and staff development program, from their present focus to a focus on personal professional growth, change teacher attitudes about staff development and their professional practices in such a way as to improve student achievement/performance?

RELATED QUESTIONS:

- Will a differentiated model of evaluation/supervision promote and foster professional growth?
- Can professional growth plans develop self-reflection and metacognitive practices in teachers?
- Will professional growth plans bring more teacher ownership to the staff development process?
- Will professional growth plans increase teacher proficiency in specifically identified professional practices?
- How will the use of professional growth plans impact student achievement?

PROFESSIONAL GOALS:

- Understand and apply the characteristics of the adult learner.
- Understand and apply the research on effective staff development.
- Understand the components and facilitate the development and growth of a learning organization.
- Model for teachers best practices research.

LEARNER-CENTERED GOALS:

- Change (teacher) attitude about professional development.
- Develop ownership and initiative on the part of teachers in their professional growth.
- Develop teachers as lifelong learners.
- Develop self-reflection and metacognition processes as they relate to professional practices.
- Develop an understanding of professional standards.

BASELINE DATA:

- Teacher attitudinal survey
- Self-assessment results over time

ACTION PLAN (INTERVENTION):

- Research adult learning, staff development issues, differentiated supervision models.
- Develop process of differentiated supervision.

(Continued)

Figure 0.4 (Continued)

- Develop process for use of professional growth plans.
- Develop procedures/guidelines for professional growth plan.
- Educate staff on both processes.
- Implement processes.

DOCUMENTATION:

- Reading log with reflections
- Log with reflections of interviews, meetings with consultants
- Copies of plan(s) development
- Final process/procedures for differentiated supervision
- Final process/procedures for professional growth plans

METHODS OF EVALUATION:
- Attitudinal survey
- Self-assessments
- IGAP scores

OBSERVATIONS:
- None

The role the "school leader" (principal, department chair, staff developer, or teacher) plays in the process distinguishes this process from other growth plans. From helping the educator identify targets for professional growth, through plan design and implementation, the school leader collaborates and actively facilitates professional learning. To be effective in leading this process, school leaders need a comprehensive knowledge of the "why and how to" of the process.

Those who will implement the Professional Growth Plan Process in a school or district are usually those same individuals who already have tremendous demands on their time. They may not have the knowledge base or the time to create a process, but they do have the knowledge, skills, and resources necessary to take an established, proved framework and customize it to their specific needs. This book provides the school leader with a thorough understanding of the Professional Growth Plan Process and how to implement it. The information in the following pages tells the school leader explicitly what to do, when to do it, how to do it, and of what to be cautious.

The role of school leader is always important to successful implementation of the growth plan process; however, the role is most critical when the process is implemented for the first time. Because few staff members (called participants in this book to include those not in traditional instructor positions) are familiar with the Professional Growth Plan Process, and many will be skeptical if not hostile about it, the school leader must be prepared to shepherd participants carefully through the entire process the first time. If done properly, the school leader can all but ensure that participants experience success. But the potential for failure increases exponentially when participants are left to develop and implement a plan on their own. To lead this process effectively and successfully, school leaders must understand and be able to articulate to participants the purpose, plan, and procedures. They must anticipate problems as well as their solutions, while aggressively supporting participants through plan development and implementation. Ideally, once participants experience the entire process, they understand the growth plan process, its purpose, and its potential for promoting professional growth, and second and third generation plans require less intensive involvement on the part of the school leader.

HOW TO USE THIS BOOK

To ensure successful implementation of the Professional Growth Plan Process, the school leader must thoroughly understand the components, procedures, and possible pitfalls of the process. Reading this book from beginning to end provides the school leader a comprehensive and necessary overview of the process. Because plan components build on one another, it is important that the school leader read the book sequentially and acquire an understanding of the critical interactive relationship of growth plan components as well as an understanding of the development of each.

The Professional Growth Plan takes school leaders step-by-step through the Professional Growth Plan Process from its introduction in the district or school through its development, implementation, evaluation, and completion.

Resources A and B provide blackline masters for use in each step of the growth plan process. The blackline masters support two audiences, the school leader and the participants. School leader blacklines (Resource A) help the school leader organize and administer the process. Participant blacklines (Resource B) guide the introduction, development, and implementation of the Professional Growth Plan, supporting both participants and the school leader. Resource B also includes a master guide that explains how to use each blackline in the Professional Growth Plan Process. Blacklines appear in the Resources, for the most part, in the order they are used in the process. References within the text help the school leader understand when to use a blackline master. The degree of support and direction required by either a participant or the school leader ultimately determines which blacklines to use. For first generation plans, it is advisable to use most, if not all, of the participant blacklines. Once the process is familiar to the school leader and participants, fewer blacklines may be necessary. Familiarity with the process also allows the school leader to customize the components and procedures to accommodate the unique needs of the learning organization.

Sample completed forms in the text illustrate what typical submissions from participants look like. These samples represent responses of the average participant who does not have a lot of time to spend completing forms. School leaders should not set unrealistic goals for the quality of their own participants' completed forms. The completed forms will not and need not be extensive, need not be written in complete grammatical sentences, and need not even represent deep thought. Participants should spend time on the growth plan process, not worrying about providing perfectly completed forms.

Because the process can seem and, indeed, can be overwhelming, the procedures offered are detailed and numerous. The intent is to err on the side of excess so as to provide as much information as possible. If the detail of procedures threatens to overwhelm, the school leader's first action should be simplification! Do what it takes to make it work!

ALL LEARNING IS LOCAL

Paraphrasing the late speaker of the house Tip O'Neill, "All learning is local." This is an important consideration when implementing the Professional Growth Plan Process articulated in the following pages. As in all learning, when implementing the Professional Growth Plan Process as a tool to promote professional growth, it is important to consider the prior experiences and background knowledge of learners as well as the climate of the learning environment and the resources available to support and sustain learning (Guskey, 2000). Schools and school leaders should adjust and modify the process to meet the unique needs of the professionals it is to accommodate. They should use both the format and forms of the process in their entirety or selectively to support the needs of learners and the learning organization. It is not meant to be a highly prescriptive, rigid, or static process. The strength and power of the process is in its adaptive ability to address the diverse needs of the individuals within a learning organization.

Professional Growth

Defining the What, Why, Who, and How

[W]hat little is invested is too often spent on forms of training aimed at improving at the margins (making conventional teachers a little better at what they conventionally do by making them more conscious of what they have been doing all along) rather than developmental programs aimed at causing teachers and administrators to think differently about their work and work differently because of what they come to think.

—Schlechty, 1990, p. 107

WHAT IS PROFESSIONAL GROWTH?

Before development of the first staff Professional Growth Plan, the school leader must understand what the Professional Growth Plan Process is, its purpose, the people involved, the conditions necessary for its success, and, of course, the definition of professional growth.

Professional growth is the most obvious goal of the Professional Growth Plan Process. But what constitutes professional growth often varies significantly with the audience defining it. Within the context of the Professional Growth Plan Process this book articulates, professional growth requires more than simply acquiring new knowledge or new skills. This book's definition of professional growth includes the continual application of the newly acquired knowledge and skills in the pursuit of improved student achievement. It also sets expectations for the transfer of new knowledge and skills to other appropriate areas of instructional practice, all the while nourishing the learning community.

Five criteria define and characterize the professional growth the Professional Growth Plan Process promotes. Each criterion is unique, yet each interacts dynamically with the other four. Within the Professional Growth Plan Process, evidence of a combination of the five criteria demonstrates professional growth.

An individual has grown professionally if he or she

- has acquired new knowledge and/or skills;
- uses the new knowledge and/or skills (when and where appropriate);
- improves student achievement;
- enhances reflective practice; and
- contributes to the learning community.

School leaders may wish to share Blackline P-1, Professional Growth Criteria, with participants to serve as an at-a-glance reminder of the criteria for successful growth plan completion as well as lifelong professional growth. The blackline also appears in Resource B.

The degree to which each criterion is represented at completion of the professional growth process varies from person to person and even with each Professional Growth Plan experience; however, evidence documenting each attribute must exist for the Professional Growth Plan to be considered a success. Chapter 6, Completing the Growth Plan Process, provides more detail about the evaluation of these criteria and professional growth.

WHAT IS A PROFESSIONAL GROWTH PLAN?

The Professional Growth Plan in this book is a staff development tool that provides a clearly articulated plan of study that, when completed, results in the acquisition and application of new knowledge, skills, attitudes, and behaviors that improve the professional proficiency of those using the plan for the purpose of improving student achievement. Growing in popularity as a professional development model, the professional growth plan concept is in use in schools across the country today. (Professional growth plans are also called professional development plans.) A variety of plan formats exist. While these other plans share a common purpose with the growth plan this book describes, the components and implementation procedures set this Professional Growth Plan Process apart.

Most growth plan formats in use today are very general, using loosely defined procedures for implementation. Components are usually limited to a topic, goals, and a brief overview of the activities to be done in association with the plan. Topic selection may be one of total participant choice, or it may be by administrative directive. Some growth plan topics must relate directly to a specific school improvement effort, whether that is a need of the participant or not. Criteria for evaluation are rarely articulated. Sometimes a growth or performance portfolio is required; other times a written summary of growth plan activity serves as an evaluation tool. Most growth plans require completion within a school year, which contrasts sharply with the growth plan process described here, in which a growth plan can span one to three years.

PROFESSIONAL GROWTH CRITERIA

You grow professionally when you

✓ acquire new knowledge/skills,

✓ apply new knowledge/skills,

✓ enhance reflective practices,

✓ improve student achievement, and

✓ contribute to the learning community.

Blackline P-1

The clearly defined interdependent components, the step-by-step procedures for implementation, professional growth targeted through use of student performance data and professional performance standards, and the participants assuming responsibility and accountability for their own learning differentiate the Professional Growth Plan presented here from most growth plans in use today.

WHAT IS THE PROFESSIONAL GROWTH PLAN PROCESS?

The Professional Growth Plan Process is a framework for staff development that uses a set of procedures in combination with a Professional Growth Plan to promote professional growth. Plan components, procedures that direct their use, and policies that guide the implementation of procedures make up the Professional Growth Plan Process.

Development and implementation of a Professional Growth Plan involve continuous self-assessment, goal setting, learning, application of the learning, self-reflection, evaluation, and refinement of the newly acquired skills. The Professional Growth Plan Process has four phases of development: (1) targeting professional growth, (2) plan design, (3) plan implementation and monitoring, and (4) plan evaluation.

1. Targeting Professional Growth: In this phase, participants recognize and clarify their needs for professional growth. Identified needs can represent any aspect of the teaching and learning process. Participants might, for example, identify a need to understand and implement differentiated instruction because they feel they are not meeting the needs of all the students they serve. They might identify the need to increase student engagement. This then requires them to understand and use interactive instructional strategies. To help identify their professional growth needs, participants conduct a needs assessment based on professional performance standards/best practices research and relevant student performance data. Discrepancies and/or deficiencies identified in the needs assessment become potential targets for professional growth. Using the insights and understandings gained through the needs assessment, participants meet with the school leader to review their findings and select an area and topic for growth plan development.

2. Plan Design: In the plan design phase, participants define a very specific plan of study and action that ensures they acquire the new knowledge, skills, behaviors, and attitudes they identified in the first phase.

3. Plan Implementation and Monitoring: These activities occur concurrently. While participants undertake plan implementation, the school leader monitors the implementation to ensure that participants make progress toward their established goals.

4. Plan Evaluation: The participant and school leader evaluate the plan throughout the process based on the participant's collection of data, artifacts, and reflections, among other pieces of information. An evaluation of the entire process and the participant's professional growth occurs at the end of the process.

Chapter 3 covers targeting professional growth, Chapter 4 describes plan design in detail, Chapter 5 discusses the implementation and monitoring phases, and Chapter 6 covers plan evaluation. (Chapter 2 addresses logistical concerns and explains how to introduce the process to staff. Chapter 7 highlights ongoing professional growth through second and third generation plans, capacity building, and sustaining the process.) Each phase has activities and components that support and help develop the specific phase as well as the entire process. While listed sequentially and separately, once established, these phases interact with each other dynamically. As participants acquire new knowledge and experiences resulting from implementation of their plan, it may be necessary and quite appropriate to revisit a phase to refine and redefine its components.

For the Professional Growth Plan Process to meet the learner's changing needs, the phases must be fluid and flexible, allowing participants to adapt the content of their growth plan as they implement it. Such adaptability provides the best opportunities for learning and for professional growth to occur, the primary purpose of the process.

WHY USE THE PROFESSIONAL GROWTH PLAN PROCESS?

The Professional Growth Plan promotes professional growth, and the Professional Growth Plan Process promotes learning that is standards driven, self-directed, inquiry based, and lifelong. The growth plan process also has the following characteristics (see Figure 1.1).

Figure 1.1   Characteristics That Promote Learning

The Professional Growth Plan Process is

- learner centered
- goal oriented
- results driven
- experience based
- collaborative
- job embedded

It also

- has flexible pacing
- promotes reflection

Learner centered—The focus of the growth plan is the needs of the learner (participant).

Goal oriented—Learner (participant) goals and student goals drive the entire process. Each component of the plan and process relates in some fashion to the attainment of the established goals.

Results driven—Participants and the school leader examine results in both a formative and summative manner to decide the next step, plan of action, or intervention. Participants collect and analyze data to determine whether they are making progress toward achieving their established goals.

Experience based—Learning is active and promoted by doing. Participants are required to read, observe, practice, reflect, and refine. They must apply their newly acquired knowledge in their job assignment.

Collaborative—At a minimal level, the Professional Growth Plan requires participants to share their experiences and the results of their growth plan activities in conversations and discussions with colleagues. Peer coaching, study groups, and mentoring relationships are growth plan activities that support and encourage collaboration. Group growth plans promote collaboration at a more intense level, where group members discuss and make decisions about instructional practices.

Job embedded—Most of the learning associated with growth plans occurs in the execution of participants' daily assignment. Applying new knowledge and skills into the context of their daily experience provides participants with a unique opportunity to obtain new insights and understanding of their practice, while making the learning relevant and meaningful.

Flexible pacing—Participants establish their own timeline for growth plan implementation based on their own learning styles and pacing.

Promotes reflection—As part of the evaluation criteria, participants document their reflective practice. For those unfamiliar or hesitant with reflection, the plan provides a variety of formal reflective prompts to help develop participants' reflective practices.

Each of these characteristics serves to strengthen the ability of the Professional Growth Plan and Process to address individual learning styles and the unique learning needs of each educator who uses them.

BUILDING ON THE FOUNDATION OF KNOWLEDGE AND EXPERIENCE

It is by design that the Professional Growth Plan Process builds on a teacher's background knowledge and experience. They become the foundation for building the new understandings, skills, behaviors, and attitudes the growth plan targets (Brooks & Brooks, 1999). The process design and growth plan activities facilitate the acquisition of new skills and knowledge. This learning occurs because growth plan activities usually relate to the specific context of the educator's assignment, resulting in job-embedded learning—learning by doing and from doing—in the course of an educator's daily practice. Participants perform many growth plan activities as part of daily instruction, which gives them ample opportunities for practice and observation. Feedback is immediate and it is real. Participants can evaluate accurately the effectiveness of the new intervention or instructional strategy.

Adjustments participants make reflect their actual experiences with students. A first-grade teacher learning to diagnose students' developmental stages in spelling can collect student work samples daily, using them to apply her newly acquired understanding of developmental spelling and the characteristics of each stage. This teacher can use the student work samples collected over time to understand better how students work through each stage of development. Similarly, a high school English teacher trying to develop students' reflective practices can provide direct instruction, monitor student work samples to determine the effectiveness of the instruction, then modify the instruction to address the needs reflected in the student work samples. Viewing work samples over time, this teacher can also identify students' growth or lack of growth. Implementing their activity as part of their normal practice also enhances participants' engagement in the process.

PROVIDING LEARNING OPPORTUNITIES

Another process design feature that supports learning is the allocation of time to learn. Established time frames accommodate the learning experiences defined in the growth plan. To provide the time necessary to acquire deeper understandings, the time frame for learning is not in allotments of hours, days, or weeks as in more traditional professional development models (Fullan, Hill, & Crevola, 2006). As they plan their own learning experiences, depending on the activities they choose, participants may find it necessary to spread the experiences and learning over a period of one to three years, thus providing adequate time to acquire, practice, evaluate, refine, and assimilate the targeted new skills and knowledge. The school leader and participants hold regularly scheduled meetings to monitor growth and progress. Details about the Progress Meetings and managing potential problems associated with the life span of the growth plan are provided in Chapter 5.

To enhance those opportunities for developing deep and transferable understandings, the entire process promotes and requires the use of metacognition. In planning, implementing, monitoring, and evaluating the Professional Growth Plan, educators develop and refine reflective practices as part of their documentation of professional growth. The inclusion of all these factors of learning into the Professional Growth Plan Process maximizes the potential for professional growth.

From this process evolves educators analytical of their own performance and committed to continuous professional growth—educators who can work independently and interdependently in the pursuit of improved student achievement. While it is critical to continuous and substantive school improvement to develop an instructional staff that strives continually to attain the highest professional standards, it is also fundamental to school improvement that instructional staff function as a learning community (Schmoker, 2006).

SHAPING A LEARNING COMMUNITY

The learning community is a group of individuals who share the common purpose and goal of promoting learning. Each member of the learning community must be committed to the acquisition of the new skills, behaviors, and knowledge necessary to support improved student achievement. The learning community promotes both individual learning, which addresses the needs of the learner, and collective learning, which addresses the needs of the whole learning community. The procedures and practices in the Professional Growth Plan Process act as catalysts not only for the professional development of the educator but for the development and growth of a professional learning community. The cement in the Professional Growth Plan Process binding these two important components of school improvement—individual professional growth and growth of the learning community—are professional teaching and learning standards.

The Professional Growth Plan Process and the learning community it nourishes are anchored in a set of established professional performance standards. Discussions of these performance standards bring a shared vision and clearer understanding of best practices teaching and learning to all members of the learning community (DuFour & Eaker, 1998). From this base of standards is built a common vocabulary and a context for discussing and describing teaching excellence between and among administration and instructional staff. While a common terminology may exist before implementation of the growth plan process, an understanding of what the terminology actually means and what it looks like in practice can vary dramatically.

Cooperative learning is a classic example. While one teacher may interpret cooperative learning as four students with their desks touching, another teacher might envision groups of carefully selected students with each group member having clearly defined roles and responsibilities. Depending on which definition one accepts, the implications for classroom management and for the design and delivery of instruction are significant. By talking about cooperative learning, by describing what it should look like in similar and different teaching assignments, everyone involved in the discussion should develop a common understanding of the term and its application in the context of the learning organization. Once they understand the process as the learning community defines it, growth plan participants can determine whether they need to study the topic further to implement cooperative learning fully and consistently in their practice.

Building on the shared vision of teaching and learning established through professional performance standards, the Professional Growth Plan Process encourages and requires staff to share, analyze, and implement their continually evolving knowledge about teaching and learning. This act of sharing knowledge and experiences encourages collaboration while also fostering a greater risk-taking environment. Sharing helps participants identify other staff members with similar experiences, concerns, or needs who may offer assistance. Honest sharing and acceptance of failures as well as successes send a strong message that the learning community does not view failure as bad, or as a result of incompetence, but rather a valued and important part of the learning experience. Removing this fear of failure frees participants to experiment and innovate. This sharing of knowledge and experiences accelerates the rate in which new information enters the learning community (Fullan, 1993). The sooner the community can acquire and assimilate information, the sooner it can use it productively. This active sharing of knowledge and experiences supports and develops a collaborative culture of inquiry so important to sustaining a learning community. The Professional Growth Plan Process promotes growth of the individual and the organization simultaneously.

WHO CAN USE A GROWTH PLAN?

With slight modification, the Professional Growth Plan Process can meet the diverse training and supervision needs of most teaching staffs; however, the new teacher still developing basic levels of proficiency or the veteran teacher experiencing difficulty may require a plan directed or prescribed by an administrator. These administrator-controlled plans can be structured to complement or support mentoring programs or remediation procedures that already exist. Using the same growth plan format, the administrator or supervisor can specifically define the growth plan's professional goals and action plan for these participants, providing the direction and focus to help these participants address performance deficiencies the supervisor has identified.

The experienced staff member with a history of demonstrated competence benefits most from the growth plan process. Competence in a classroom or one's job assignment suggests a certain level of responsibility and self-direction—both important for successful use of the growth plan process. This competence also suggests a degree of professionalism that includes a commitment to high student achievement, collaborative efforts, reflective practices, and lifelong learning. Using these personal characteristics and the knowledge base they have acquired through experience, competent staff members can use the Professional Growth Plan Process to help them realize their professional potential effectively and efficiently while accepting and welcoming responsibility and accountability for their own professional growth.

The use of this Professional Growth Plan is not limited to instructional staff (see Figure 1.2). The process can be adapted for the entire learning community by using the professional performance standards that match the position. The Professional Growth Plan Process requires few other changes for effective use in a noninstructional position. From superintendent to classroom teacher, from speech pathologist to social worker, from driver's education teacher to board of education member, the process works well. The bonds within a learning community strengthen when the majority of its constituents are part of the same professional growth process.

Figure 1.2   Anyone Can Use a Professional Growth Plan

- Teacher
- Specialist
- Staff Developer
- Administrator
- Board of Education Member

GROUP GROWTH PLANS

Social interaction enhances learning (Brandt, 1998). Capitalizing on this understanding, the format of the Professional Growth Plan easily accommodates and encourages collaborative plans. Individuals with common needs and interests can develop a group growth plan. Not only do staff members learn together as they discuss, analyze, and experiment with targeted classroom practices and the resulting impact on student achievement, but they also participate in mutual decision making as they seek to resolve their real problems relating to their real students. Group growth plans, with only slight modification, follow the same format and process as the individual growth plan. A group growth plan ideally serves two to four staff members, usually individuals from the same grade level, discipline, or specialty area, who have chosen to work together because of a common need or interest. Cross-grade, cross-discipline, or multispecialty teams are possible, although less frequent. In a group plan, members share the same plan components, and while the Action Plan may be the same for all, different group members may assume responsibility for different tasks. It is important to note that each member is still individually accountable for his or her own professional growth and the documentation of that growth.

From a school leader's perspective, the group growth plan is no more difficult to facilitate than an individual plan and in some ways is less demanding of his or her time—three people working on a single plan means designing one plan instead of three, scheduling one Progress Meeting instead of three, ordering one set of resource materials, and so on. Additionally, and more importantly, the group growth plan develops the professional relationships and common learning experiences that advance the development of the learning community. Chapter 4 provides a comprehensive discussion of group growth plans.

WHO CAN LEAD THE PROFESSIONAL GROWTH PLAN PROCESS?

Most critical to the entire Professional Growth Plan Process is the individual who leads its development and implementation. This individual's role is especially critical when the Professional Growth Plan Process is first introduced and implemented because its purpose and format are new and foreign to staff. Just as a classroom teacher works diligently to manage all the variables that impact learning in the classroom, the school leader must manage the variables within the school organization that impact professional growth. If the school leader manages the variables well, conditions for optimal learning materialize. At that point, the learners, regardless of age or position, must assume responsibility and accountability for their learning and growth. However, if the school leader manages the variables poorly, meaningful learning opportunities do not materialize. The learning experience becomes frustrating or overwhelming. If opportunities for learning are not present and produce nothing but frustration, not only is professional growth unable to occur, but the learning community's attitudes and beliefs about professional growth become negative and create obstacles to future professional growth efforts. Therefore, the success or failure of the entire process rests substantially with the school leader.

The school leader responsible for the Professional Growth Plan Process is not defined by position, though building principals most often assume the role. Superintendents, principals, department chairpersons, staff developers, team leaders, and even teachers can lead the Professional Growth Plan Process effectively (see Figure 1.3).

Figure 1.3 Who Can Lead the Professional Growth Plan Process?

- Superintendent
- Principal
- Department Chair
- Staff Developer
- Team Leader
- Teacher*

NOTE: *A teacher must be able to access resources to support implementation and have time set aside from his or her regular assignment to administer the process.

More important than position are the personal and professional attributes the individual brings to the role of school leader (see Figure 1.4). Because the basis of the entire Professional Growth Plan Process is trust, the attributes of personal and professional integrity are crucial (Costa & Garmston, 2006). Activities and experiences requiring trusting relationships between participants and the school leader are woven throughout the process. The needs-assessment component, for example, requires participants to identify and acknowledge weaknesses in their performance. To be truly honest in the assessment, participants must trust that the information they share with the school leader will not be used against them. Instructional staff decide when, where, and how they implement their growth plans, and the school leader must trust that staff will do this without close and intense monitoring. Confidentiality breached, a promise broken, or credibility compromised can quickly and effectively destroy the entire process and possibly cause people harm.

Figure 1.4   Essential Attributes of the School Leader

- Personal and professional integrity
- Thorough understanding of the purpose and procedures of the Professional Growth Plan Process
- Comprehensive working knowledge of curriculum and instruction
- Competent cognitive coaching skills
- Understanding of and ability to articulate professional performance standards and best practices
- Organizational skills

The school leader can learn or develop all the other attributes required to lead the Professional Growth Plan Process. (In fact, a school leader may recognize a need for additional background in a particular area, such as cognitive coaching, and seek that background before beginning the process. Of course, the school leader who already possesses these attributes is most desired.) A thorough understanding of the purpose and procedures of the process is necessary to direct others in the development of growth plans. This knowledge also establishes a solid base from which the school leader can make decisions regarding any unanticipated management and implementation issues. For example, understanding the issues related to a group growth plan helps the school leader assess the effects of the prolonged illness of one group member on the group's progress as well as on the individual, and the school leader can then make the necessary accommodations. Understanding the need for time to collaborate helps the school leader recognize opportunities to free up staff to work together.

The school leader must have cognizance of the relevant curriculum and instructional strategies, and be able to articulate professional performance standards and best practices as they relate to an individual participant's job assignment. To lead these discussions and all the other discussions that are part of the growth plan process, the school leader must have at least basic cognitive coaching skills. To be effective as a cognitive coach and administrator of the process, the school leader must be nonjudgmental, an active listener, and accessible (Costa & Garmston, 2006). Before agreeing to lead this process, an individual should thoroughly understand the responsibilities associated with the role and all that responsibility implies. Chapter 2 details the considerations and concerns the school leader faces as manager and facilitator of the process.

If implementation of the growth plan process takes place districtwide in a number of different schools, it is wise to ensure consistent implementation of the process. The district should provide common training opportunities for school leaders—formation of study groups using this text would be a sufficient start. This study group would allow school leaders to share information and problem-solve together, perhaps as a growth plan of their own.

HOW TO IMPLEMENT THE PROFESSIONAL GROWTH PLAN PROCESS SUCCESSFULLY

A competent school leader to oversee the process is one of five factors that can significantly impact the success or failure of the entire Professional Growth Plan Process. The remaining four factors are administrative support, a climate of trust, availability of resources, and consequences for incomplete or unsuccessful growth plans (see also Figure 1.5). Careful consideration of each factor can help determine whether the conditions necessary to support the process exist within the organization.

Figure 1.5   Conditions Critical to Growth Plan Process Success

- Competent school leader
- Administrative support for finances, policies, and structures
- Climate of trust
- Availability of resources (including materials, workshops, and other training opportunities) and time
- Established consequences for incomplete or unsuccessful growth plans

Administrative Support

While Professional Growth Plan Process implementation occurs typically at a building level, support from the central office, including the superintendent and board of education, is essential. These individuals control the policies, money, and structures (school calendar, teacher workshop days, early dismissals, etc.) necessary to make the growth plan process work. The support does not have to be unconditional, but they must at least agree to provide an opportunity for the process to work. The process requires at least a three-year commitment to have any chance at success. To have a central office and a board of education support the process at the outset significantly increases its chance of succeeding; their support will strengthen as they witness the results. A number of different political factions must be on board at least minimally. The school leader may have to play a significant role in garnering their support, such as getting a board of education to accept the process as an alternative model of staff development and perhaps as part of an evaluation. District unions must also support the process, and this support may require modification of the existing master contract.

A Climate of Trust

Closely tied to the school leader factor is the factor of trust. When implemented effectively, the Professional Growth Plan Process contributes significantly to building and sustaining a climate of trust within the learning community. Productive organizations are built on a foundation of trust as it fosters many of the attributes essential to the growth and improvement of the organization. These attributes so important for organizational growth, such as open and free-flowing communication, critical examination, honest evaluation, risk-taking, and innovative initiatives, also contribute to the growth of the individual. If learning communities are to develop and grow to their potential, they must build and sustain an atmosphere of trust. A lack of trust within a learning organization should not prohibit the use of the Professional Growth Plan Process but rather encourage it.

Those who determine whether this process is appropriate for their organization—such as administrators, board of education members, teachers, and union representatives—must conduct a thorough assessment of the existing climate of trust within the organization before beginning the process. Understanding the existing climate makes for better decisions by the school leader regarding implementation of the entire Professional Growth Plan Process as well as the designing of individual growth plans. For example, if a high degree of trust exists within an environment, if competition is minimal or nonexistent, and if collegial relationships are supportive, the school leader might share the first growth plans that are developed with the entire staff to serve as examples to others in the growth plan design and development stage. The school leader may even ask those staff members who have completed their growth plan design to share their experiences and thoughts about the process with staff members. If, however, the environment lacks trust, if a high degree of divisiveness, jealousy, or suspicion exists among staff, selecting a few staff members to share their plans or experiences may not serve the process or those staff members well. Sharing plans and their development in such a fashion may, unfortunately, be misinterpreted as administrative favoritism. Knowing the environment is lacking in trust, the school leader may choose to work individually or within the fractionalized groups to develop their plans instead of risking further division among the staff.

Resources

For Professional Growth Plans to meet their potential as tools of professional growth, they must be supported with adequate resources. If resources are not available to support the activities associated within each growth plan, the process should not be implemented. To do so would set participants up for failure. The obvious resources such as books and training opportunities should be available, but also hidden resources such as the commitment of time set aside specifically for growth plan work should be available. Time to work on growth plans is fundamental to success. If educators must complete growth plans in addition to meeting all the other demands in their work day with no provision of additional time, the process will certainly fail. Implementation of the Growth Plan Process requires school or district administrators and the school leader to look at the time allocated for workshop days, early dismissals, and late starts as well as other time-related structures, such as planning/prep time, to find the time for participants to work on their growth plans.

It is the school leader's responsibility to advocate aggressively and creatively for the acquisition of all manner of resources to support growth plans.

Consequences

A final factor to consider is the issue of the consequences for incomplete or unsatisfactory growth plans. Consequences need to be clearly defined and understood by everyone before the process begins. To get into the process without providing for the possibility of unsuccessful completion would make resolving the issue even more difficult as well as threaten the viability of the process. Predetermined consequences ensure the fair and equitable treatment of all participants, establishing the integrity of the process. If each case is treated independently and perhaps differently, with participants receiving different consequences, the accusation of favoritism or partiality can surface, compromising the integrity of the process. If the process is perceived as unfair, support for the process diminishes if not disappears. Similarly, the specified consequences must be enforced to preserve the integrity of the entire process (DuFour & Eaker, 1998). To have consequences in place before beginning the process conveys careful planning and concern for the integrity of the process and for those who are participating in it.

Of course, defining consequences involves defining the factors that determine whether a growth plan has been completed successfully. Ideally, these consequences are defined through a joint effort of administration and staff. In some circumstances, however, consequences may be part of contract language or may be defined totally by administration. Consequences vary, of course, by school or district. In a differentiated supervision model, for example, consequences might place a participant in a more closely monitored supervision strand. If the growth plan is not part of a supervision model, the administration might require a participant to attend specified workshops instead of using a workshop day to work on growth plan activities. Participants might have to complete a new, prescribed growth plan that involves close and direct supervision. Participants may not be eligible to move a step on the salary schedule or receive incentive pay.

A thorough analysis of each of the conditions critical to success can help determine whether the Professional Growth Plan Process is viable for the learning organization. The decision to adopt the process is then made from an informed position.

ENCOURAGING NEW TRADITIONS IN PROFESSIONAL GROWTH

The Professional Growth Plan Process modifies and alters traditionally held rules, roles, relationships, and responsibilities of all those involved in the process. Historically, the administration has determined the needs of an instructional staff and how and when to meet those needs. With this Professional Growth Plan, instructional staff members identify their own needs and decide how and when to meet them. Typically, educators must implement new instructional practices in isolation with little collaboration among staff. The Professional Growth Plan encourages collaboration on new practices through such vehicles as peer coaching, study groups, and group growth plans. The Professional Growth Plan Process represents a radical departure from traditional staff development programs. Through this process, staff members assume primary responsibility for their professional growth and for providing evidence that professional growth has occurred.

With the initial design of their Professional Growth Plan complete, participants begin to assume ownership and responsibility for their professional growth saying, "This is what I need to know and be able to do. This is how I am going to learn it. And this is how we will know that I have." When the growth plan process is complete, so, too, is the transfer of responsibility and accountability for professional growth from the school leader to participants. The administrative/supervisory role becomes more facilitating as staff members assume more responsibility and accountability for their professional growth.

2

Managing the Professional Growth Plan Process

Failure to take time in the beginning usually results in the need to take corrective time in the middle and frequently leads to the abandonment of a good idea because "we didn't like it" or "it didn't work here." Time spent doing things right is not wasted; it is time saved.

—Schlechty, 1990, p. 104

OPERATIONAL ISSUES

The school leader must address a range of operational issues that surface throughout the growth plan process. Some issues will arise sooner, some later, and some the school leader must consider before the Professional Growth Plan Process even gets underway. This chapter discusses these initial areas of consideration: locating resources, including time; organizing people, events, and information; and introducing the growth plan process to staff. Chapters 3 through 6 address common operational challenges that arise during plan implementation. Figure 2.1 identifies some operational issues the school leader will face as administrator of the Professional Growth Plan Process.

Figure 2.1 Operational Issues

- Allocating Resources
- Creating Time
  - to Plan
  - to Implement
  - to Share
- Organizing People, Events, and Information
- Monitoring and Facilitating Plan Progress
- Resolving Personnel-Related Issues
  - Family Leaves
  - Transfers/Changes in Position
  - Extended Illness
  - Group Dynamics
  - Lack of Progress
- Balancing the Needs of Individuals With Needs of the Learning Organization
- Keeping Focus on Growth, Not on Bureaucracy and Administrivia

ALLOCATING RESOURCES

Among the questions the school leader must answer are, Who gets what? Is it equal? Is it fair? Does it matter? Rarely in education do enough resources exist to support the needs of staff development programs completely.

Unfortunately, the Professional Growth Plan Process does not require any fewer resources than traditional staff development programs and structures. However, the Professional Growth Plan Process does advance a different perspective on the allocation of resources. Unlike the one-size-fits-all staff development programs that distribute cost allocations evenly among staff because everyone attends the same presentation or workshop, the resource needs reflected in individual professional growth plans vary significantly from plan to plan. The distribution of costs among participants will not be the same. To allocate money or other resources equally may be an equal treatment of each participant in the process, but it is not necessarily a fair treatment of each participant.

Because the structure of each growth plan meets the unique needs of the individual, each growth plan has unique resource needs. Some plans require more resources than others. To allocate the same resources for each plan would not allow for an equal degree of implementation of each plan, and could result in unequal professional growth opportunities and affect professional growth. While equity is certainly a consideration—a few plans should not consume all the available resources at the expense of other plans—exact equity in resource allocation cannot dominate the allocation of resources. This is not to say that growth plans should be designed without consideration of available resources; that, too, would be irresponsible.

It is necessary for school leaders and participants to have realistic expectations of resource support for the activities and tasks they select for their growth plan. A district or central office may allocate funds per school or per department in very large schools, leaving the school or department to set the guidelines for how to spend the money. If the money comes with certain distribution parameters, participants should know what these are. Understanding these allocation guidelines and the reasoning behind them before beginning the growth plan process provides participants with direction as they design their growth plans.

The school leader retains ultimate control of resource allocation. However, growth plan participants—or the entire learning community if most staff members are involved in the process—and the school leader should set and agree on guidelines for resource allocation. Guidelines reached through consensus of staff under the guidance and direction of the school leader help clarify the reasoning behind allocation decisions and best serve the process and the learning climate, providing support and acceptance of those decisions by everyone.

RESOURCE ALLOCATION CONSIDERATIONS

Resource allocation topics of most concern are those related to attendance at workshops and conferences because these activities typically require significant expenditures. School leaders and participants must ask questions to determine whether workshops and conferences match growth plans:

- Are the workshop/conference presenters reputable organizations or experts noted in the field?
- How closely does the workshop support the growth plan?
- What are the associated costs of participation?
- Are other workshop options less expensive?
- Can other growth plan participants use workshop materials, or can participants share the materials with the entire learning community as a resource?
- Does the workshop require a follow-up session?
- How far away is it? What are transportation/lodging needs?
- How many days of substitutes are required?

Obviously the success of any growth plan should not depend on attendance at a particular workshop or conference, unless funding is not a problem.

Group growth plans, a growth plan two or three participants work on together, can present unique issues. If a workshop is deemed valuable, who goes to the workshop? Do all members of the group attend and acquire a common experience and knowledge base from which future discussions and decisions stem? Or should one member of the group attend and share the information, knowledge, and skills the workshop offers with the rest of the group? If participants present requests of equal worth, but resources exist to fund only one request, should the group hold a lottery? Should the school leader meet requests on a first-come, first-served basis? Additionally, what about changes in resource needs once implementation of a plan has begun? How does the school leader provide for new needs? These are just a few of the concerns and problems that can arise when allocating resources.

Because it is difficult to predict every issue that might arise, the school leader can modify the resource allocation guidelines to address problems and concerns that the learning community may not have anticipated when establishing the guidelines. Willingness to modify guidelines demonstrates to participants a commitment to the fair treatment of everyone. The school leader must ensure during both the design and the implementation of a growth plan that gross inequities do not occur because that would compromise the integrity of the process. Generally, if participants feel they have been treated fairly in the allocation of resources, equity does not become an issue.

AVAILABLE RESOURCES VERSUS NEEDS— A BALANCING ACT

As the person responsible for allocating resources, the school leader should have a comprehensive understanding of all the resources available within the school, district, and community and their capacity to support professional growth plan activities. It is equally important to project resource needs of each growth plan at the design stage and understand the impact those resource demands will have on total resources available within the school or district. For the school leader assisting in the design of growth plans, it is a true balancing act. To approve a growth plan that does not have resources available to support full implementation is counterproductive to the growth plan process. The frustration resulting from a partially implemented plan, whose progress halts due to a lack of resources, will destroy any enthusiasm or sense of commitment a participant may have for the growth plan process. A shortage of resources to support growth plans in progress can quickly short-circuit the entire growth plan process.

TYPICAL RESOURCE NEEDS

As stated previously, the allocation of staff development resources can change in the Professional Growth Plan Process. Historically, the majority of staff development monies have been large, one-time expenditures for consultant fees, accrued when the district or school brought in regional or national consultants for workshops or other one-time trainings. Those monies may be reallocated in smaller amounts to provide for individual needs defined within growth plans. For example, these monies may be used on print materials, media, or other instructional materials to support new instructional strategies. While school leaders address needs on an individual plan-by-plan basis for the most efficient use of resources, they should review growth plans within a school and/or district to identify common needs that can share resources. Sharing resources not only conserves resources but also provides another opportunity for collaboration and sharing of ideas and information within the learning community.

The resource needs of professional growth plans vary; however, many of the resources fall into the following categories: (1) training, (2) print materials, (3) instructional materials/supplies, (4) technology, (5) clerical supplies, (6) substitutes, and (7) miscellaneous. While not all-inclusive, these categories do provide a basis for budgeting considerations. Most resource costs associated with professional growth plans already exist within school and district budgets, though they are not always found in staff development line items. For example, college courses requiring tuition reimbursements and book fees are common items in school budgets. So are costs associated with workshops, conferences, and site visits, including registration fees, travel, food, and lodging. Professional materials, instructional materials, technology, and substitute wages are also common budget items.

Budgeting for the first year of the Professional Growth Plan Process is most difficult because participants have not yet defined their needs. Budgeting becomes easier in subsequent years as growth plans are in place and have a history of associated costs. Requiring participants to complete a Resource Request Budget Form, Blackline P-23, helps the school leader project costs associated with all growth plans, helping to define future budgets. A sample completed Resource Request Budget Form appears on pages 22 and 23, and a blackline master appears in Resource B.

Another valuable budget management form for school leaders is the Annual Growth Plan Projected Budget, Blackline SL-2. A sample appears on page 24; the blackline appears in Resource A. Compiling all the individual growth plan budgets submitted by participants assists in budget building. Because participants work on their plans throughout the year, a totally accurate budget projection is not possible. But school leaders can make a fairly accurate estimate from the growth plan budgets submitted as they reflect the primary needs of the growth plans. The more experience school leaders have with professional growth plan budgets, the more accurate the budget building process becomes.

ACQUIRING ADDITIONAL RESOURCES

Additional monies to support growth plan activities are always useful. Parent organizations, education foundations, and some civic and service organizations are more open to supporting professional development activities for school staff. Asking for specific items such as a plane ticket, workshop registration fees, hotel accommodations, or any other item that would help offset the cost of a training activity often receives a favorable response. Likewise, requests for print materials, specific instructional materials, or computer software may find support in those organizations. It is also worth remembering that these organizations may receive teacher requests more warmly than requests from administrators. Universities and community colleges, public and private museums, and public libraries often have access to state and federal grants that include partnerships with schools. Business partnerships are another possible source for funds. Additional sources of funding do exist for those who are creative and committed to seeking them.

Build a Professional Library

As a school acquires resources over time that support professional growth plans, many of those resources can be placed in professional libraries. Training media, professional books, and even products of growth plans themselves placed in professional libraries can support future growth plans.

WHO HAS THE TIME?

The resources always in greatest demand are time and money. Time is most often in shortest supply, although time often equates with money. Fortunately, the participant's job assignment often provides the opportunity—and thus the time—to apply, practice, and refine new knowledge and skills. By design, much of the learning that

RESOURCE REQUEST BUDGET FORM

Projected Expenses for Fiscal Year 2006–2007

Professional Growth Plan: Cooperative Learning

Participants: Jim H., Ron L.

Projected Completion Date: 4/07

TOTAL $ 300.00

Workshop/Conference/Site Visit:

Title/Sponsor	Date	Fee	Expenses
Visit Ted Brown's 7th and 8th grade classroom at Edison Middle School	10/14	NA	Travel: Food: Hotel:
			Travel: Food: Hotel:

Total Workshop/Conference: $ 0

Print Materials:

Title/Author	Amount
Cooperative Learning/Smith, R., and Jones, Y.	
2 @ $ 50.00	100.00

Total Print: $ 100.00

Supplies:

Item	Amount
Posterboard, markers, Post-it Notes for 2 classrooms	25.00
2 Binders (3-ring D)	10.00
Audiotapes	15.00

Total Supplies: $ 50.00

Blackline P-23 (Page 1 of 2)

Media/Software:

Title/Publisher	Amount

Total Software: $ _____ 0 _____

Substitutes:

# of Days	Projected Date(s)	Amount
2	2 subs for Oct. 14th visit	150.00
	2 @ 75.00	

Total Substitutes: $ _____ 150.00 _____

Miscellaneous:

Item	Amount

Total Miscellaneous: $ _____ 0 _____

Grand Total*: $ _____ 300.00 _____

Comments:

*Please remember to include shipping and handling costs in your figures.

ANNUAL GROWTH PLAN PROJECTED BUDGET

Fiscal Year 2006–2007

Topic/Contact Person	# in Plan/Grade	Workshop	Print	Supplies	Media	Substitutes	Misc.
Phonemic Awareness/Sandy	(3)/K		150	25			25
Dev.Spelling/Becky	(3)/1st	500	200	20		150	
PE Assessment/John	(1)	20	70	50	75		
Writing Prompts/Elaine	(3)/4th			40			
Coop. Learning/Sally	(2)/5th		100	50		150	
Level Books/Mary	(1)/Reading Sp.		75	25			250
Pay-based Assess./Alice	(1)/Speech	125	75	25			
TOTAL		645	670	235	75	300	275

Blackline SL-2

occurs during the Professional Growth Plan Process is job embedded, making demand for time to practice new skills one that is most easy to accommodate.

More challenging, but as critical to the success of the Professional Growth Plan Process, is providing time for study, training, collaboration, planning, and evaluation. A few schools build these windows of opportunity into their daily instructional programs. One such example is block scheduling, increasingly used in schools today. It provides teachers of a common grade or discipline with planning time every day or every other day. But far more schools do not provide opportunities within the instructional program for staff to study, train, collaborate, plan for new and different instruction, and evaluate instructional activities comprehensively.

If the Professional Growth Plan Process is to realize its potential for promoting professional growth and building a productive learning community, school leaders must become proactive in making time for participants to grow professionally. To ask staff to implement professional growth plans in addition to all their other job-related responsibilities without providing the additional time to work on growth plan activities is totally unrealistic. It shows a lack of understanding of the learning process as well as a lack of understanding of the demands already placed upon instructional staff (DuFour & Eaker, 1998; Fullan, 1993).

Additional time is rarely found—it must be created. Examining present structures for new uses is the best way to find time. Modifying the school day schedule on a regular basis by providing late starts or early dismissals can help provide growth plan work time. Many schools already use this practice for school improvement activities. The late start or early dismissal occurs once or twice a month, usually on a specified day of the week, such as the first Wednesday or the first and third Fridays of the month. If announced far enough in advance to allow parents adequate time to make child care accommodations, or if child care accommodations exist within the school, the scheduling meets with minimal resistance from parents. Schools serving older student populations experience little, if any, parent resistance. As long as parents feel the staff is really spending the time improving competency, they accept changes in the school day schedule readily.

Rearranging schedules to provide common planning times or using floating substitutes within the school day can also help. The use of substitutes, however, is not always the best way of providing time as it takes staff extra time to prepare for a substitute and often more time to clean up after the substitute. Additionally, substitutes rarely deliver the same quality of instruction as the assigned teacher. Finally, the expense of frequent use of substitutes can also be prohibitive. The best use of substitutes is for staff absences due to attendance at workshops or conferences or site visits.

A structure already in place in most districts and one that carries little or no expense is the option to allow staff members to use teacher workshop/inservice days for their own Professional Growth Plan activities. Instead of having large group presentations or even smaller topic-oriented presentations, staff members are free to use the entire day on activities defined in their growth plan. On these days, participants can conduct site visits, do research at university libraries, or work with group members on their growth plan. Use of a workshop day provides large uninterrupted blocks of time for study, collaboration, planning, and evaluation. Completing a sufficient quantity and quality of work on these days can provide participants with the sense of accomplishment and positive feedback necessary to fuel the momentum and sustain their enthusiasm and commitment to plan completion. Allowing participants to use workshop days in this fashion also supports the transfer of responsibility for professional growth from the school leader to participants. See the section Monitoring the Process in Chapter 5 for advice on having participants use blacklines in Resource B to share their work and progress from workshop days with the school leader.

ORGANIZING PEOPLE, EVENTS, AND INFORMATION

How does the school leader keep track of everyone and everything? Management of the Professional Growth Plan Process can be a very formidable task for any school leader. Initially, as with anything new, the process is extremely time consuming and can be quite overwhelming with details. One significant factor in determining the success or failure of the Professional Growth Plan Process may very well be the school leader's ability to manage the process effectively.

Managing the process requires a variety of skills and abilities. In addition to cognitive coaching skills, organizational skills are vital. The ability to manage the process effectively is directly related to the school leader's ability to organize and coordinate people, events, and information. Fundamentally, the school leader needs to have a fairly accurate understanding of where each participant is in the Professional Growth Plan Process as well as an understanding of the condition of each individual's growth plan. Monitoring participants' progress toward the defined goals allows the school leader to anticipate problems and assist in solving them before they become major obstacles.

Sometimes staff members do not recognize the magnitude of an obstacle they encounter. For example, if adequate resources are not available to acquire information on a specific topic, it becomes a counterproductive use of participant time to continue pursuit of the information. The lack of quick access to information may indicate that not enough information is available to support a growth plan topic. Careful monitoring of growth plans alerts the school leader to an obstacle. Aware of the difficulty, the school leader can then meet with the participant and determine whether changes in the growth plan are necessary to address an obstacle. Early intervention by the school leader can reduce participant frustration and sustain the movement toward the established goals. Tracking the status of all plans also enables school leaders to prioritize topics for meetings with participants for the most effective use of everyone's time. It also helps them prioritize the allocation of available resources to meet the changing needs of participants as they work through their plans. Tracking allows school leaders to project and anticipate needs.

FORMS—HOW CAN THEY HELP?

If tracking is so important, how then do school leaders keep track of everyone's status? Forms. Forms serve multiple beneficial purposes in the organization and management of the Professional Growth Plan Process. Forms can facilitate communication, ensure expedient use of time, and provide efficient documentation of needs, information, data, and events.

This book includes a variety of forms that support the organization and management of the growth plan process. They appear as reproducible blackline masters in the resources. These hard copies transform easily into an electronic format. Forms designed for school leader use appear in Resource A. While these forms are rather generic, school leaders can create forms to meet their specific needs by either adapting the existing forms or developing entirely new and different forms. The need for a particular form may not become apparent until the growth plan process is well underway. (See also "The Role of Participant Blacklines" later in this chapter.)

FORMS TRACK THE GROWTH PLAN PROCESS

Three management forms can provide a quick reference for school leaders. School leaders should complete the first form, Growth Plan Tracking Chart, Blackline SL-4, for every participant and growth plan. A sample completed form appears on page 28, and the blackline appears in Resource A. Information on this chart provides a time line of target dates for various tasks associated with a particular growth plan. Keeping a chart for each participant gives school leaders a quick reference describing the status of each participant's growth plan.

Two other management forms help with planning and scheduling specifically. They help categorize the activities associated with the Professional Growth Plan Process. A sample completed Monthly Tracking Chart, Blackline SL-5, appears on page 30, and a sample Annual Tracking Chart, Blackline SL-6, appears on page 31. (Resource A contains blacklines of both forms.) Because a basic time allotment is associated with each growth plan activity, school leaders can use the information on the charts to estimate the time required to support the Professional Growth Plan Process. This information can help the school leader make more informed scheduling decisions. The charts can provide time allocation estimates for individual growth plans as well as an estimate for all growth plans collectively, giving school leaders a good idea of the total amount of time they spend on the growth plan process.

A composite form of school leader checklists, Blackline SL-1, appears in Resource A. For reference, the checklist appears on pages 32–33. This master list of school leader checklists, divided and listed sequentially by components of the growth plan process, guides the school leader through the growth plan process.

FORMS FACILITATE COMMUNICATION

Other forms facilitate communication between the school leader and the participant, such as the Request for Assistance, Blackline P-25 (see page 34 for a completed sample). Communicating in writing, hardcopy or electronically, can save time for everyone, often eliminating unnecessary meetings and reducing the amount of time spent in the necessary meetings. If the school leader can address the situation or resolve the problem based on a written request from a participant without holding a meeting, they both save time. If the problem or situation does require a meeting, the participant will have defined the problem and the school leader comes to the meeting better prepared, requiring less time to define and, possibly, resolve the problem or situation.

FORMS PROVIDE DOCUMENTATION

Collected over time, forms can provide a trail documenting the successes, as well as the problems and obstacles, encountered during growth plan implementation. If the successful completion of a growth plan is questioned, this record of progress becomes very important. These forms become evidence to substantiate or explain the reason for

GROWTH PLAN TRACKING CHART

Name(s): <u>David Cunningham</u>

Plan Topic: <u>Reflective Thinking</u>

Projected Completion Date: <u>4/15/09</u>

	Target Completion Date	Task Date Completed
Explanation of Growth Plans/ Components Handout	10/06	10/1/06
Self-Assessment/Handout	10/06	10/15/06
Needs-Assessment Conference	10/06	10/24/06
Growth Plan Draft/Final Draft	11/06	11/16/06
Progress Meetings Year 1—1, 2, 3	1. 2/07 2. 5/07 3.	1. 2/20/07 2. 5/17/07 3.
Interim Sharing	9/07	9/13/07
Progress Meetings Year 1—1, 2, 3	1. 11/07 2. 2/08 3. 5/08	1. 11/16/07 2. 2/8/08 3. 5/11/08
Interim Sharing	5/08	5/20/08
Progress Meetings Year 1—1, 2, 3	1. 10/08 2. 1/09 3.	1. 2. 3.
Interim Sharing	1/09	
Completion Date	4/15/09	
Growth Plan Summary Due Date	5/15/09	
Growth Plan Summary Conference	5/20/09	
Final Sharing	5/09	

Blackline SL-4

the failure of the growth plan. The forms may reflect a lack of effort or problem-solving attempts on the part of the participant. They may also, however, document a lack of support or assistance from the school leader in resolving problems that led, ultimately, to the failure of the growth plan. In this situation, the school leader must assume some of the responsibility for failure of the growth plan. The forms become a safeguard for participants. Participants cannot be held totally responsible for failure of their plan if they did not receive the support necessary to implement it successfully. This is an example of the need to establish policies and consequences for growth plans that fail (see Chapter 1, Consequences). What happens if the school leader does not provide the necessary support? How does the participant address the situation? Policies must be stated clearly before plan implementation in the event that a school leader's incompetence results in the failure of a growth plan. Used for this purpose, forms can provide a fairly accurate overview of growth plan activity and participation.

THE PROBLEM WITH FORMS

While forms can solve many problems for the school leader, they can create a few, too. Procedures for distributing, collecting, processing, and organizing forms are necessary to maximize their effectiveness. School leaders must define, share, and use these procedures. It is difficult to anticipate all needs before beginning the growth process, but a few simple guidelines can eliminate some confusion.

School leaders need first to determine what forms to use. Next, they need to determine the most effective way to share and explain the forms.

- Will participants have copies of all forms, either hard copy or electronic?
- Will participants have copies of some forms, but ask for other forms?
- If they request forms, who receives the request? Under what time frame?
- How do they submit completed forms?
- Do certain forms have time frames for completion and return to the school leader?
- Must participants complete forms at a certain point in the growth plan process?
- Can participants expect a response from the school leader within a specified period of time?
- Do participants need to keep copies of completed forms?
- Does the school leader make copies of the completed forms?
- Who keeps the original?

Thinking through these procedural questions can make implementation of the process proceed more smoothly.

Electronic folders, three-ring binders, or file folders indexed alphabetically by participant provide a simple and effective means for organizing completed forms. The school leader needs to determine the purpose of the form, how frequently the information needs to be accessed, and the importance of the form to the documentation process. These factors, among others, can help define the organizational structures and procedures needed to manage the paperwork generated from use of forms.

Only after the Professional Growth Plan Process is implemented can the school leader fully understand what and how he or she needs to organize and design structures to meet these organizational needs. Not thinking about them in advance, however, is very shortsighted and can create unnecessary obstacles to implementation.

(Text continues on page 35)

MONTHLY TRACKING CHART

NEEDS-ASSESSMENT CONFERENCES Date/Practitioner(s)	PLAN DESIGN MEETINGS Date/Practitioner(s)	PROGRESS MEETINGS Date/Practitioner(s)	SUMMARY CONFERENCE MEETINGS Date/Practitioner(s)
10/14 Deanna Smith	10/3 Ellen White	10/12 1st grade Karen Rock Beth Joos Mary Meeks	10/21 Brian Merrill
10/28 Nick James			

MONTH: _____

Page _____ of _____

Blackline SL-5

30

ANNUAL TRACKING CHART 2006–2007

NEEDS ASSESSMENT/ PLAN DEVELOPMENT	PLAN DEVELOPMENT ONLY	PLAN IN PROGRESS	PLAN SUMMARY CONFERENCES
Millie M.	Marty R.	Becky D.	Beverly M.
Donna L.	Amy T.	Dave A.	Brian J.
Betty H.		Ed P.	Joyce K.
Randy L.		Susan E.	Mike D.
		Rita N.	George D.
		Valerie S.	Amanda K.
		Julie H.	
		Sandy P.	
		Linda J.	
		Abbie K.	
		Steve G.	

Page ___ of ___

Blackline SL-6

SCHOOL LEADER CHECKLISTS

Topic Selection

- ❑ Is the topic relevant to the participant's assignment?
- ❑ Do professional performance standards and best practices research support the topic?
- ❑ Can it impact student achievement?
- ❑ Are resources readily available to support study and practice?
- ❑ Does the participant have the background knowledge and skills necessary to pursue this topic successfully?

Participants in a Group Growth Plan

- ❑ Do the personalities of each group member mesh?
- ❑ Is one member a dominating force who will control or limit the potential learning of others?
- ❑ Do the experience, skills, and knowledge of the participants contribute to the functioning of the group?
- ❑ Will group members have an opportunity to meet and work together?
- ❑ Do group members have any hidden agendas?
- ❑ Are there too many in the group to allow full participation of all members?

Professional Goals

- ❑ Does the participant already have this knowledge or this skill?
- ❑ Are the goals attainable?
- ❑ Will achieving the goals result in professional growth?
- ❑ Are the goals assessable?
- ❑ Do the goals link to improved student achievement?
- ❑ Do the goals support school improvement directly?
- ❑ Is the number of goals appropriate?

Learner-Centered Goals

- ❑ Does a clear link exist between the Professional Goals and the Learner-Centered Goals?
- ❑ Can these goals impact student achievement?

- ❑ Do the goals support school improvement efforts?
- ❑ Can participants document these goals fairly easily?

Essential and Related Questions

- ❑ Does the Essential Question have a known answer?
- ❑ Is it possible to answer the Essential Question?
- ❑ Do the questions require more than a yes or no answer?
- ❑ Does the Essential Question support the Professional Goals?
- ❑ Do the Related Questions support the Professional Goals?
- ❑ Will answering the Related Questions help answer the Essential Question?
- ❑ Will professional growth result from pursuing answers to the Essential and Related Questions?
- ❑ Does the Essential Question define a manageable scope of study?

Action Plan

- ❑ Do the activities outlined in the Action Plan address Professional Goals and Learner-Centered Goals?
- ❑ Do the activities cover each phase of the learning cycle: exploration, application, evaluation, reflection, refinement?
- ❑ Are resources available to support the plan?
- ❑ Is the participant capable of completing the task and activities?
- ❑ Is the time frame realistic?

Documentation

- ❑ Does the practitioner understand what artifacts are and the purpose of documentation?
- ❑ Does the targeted documentation represent the growth plan?
- ❑ Does an adequate amount of documentation exist from which to select Baseline Data and evaluation data?

❑ Are the resources and supplies needed to support the documentation available?

❑ Has the participant targeted enough artifacts to document each professional growth criterion adequately?

❑ Does the practitioner have a plan for organizing the artifacts?

Baseline Data

❑ Do Baseline Data exist to show a beginning point?

❑ Can the data selected provide a basis for comparison and analysis of comparable data collected after the intervention?

❑ Can the data document professional growth: new knowledge or skill, change in practice, ability to reflect, contribution to the learning community, or improvement in student achievement?

❑ Are the data and the data collection and interpretation process simple enough for participants to manage?

Methods of Evaluation

❑ Does the participant address each Professional and Learner-Centered Goal?

❑ Can the artifacts in the growth plan document growth?

❑ Are the evaluation methods reasonable and doable?

❑ Does everyone understand and agree what professional growth in this plan will look like?

❑ Is a Method of Evaluation present for each of the criteria that characterize professional growth?

Resources

❑ Will the resources help the participant reach his or her goals?

❑ Are the resources readily available?

❑ Does the success of the plan depend on access to a particular resource?

❑ Can the school provide the resources?

❑ If not, are there other sources to acquire the resources?

Sharing With the Learning Community

❑ Does the format selected facilitate sharing of the growth plan information?

❑ Is the purpose for sharing clear?

❑ Is the forum/audience appropriate?

❑ Does the format or presentation encourage "bring and brag"?

❑ Is the content of the growth plan experience and its significance (not the step-by-step procedures) the focus of sharing?

❑ Do the skills, abilities, and talents of the participant complement the forum and format?

Progress Meetings

❑ Is the participant making adequate progress?

❑ If it is a group plan, are all participants contributing actively?

❑ Is documentation adequate?

❑ Does the plan require modification?

❑ Is the reason for modification reasonable?
  • New knowledge or understandings
  • Insurmountable obstacles
  • Lack of resources or information

❑ Do all parties agree that modification is necessary?

Summary Conference

❑ Did the participant achieve the Professional Goals?

❑ Did the participant achieve the Learner-Centered Goals?

❑ Did the participant address the Essential Question?

❑ Does evidence exist to document all five professional growth criteria?

❑ Can the participant articulate the growth he or she has experienced?

❑ Has the participant made a contribution to the learning community?

❑ Do you agree with the participant about the growth that has occurred?

Blackline SL-1 (Page 2 of 2)

REQUEST FOR ASSISTANCE

Person(s) Requesting Assistance: Amy K., Marian A., Millie P.

Date Submitted: 11/13/06

Date Needed: ASAP!

Request: We need to meet with you as we have run into a real problem. The workshop we were signed up to attend has been cancelled. We were counting on that workshop to provide us an overview of the whole topic of concept-based instruction. Now what do we do?

Facilitator Response: Are you available after school Thursday? Don't panic!

Date: 11/14/06

(Text continued from page 29)

As the process and its procedures become more firmly embedded in the learning community and the school, as participants better understand the process and its procedures, as the time frames for each growth plan become more spread out, as the goals of the Professional Growth Plan Process are achieved and the learning community flourishes, management of the process requires far less time and effort. Management of the process becomes a professionally rewarding experience for the school leader.

INTRODUCING THE PROCESS TO STAFF

Once the conditions critical to growth plan success (see Chapter 1) are in place and the school leader has begun addressing operational issues, introduction of the Professional Growth Plan Process to staff can occur. Participation in the initial implementation of the growth plan process should be voluntary, and the number of plans should be limited to a manageable number. Three to five plans are ideal to start as far more than three to five staff members could be involved if the staff chooses to participate in group plans. To provide the school leader with a range of management experiences, the initial implementation should include individual plans and group plans. Beginning on a small scale helps ensure successful implementation. The school leader and participants can then identify problems more easily and resolve them more quickly. Once the initial participants are fully familiar with the process, they can offer help and advice not only to other new process participants but also to the school leader.

Given the unique dynamics of each school, the school leader may choose to target particular individuals, grade levels, or departments for participation. Characteristics of those who participate in the initial startup of the process include an openness to change, ability to deal with uncertainty, and flexibility. All involved initially must also be committed to the process, understanding that problems are inevitable and that the process requires them to identify and analyze the problems as they occur. Participants must also understand that they have a responsibility to solve problems, not just identify them. The school leader assumes the greatest responsibility for making the process work, for keeping lines of communication open and flowing, and for encouraging participants in their work.

When introducing the Professional Growth Plan Process to school staff, it is important that the school leader not only describe the Professional Growth Plan Process but also explain its purpose and the potential impact successful implementation can have on individuals, student achievement, and the learning community. An at-a-glance list of growth plan benefits, Blackline P-2, appears on page 36 and also in Resource B.

During this presentation, the school leader should describe implementation timelines, consequences of participation or lack of participation, and any contract and/or supervision issues that may be of concern. For example, participation in the growth plan process may mean a staff member no longer participates in the traditional evaluation process or has a reduced number of observations. Participation may make staff eligible for incentive pay or it might be part of the criteria for movement on the salary schedule. Participation in the growth plan process may release participants from attending districtwide or schoolwide staff development sessions. On the other hand, the consequences for not participating once the process is institutionalized may include attending all district- and school-sponsored staff development sessions,

GROWTH PLAN PROCESS BENEFITS

The Professional Growth Plan Process Benefits You, Your Students, Your School

✓ You develop the skills, knowledge, attitudes, and behaviors that increase your professional competence.

✓ You assume control and responsibility for your learning.

✓ You choose
- what you learn,
- how you learn it, and
- the time frame for learning.

✓ You improve student achievement.

✓ You support school improvement.

✓ You build collegial relationships and strengthen your learning community.

undergoing a traditional evaluation procedure, and forfeiting eligibility for incentive pay or movement on the salary schedule.

The school leader may not be able to address all issues until implementation is underway, but it is important that he or she acknowledges this situation honestly. The building of a climate of trust begins with the first school leader presentation.

SOLICITING PARTICIPANTS

After making an initial presentation, the school leader should seek volunteers to participate in the inaugural growth plan process. Within every staff exist individuals who like to be on the cutting edge and are always ready to try something new. These staff members are the most obvious candidates. Other candidates include those who already have done some work on their own and welcome the additional support the process offers. A school leader who feels very confident in his or her ability to make the growth plan process work might solicit a staff member who is uncertain of the process and very vocal with reservations. If this candidate, through a positive growth plan experience, becomes an advocate for the process, the additional time and support the school leader invests in this individual may pay significant dividends in the long term. Advocacy of the process by a vocally reticent participant can ultimately help sell the process to other staff members, substantially reducing the time a school leader spends selling the process.

To give the volunteer participants an overview of the growth plan process, the school leader can provide them with the Professional Growth Plan Participant Blackline Master Guide as well as the following blacklines:

- Professional Growth Plan Process Participant Checklist, Blackline P-3
- Professional Growth Plan Format, Blackline P-4
- Explanation of Professional Growth Plan Components, Blackline P-5

Participants should have ample opportunity to review these blackline masters before the school leader meets with them to walk them through the process. It is important to remember that questions will be numerous, and the school leader will not always have the answers. Again, this is a trust-building activity. A brief description of the master guide and the overview blacklines and their use follows. The guide and the blacklines appear in Resource B.

PROFESSIONAL GROWTH PLAN PARTICIPANT BLACKLINE MASTER GUIDE

The master guide lists all the participant blacklines and briefly describes their purpose and when to use them. Participants can use the guide to determine which blacklines might help at a particular stage in the process. School leaders can use the guide as an at-a-glance reminder of a blackline's role in the process. Like all the blacklines, this guide can easily be adapted and even expanded to meet the needs of all participants.

Professional Growth Plan Process Participant Checklist

The Professional Growth Plan Process Participant Checklist, Blackline P-3, on page 39 is a checklist of the steps of the growth plan process to help guide participants through the process. The school leader can easily adapt the sequence of activities this checklist offers to the particular needs of a school or district. For example, the first step in the process is a formal needs assessment based on established professional performance standards and student performance data. While important to the growth plan process, and strongly recommended, formal needs assessment is not essential to its success. Schools lacking adopted professional performance standards or school leaders lacking time to conduct the needs-assessment process may choose to skip this component.

The checklist also provides a quick but complete overview of the entire Professional Growth Plan Process and its four phases: (1) targeting professional growth, (2) plan design, (3) plan implementation and monitoring, and (4) plan evaluation. A blackline master is in Resource B.

THE PROFESSIONAL GROWTH PLAN FORMAT

Various components combine to create the Professional Growth Plan design. The growth plan format provides structure, continuity, and cohesiveness to the professional growth experience. Adapted from one originally designed and used in *Designing Professional Portfolios for Change* (Burke, 1997), the format presented here has evolved over time and through use to accommodate the change in focus and purpose from professional portfolios to professional growth plans. See page 40 for a reproduction of the Professional Growth Plan Format, Blackline P-4.

EXPLANATION OF PROFESSIONAL GROWTH PLAN COMPONENTS

Each component of the growth plan plays a role in defining the professional growth experience. Explanation of Professional Growth Plan Components, Blackline P-5, explains each component; the first page appears on page 41 for reference. Questions that accompany each explanation provide participants with support and direction to complete each component. By answering the questions, participants can compose a first draft growth plan.

The plan components appear in a sequence; however, the actual defining of each component is less sequential and far more interactive. Each component of the format is like a puzzle piece that must fit with all the other pieces to complete the growth plan puzzle. Participants may develop one component, then after considering a subsequent component, they may find it necessary to go back and revise the earlier component. Back and forth design and revision builds a cohesiveness between components that strengthens the overall growth plan design.

The format of a growth plan should always be flexible. After acquiring some experience with growth plan design, the school leader may choose to change the sequence or components of the growth plan format to better meet the needs of participants. Because the school leader works with the development of many plans, he or she may be the first to recognize a need to change the growth plan format.

(Text continues on page 46)

PROFESSIONAL GROWTH PLAN PROCESS PARTICIPANT CHECKLIST

Phase 1: Targeting Professional Growth

- ❑ Review and understand professional performance standards and best practices research.
- ❑ Perform professional performance standards self-assessment.
- ❑ Analyze available student achievement data.
- ❑ Look for correlations between practices and student performance.
- ❑ Participate in Needs-Assessment Conference.
- ❑ Choose plan Topic.
- ❑ State Rationale for Topic Selection.
- ❑ Identify Participants if a group plan.

Phase 2: Plan Design

- ❑ Establish Professional and Learner-Centered Goals.
- ❑ Create Essential and Related Questions.
- ❑ Design Action Plan.
- ❑ Determine modes of Documentation.
- ❑ Identify Baseline Data.
- ❑ Define Methods of Evaluation.
- ❑ Identify Resource Needs.
- ❑ Choose Method of Sharing Results with the Learning Community.

Phase 3: Plan Implementation and Monitoring

- ❑ Implement Action Plan.
- ❑ Conduct Progress Meetings.
- ❑ Participate in interim sharing of growth plan.

Phase 4: Plan Evaluation

- ❑ Summarize growth plan activities.
- ❑ Participate in growth plan summary conference.
- ❑ Conduct growth plan self-evaluation.
- ❑ Complete growth plan summary reflection guide.
- ❑ Share results with the learning community.

Blackline P-3

PROFESSIONAL GROWTH PLAN FORMAT

Name: Date Submitted:

Topic Selected:

Rationale for Selecting Topic:

Participants:

Professional Goals:

Learner-Centered Goals:

Essential Question:

Related Questions:

Action Plan/Time Line:

Documentation:

Baseline Data:

Methods of Evaluation:

Resource Needs:

Method of Sharing With the Learning Community:

Projected Completion Date:

Progress Meeting Dates:

Plan Approved Date:

Plan Administrator's Signature:

Participant's Signature:

Blackline P-4

EXPLANATION OF PROFESSIONAL GROWTH PLAN COMPONENTS

The following explanation of growth plan components endeavors to help you develop your Professional Growth Plan. This guide helps you define (1) what you want to know or be able to do at the end of the plan, (2) how you will acquire that knowledge and skill, and (3) how you will know that professional growth has occurred.

First, talk through your plan with the plan administrator/school leader or a colleague to help you clarify what you want to do and ensure that the scope of your plan is narrow enough for you to attain without unnecessary frustration. Simplicity is the key to the Professional Growth Plan.

PROFESSIONAL GROWTH PLAN COMPONENTS

NAME: _____   DATE SUBMITTED: _____

TOPIC SELECTED

Identify the focus of your plan.

- What is the general subject, content, focus of your plan (e.g., personal fitness, emergent literacy, play-based assessment, writing prompts)?
- What would you choose as a title for your plan?
- Under what subject would you look for information in the library?

RATIONALE FOR SELECTING TOPIC

Explain your reason for choosing this topic.

- Why have you chosen this area as the focus of your plan?
- Why should you investigate this area?
- What problem or issue would you like to resolve?

PARTICIPANTS

- Identify the plan participants by name and position.
- Is this an individual plan or are you working with a colleague?
- If you are working in a group, who are the participants?

PROFESSIONAL GOALS

These goal statements represent the professional growth you would like to experience on plan completion. It is important to focus the goals and not try to do too much. Keep goals manageable and realistic.

- What do you want to know or be able to do at the completion of this plan that you do not know or cannot do today?
- How will you be a more proficient educator when you have completed this plan?

Blackline P-5 (Page 1 of 5)

EXPLANATION OF PROFESSIONAL GROWTH PLAN COMPONENTS (Continued)

LEARNER-CENTERED GOALS

These goal statements represent the growth in student achievement or performance that will occur on completion of the plan. It is understood that not all students attain these goals, but the majority of students should attain them. Again, it is important to keep a narrow, clearly defined focus that produces manageable and realistic goals. Be as specific as possible about how your plan will improve student achievement. This achievement may not be immediate; it may take a year or two to see results. However, if you cannot link your efforts to an improvement in student achievement, you need to rethink your plan.

- What will students know or do better as a result of this plan?

ESSENTIAL QUESTION

Establish a question, which when addressed, helps you meet your established Professional and Learner-Centered Goals. Keep the question as focused as possible.

- What do you want to know?
- Does this question have an answer?
- Is the question too narrow or too broad?
- Can you think of other questions you need to address first to answer this question?
- Do you know the answer to this question?

RELATED QUESTIONS

The answers to these questions help answer the Essential Question. You might want to think of them as subquestions.

- What else do you need to know to answer the Essential Question?

ACTION PLAN/TIME LINE

List the tasks or activities you need to complete and a time line of when you will complete the task or activity. Merely approximations, these times serve as benchmarks to ensure that you are progressing toward plan completion. Use action verbs to write your tasks (e.g., research play-based assessment, read, interview, visit where it is in use; conduct a survey of area schools that have personal fitness plans as part of the curriculum; and create writing prompts that support the curriculum). The more details you provide, the better the direction you will have to begin your plan. Details also help you identify what resources you may need to support your plan.

- What sequential steps will you follow to complete your plan?
- What resources will you review?

- Whom will you interview?
- What will you create?

Example Action Plan Time Line statements:

By November '06
Identify and clarify for the purpose of instruction the characteristics of narrative, persuasive, and expository writing and writing prompts.

By December '06
Map the third-grade curriculum by topic/unit/activity.

By January '07
Complete a student attitude survey regarding personal fitness plans.

By March '07
Solicit from local high schools personal fitness plans that are part of their curriculum.

DOCUMENTATION

The sum total of your documentation constitutes your Professional Growth Plan portfolio. The documentation demonstrates your work on the plan and the professional growth you have experienced as a result of completing the plan. Each piece of documentation (artifact) should relate closely to your Professional Growth Plan; each piece is unique to you and your plan. Self-reflection and metacognition (evaluating what you know, how you know it, and why you know it) are critical components of the documentation process. Collecting documentation may be one of the most important tasks you do related to your professional growth. It is important to outline at least the basic contents or potential artifacts you will include in your portfolio before you implement your plan. Common artifacts are a reading log and reflections or comments about your readings, samples of student work, lesson plans, units developed, a work log, or any other items that are important in the completion of your plan. Once you get into the process, you may add or delete particular items. You may even include a "Portfolio Rejection Log" containing artifacts you chose not to include and reasons why.

- What data or artifacts are you going to collect and why?
- What artifacts will help demonstrate your work, activities, reflection and metacognition, learning, and application of learning associated with the Professional Growth Plan?

BASELINE DATA

Collected at the beginning of your plan, this information gives you a basis of measurement to determine whether growth has occurred. The data does not necessarily have to include numbers or quantified test results. Baseline data can come from an observational checklist, attitudinal survey, or a combination of quantitative and subjective data. If you cannot measure growth, your plan may not have enough focus or specificity.

- What information can you collect before you begin your plan that reflects your beginning point?
- Can this information provide a basis for comparison of information collected after your action or intervention plan?
- Can this information demonstrate growth or change, should they occur?

Blackline P-5 (Page 3 of 5)

EXPLANATION OF PROFESSIONAL GROWTH PLAN COMPONENTS (Continued)

METHODS OF EVALUATION

Explain what you will do to provide evidence that you have addressed your Essential Question and attained your goals at completion of your plan. (You may want to refer back to your baseline data to determine how you will evaluate the plan's effectiveness and the attainment of your established goals.) These methods do not have to be statistically pure, but they need to demonstrate that you have achieved the goals. Your professional development portfolio should demonstrate your professional growth and the attainment of your Professional Goals.

- How will you determine whether growth has occurred (yours and your students')?
- How will you determine whether you implemented your growth plan effectively?
- Did you attain the Professional and Learner-Centered Goals you established?
- What documentation will show new knowledge or skill?
- What documentation will show changes in instructional practices?
- What documentation will demonstrate increased reflection skills?
- What documentation will show your effort?
- What documentation will show a contribution to the learning community?
- What documentation will show improvement in student achievement?

RESOURCE NEEDS

Identify the types of support you need to complete your plan. Be as specific as possible, listing workshop titles, dates, and sponsoring agencies; book titles, authors, and publishers; and so on. If possible, attach anticipated costs associated with each item. Your needs may change once you implement your plan.

- What resources do you need to complete this plan?
- Do you need access to a computer and the Internet?
- Do you need particular books, videotapes, or audiotapes?
- Do you need release time to visit other programs or observe other teachers?
- Do you need to attend a specific workshop or training?
- Do you need to find an expert who can provide you with the training?

METHOD OF SHARING WITH THE LEARNING COMMUNITY

Explain how you will share your growth plan experience with your learning community.

- Who might benefit most from your new knowledge and skills?
- What forum and format will you use to share your growth plan experience?
- When do you think you will have something to share?

Blackline P-5 (Page 4 of 5)

PROJECTED COMPLETION DATE

Specify the month and year you anticipate completing your plan. Be as realistic as possible, but also know you can adjust the time frame if necessary.

- How much time will you need to complete your plan?

PROGRESS MEETING DATES

Identify dates to meet with the plan administrator to monitor progress toward goals.

PLAN APPROVED DATE:

PRACTITIONER'S SIGNATURE:

PLAN ADMINISTRATOR'S SIGNATURE:

Blackline P-5 (Page 5 of 5)

(Text continued from page 38)

However, participants may also recognize a need to change the format as they work through the process. It is not advisable to use different formats with different participants. The resulting inconsistencies could cause a number of logistical and management problems at the very least. Trying to keep straight the format each participant is using adds an unneeded level of complexity to the school leader's already difficult task of managing the process. Some might also interpret the use of different formats for different participants as holding different expectations and requirements for different individuals or groups. Whether true or not, such a perception opens a political can of worms that should remain shut.

Of course, before explaining the Professional Growth Plan Process or assisting participants in the design of growth plans, the school leader must thoroughly understand the function of each component of the growth plan process. A detailed explanation of each component appears in Chapters 3–6.

THE ROLE OF PARTICIPANT BLACKLINES

At this point the school leader may choose to share more blackline masters with participants. Knowing the strengths, weaknesses, and levels of understanding of the participants and the availability of time to support design activities determines which blackline masters to use. Some participants might prefer to have all the blacklines at the beginning of the process so they have a better sense of the tasks they must complete and can prepare for the next step. Others might prefer to receive each blackline as they need it so they do not feel overwhelmed with all the tasks ahead. The school leader should take care to reach a balance between providing enough information to answer questions and support participants' design needs and overwhelming participants with blackline masters and directions. For some, particularly those new to the process, receiving all the blackline masters used in the process would confuse more than clarify the process. Some participants need the school leader to lead them step-by-step through each blackline as they need to use it. On the other hand, distributing all the blacklines in a packet of sorts to the independent workers allows them to work at their own pace.

School leaders should also consider individual participant characteristics when reading the completed forms. Completed forms are not polished products, and school leaders should not expect them to be. The forms are working documents and their quality will reflect that.

Resource B contains all the participant blackline masters. This resource also contains a guide to using the blackline masters, which the school leader might distribute to those participants who receive all the blacklines at once. Figure 2.2 lists the participant blackline masters in the general order school leaders might distribute them and as they appear in Resource B. Figure 2.3 summarizes the school leader's responsibilities before the Professional Growth Plan Process even begins. After the school leader has completed these tasks, development of growth plans can begin, with the participants identifying their professions.

Figure 2.2   General Order of Use of Participant Blackline Masters

Introducing the Professional Growth Plan Process

    P-1   Professional Growth Criteria

    P-2   Growth Plan Process Benefits

    P-3   Professional Growth Plan Process Participant Checklist

    P-4   Professional Growth Plan Format

    P-5   Explanation of Professional Growth Plan Components

Designing the Professional Growth Plan

    P-6   Growth Plan Topics

    P-7   Action Plan Learning Experiences

    P-8   Artifacts for Documentation

    P-9   Anecdotal Record

    P-10   Work Log

    P-11   Reading Reflection Guide

    P-12   Activity Reflection Guide

    P-13   Observation Reflection Guide

    P-14   Documentation Artifacts Map

    P-15   Reflection Basics

    P-16   When You Document, You . . .

    P-17   Growth Plan Evaluation Criteria

    P-18   Growth Plan Evaluation

    P-19   Methods of Evaluation Plan Sheet

    P-20   Artifact Organizer

    P-21   Evaluation Artifact Organizer

    P-22   Resource Survey

    P-23   Resource Request Budget Form

    P-24   Forums and Formats for Sharing With the Learning Community

Implementing the Professional Growth Plan

    P-25   Request for Assistance

    P-26   Work Day Plan

    P-27   Work Day Summary Reflection Guide

    P-28   Progress Meeting Questions

Evaluating and Summarizing the Professional Growth Plan

    P-29   Growth Plan Summary Activities

    P-30   Growth Plan Self-Evaluation

    P-31   Growth Plan Summary Reflection Guide

    P-32   Sharing With the Learning Community

Figure 2.3   Preparing for the Growth Plan Process

Before implementing the Professional Growth Plan Process the school leader must take the following steps:

1. Address all school and district political considerations such as board of education and union support for the process.

2. Hone the essential attributes of the school leader such as cognitive coaching skills and complete knowledge and understanding of the growth plan process.

3. Identify potential resources.

4. Provide school staff with an overview of the growth plan process and clarify its purpose.

5. Solicit volunteer participation.

6. Using the blacklines, conduct a walk-through of the growth plan process for all volunteer participants.

THE SCHOOL LEADER AS COACH AND ADVISOR

The school leader must work diligently to alleviate participant anxieties. Because the Professional Growth Plan Process is likely to be completely new to staff, anxiety can be quite high. One concern will be a fear of failure. The school leader must offer constant reassurance that everyone will receive careful guidance through each step in the process design and implementation, so only lack of participant effort can result in failure. Patience, understanding, and enthusiasm are characteristics that serve the school leader well.

3

Identifying Areas for Professional Growth

By examining their practices and by critically reflecting on the reasons for them, teachers push themselves to give good reasons for what they are doing. This in turn prompts them to change their practice when they find it wanting.

—Fullan and Hargreaves, 1996, p. 70

THE FIRST OF FOUR PHASES

After the school leader has introduced the Professional Growth Plan Process, it is time to begin the first phase of the process. The Professional Growth Plan Process has four phases: (1) targeting professional growth, (2) plan design, (3) plan implementation and monitoring, and (4) plan evaluation. This chapter describes the first phase, targeting professional growth; Chapter 4 covers the second phase, plan design; Chapter 5 covers implementation and monitoring; and Chapter 6 discusses plan evaluation. Figure 3.1 highlights the steps from the Professional Growth Plan Process Participant Checklist, Blackline P-3 (Resource B), that take place in the first phase, Targeting Professional Growth.

Figure 3.1 Professional Growth Plan Process Participant Checklist

---

Phase 1: Targeting Professional Growth

- Review and understand professional performance standards and best practices research.
- Perform professional performance standards self-assessment.
- Analyze available student achievement data.
- Participate in self-assessment conference and complete self-assessment conference record.
- Choose plan topic.
- State rationale for topic selection.
- Identify participants if a group plan.

TARGETING PROFESSIONAL GROWTH

Targeted professional growth drives the growth plan process. To ensure that the targeted growth has relevancy and meaning to sustain a participant's interest in and commitment to a Professional Growth Plan, participants must first identify and understand the areas in which they may have deficiencies and their need for professional growth. This recognition, so important to learning, is best developed through a needs-assessment process anchored in professional performance standards and relevant student performance data. Such a process helps participants identify what they need to know and be able to do, to improve student achievement, thus becoming the participant's targets for professional learning and growth.

CONDUCTING A PERSONAL NEEDS ASSESSMENT

If the learning promoted through the Professional Growth Plan is based on the participant's perceived need to acquire new knowledge, skills, beliefs, and/or attitudes, then the needs-assessment component of the process forms the cornerstone of the entire Professional Growth Plan Process. The activities associated with needs assessment require participants to (1) compare their professional practices to established professional performance standards, (2) examine and document relevant student performance data; and then after completing the first two activities, (3) look for relationships between their practice and student performance. The discrepancies and deficiencies revealed through these activities highlight to participants areas within their practice in need of professional growth.

A growth process in itself, the needs assessment has key features that advance learning and encourage change. Its structure and content, through the comparison method, create within the participant a need for learning. The activities require participants to think critically about how their practice impacts student achievement, sometimes a missing link in staff development activities (Fullan, Hill, & Crevola, 2006).

Also by design, the knowledge, skills, beliefs, and attitudes ultimately targeted for professional growth and plan development are grounded in established professional performance standards and best practice research. The needs-assessment procedures promote reflective thinking, while building or reinforcing a climate of trust, risk taking, and professionalism. And perhaps most important, this initial step of the Professional Growth Plan Process begins the transfer of responsibility and accountability for professional growth from the administrator to the participant (see Figure 3.2).

Figure 3.2   The Purpose of Self-Assessment

- Targets areas for professional growth
- Builds and strengthens professional relationships
- Begins the transfer of responsibility and accountability for professional growth to the participant

COMPARING CURRENT PRACTICES TO ESTABLISHED PROFESSIONAL PERFORMANCE STANDARDS/BEST PRACTICES RESEARCH

The purpose of the Professional Growth Plan Process is staff development aimed at improving staff knowledge, skills, and attitudes to support best practices and standards-based instruction. The first needs-assessment activity requires participants to examine and reflect on their own professional practices, identifying their strengths and their weaknesses in relation to established professional performance standards. These professional performance standards exemplify the best practices of teaching and learning. Best practices generally refers to those instructional practices research shows to be most effective.

REVIEWING AND UNDERSTANDING PROFESSIONAL PERFORMANCE STANDARDS AND BEST PRACTICES RESEARCH

Before participants can compare their practices, they must have at least a cursory understanding of the professional performance standards on which the comparison is based. Most staff members are familiar with the standards terminology, but some may need more explanation regarding what the standard looks like in their practice. Through this careful examination, participants identify and, one hopes, internalize discrepancies that may exist between their practices and those described in the established performance standards.

The Standards-Based Self-Assessment Tool

Participants can use a variety of professional performance standards that currently exist for the purpose of self-assessment. The National Board for Professional Teaching Standards has identified standards for many areas and grade levels of instruction. These standards are used as a basis for National Board Certification. Many states and school districts have established performance standards that can serve as a basis for comparison. Discipline specific professional performance standards compiled by professional organizations such as the National Council of Teachers of Mathematics also serve as a good tool.

If performance standards comprehensively address the complexity of teaching, they then inherently have the potential to overwhelm and intimidate participants with their number and scope of performance expectations. For this reason, the school leader may choose to limit the number and/or scope of standards used in the self-assessment tool. Limiting the number and/or scope of professional performance standards expedites the self-assessment task and directs participant attention to those areas of their practice that most directly impact student achievement. Standards addressing content knowledge, planning for instruction, instructional delivery, the learning environment, and assessment typically bring such a focus.

Regardless of the source of standards, any performance standards used for this comparison activity need to be explicit enough to provide educators with a clear understanding of what the target behavior, skill, knowledge, or practice looks like in their own practice (Fullan, Hill, & Crevola, 2006). Depending on the standards selected and the degree of detail supporting them, it may be necessary to provide participants with supplemental lists of best practices that further explain how a standard translates into classroom practice. Such a list may already exist within a school or district. Professional organizations usually have lists of best practices as they relate to their discipline. A number of authors deal with best practices in a user-friendly fashion, including Zemelman, Daniels, and Hyde (2005). Ideally, conversations within the learning community about performance standards occur before the use of those standards in the self-assessment tool. These discussions help each member of the learning community develop a common vocabulary and a common understanding of what the standards look like in practice. This common knowledge base then enhances the validity and reliability of the self-assessment process for all participants.

If participants do not have the opportunity to discuss the standards, the school leader must help participants interpret what the standard looks like in their assignment. This need may arise as participants are completing the self-assessment tool and come upon a standard they do not understand, or it may occur during discussion of a particular standard within the needs-assessment conference.

The self-assessment tool must use a ranking or rating system for each standard. This format allows participants to determine the proximal relationship between their performance and the established standard. The ideal tool provides not only an opportunity to rank or rate the performance but space for participants to defend or comment on their marking. The more user-friendly the tool, the more accurate the self-assessment. The more accurate the self-assessment, the more accurate the areas targeted for professional learning and growth, a critical factor in growth plan development.

Finally, to encourage honesty and openness in the completion of the document, it is important that the school leader ensure that any information participants provide is never used for evaluation purposes. Participants perform the ranking or rating for the purpose of comparison and self-assessment. It is not a ranking for a supervision evaluation. The school leader's position is totally nonjudgmental and nonevaluative. Such use would discourage any future honesty on assessments, undermining the potential for professional growth and the viability of the Professional Growth Plan Process itself (see Figure 3.3).

Figure 3.3   Needs-Assessment Component

Characteristics of the needs-assessment component:

- It uses a standards-based diagnostic tool.
- It links classroom practices to student achievement data.
- The school leader is nonjudgmental.
- The accuracy of the assessment varies with the individual's ability to self-assess and reflect.
- It can never become part of a formal evaluation.

Completing the Self-Assessment Activity

To complete the first activity participants mark the tool making notations when they feel appropriate or where discrepancies between their practice and established standards exist. Participants should be encouraged not to labor over any rating or spend too much time working on the tool. Twenty to thirty minutes is a typical timeframe for completion. (This should not become a burdensome activity. If allowed to do so it will immediately discourage participant support of the growth plan process.) Once completed, participants summarize their findings by creating a simple listing of the strengths and weaknesses they identified within their practice. Because the list is for the participants' reference during the remainder of the needs-assessment phase, draft quality is quite appropriate. This listing, along with a similar listing of strengths and weaknesses generated from the next activity, and the examination of relevant student performance data, will be used by the participant to look for possible links between the participants' practices and his or her students' performance.

EXAMINING RELEVANT STUDENT PERFORMANCE DATA

In this second step of the needs-assessment phase attention shifts from what participants do in their classroom practice to an examination of what those classroom practices produce in the form of student achievement. The purpose of this activity is to help participants make the connection between what they do in their classroom practice and how that practice impacts student achievement, both good and bad. Because analysis of student performance data often suggests needed changes in professional practices or curriculum, changes that can become the focus of a professional growth plan, this review of student data essentially reveals to participants areas in need of professional growth.

Quality data with quality analysis generate excellent indicators of areas in need of professional growth. Most schools today regularly audit student performance data as part of their school improvement process. These data serve as the basis of this needs-assessment activity. The data collected and the methods of data examination and analysis used are unique to each school. Similarly the quality of the collected data, and the quality of the data interpretation, vary significantly from school to school. Because participants use the results of this data analysis to draw inferences about the effectiveness of their own instructional practices, curriculum structure and/or content for the purpose of targeting professional growth topics, it is important that the data they analyze accurately represent student knowledge and understanding (Popham, 2001). If student data represent multiple sources of information, if they present reliable trend data, if they produce accurate inferences about student achievement and program concerns, then they can and should play an important role in targeting professional growth. If, however, the quality of the data and/or their interpretation is lacking or poor, then their use in identifying areas in need of professional growth should be limited.

Once the student performance data are analyzed, participants compile their findings into a listing of areas of strong student performance and weak student performance. Any possible explanations or hypotheses a participant might have about a particular performance should be included in the listing. Again as with the self-assessment list, rough draft quality is quite appropriate as the documentation is only for the participant's future reference.

FACILITATING DATA ANALYSIS

During this second stage of needs assessment, the school leader should continue to focus on trust building while also facilitating the data analysis process. As part of that analysis, the school leaders need to ensure that participants examine and include strong student performance in their analysis as well as poor performance. To accept responsibility for poor student performance, participants must feel confident that in acknowledging a lack of skills, knowledge, and/or the use of poor instructional practices they will not be penalized with poor performance reviews or evaluations (Schmoker, 2006). This is an opportunity for the school leader to deliver on this assurance and further foster an environment of trust.

Because data analysis can be a daunting task for many, the school leader must act proactively to make available to participants data assembled in a user-friendly format. Equally important to the interpretation process would be individuals to help struggling participants interpret the data accurately and efficiently. (This activity in and of itself could result in professional growth!) Becoming bogged down in data quickly dampens anyone's enthusiasm for the growth plan process. It also needlessly consumes precious time. Data assembled in a user-friendly format and/or thoroughly explained helps those less skilled in data analysis interpret and make more accurate connections between student performance and their practice—important connections in promoting professional growth (Fullan, Hill, & Crevola, 2006).

And finally, the school leader must emphasize the importance of looking critically at and documenting the reasons for strong student performance as part of the data analysis process. Including strong student performance in the data analysis serves two purposes. First, it affirms effective current practices, acknowledging and affirming a participant's competencies while also building the participant's confidence. Then, later in the process, as participants reflect on the relation between student performance and their practice, it provides the opportunity to identify those effective skills, strategies, and beliefs that may transfer in some fashion to other, less effective areas of the participant's practice. This act of transfer, applying the skills, strategies, or beliefs used in one area to another area of classroom practice, could well become the targeted growth of a participant's growth plan.

LINKING PRACTICE AND PERFORMANCE

Linking student performance data to professional performance standards and best practice research can make a strong case for change. When participants begin to understand, through their own analysis, how their knowledge, skills, practices, and beliefs compare to professional performance standards and best practices research, and then how those practices impact student achievement, an even stronger case for professional growth is made and potential areas for professional growth are identified. This important understanding develops in the next needs-assessment activity as participants examine and compare the lists and observations they generated through the first two needs-assessment activities.

Using the completed lists, participants look for possible links between the strengths and weaknesses they identified in their practice and the strengths and weaknesses revealed in the analysis of their student data. Any possible links (both good and bad) they discover, and any explanations they may have for them, should be documented. Again, draft quality documentation is appropriate. After completion of this third task, participants are ready to target professional growth.

Addressing Deficiencies and Discrepancies

Each of the first three Needs-Assessment activities produces a listing that reveals potential professional growth targets. These lists identify (1) discrepancies between current practices and established professional performance standards/best practices, (2) poor student performance, and (3) possible correlations between practices that do not meet with established standards and poor student performance. Items from any of these three lists can become targets for professional growth and topics for growth plan development. The participant, after reflecting on the discrepancies and deficiencies identified, prioritizes a list targeting areas or topics for professional growth. These topics and how they were chosen and prioritized become the focus of the Needs-Assessment Conference with the school leader.

NEEDS ASSESSMENT AND THE SCHOOL LEADER

The needs-assessment activities give participants an opportunity to identify areas of professional strength and weakness by comparing their practices with established professional performance standards and with student performance data. This need to identify and understand areas of strength and deficiency is as important to the school leader as it is to the participant. For the school leader, the needs assessment provides an opportunity to develop a thorough understanding of participants' perceptions about teaching and learning, about their professional practices, and about their values and goals, their learning styles, and their personality type (Costa & Garmston, 2006). To facilitate the effective development and implementation of the Professional Growth Plan, it is essential for the school leader to have these understandings.

In addition to identifying strengths and weaknesses and helping establish a common understanding of professional performance standards, the needs assessment also offers the opportunity to introduce or reinforce reflective thinking skills. While reflection activities are embedded throughout the Professional Growth Plan

Process, the needs assessment is the first occasion that requires participants to think critically about what they do, why they do it, and the consequences of the practice. It then asks participants to be prepared to articulate their thinking. For those unfamiliar with reflective practices, this task can be very uncomfortable and intimidating. The school leader must understand and be prepared to address participants' feelings on the subject when facilitating the needs assessment. More on this topic appears in the discussion of the needs-assessment conference.

The ability to conduct a needs assessment or reflect on professional performance accurately varies with the individual participant (Costa & Garmston, 2006). Regardless of the accuracy of the participant's assessment, the assessment probably represents the participant's perception of reality—a reality the school leader must understand to facilitate growth plan development effectively. The school leader should know the participants and their work well enough to know when a discrepancy exists between their perceptions and what the school leader views as reality. Through skillful questioning—asking for specific examples of the participants' techniques, asking for evidence to support their statements, and so on—the school leader can help participants view their work realistically. For further discussion on this topic, see the section Common Needs-Assessment Conference Problems in this chapter.

THE NEEDS-ASSESSMENT CONFERENCE

Though the needs-assessment conference serves many purposes, its primary goal is to help participants target areas for professional growth. From these targeted areas come possible topics for Professional Growth Plan development.

As a professional dialogue between the participant and school leader about the completed needs assessment, the needs-assessment conference gives the participant an opportunity to discuss and explain his or her practices and beliefs in comparison with established standards and best practices, and the way those practices may impact student achievement, possibly revealing areas for professional growth. It gives the school leader an opportunity to affirm and recognize those professional performance standards and best practices that the participant meets or exceeds in his or her assignment. This recognition of demonstrated competence and excellence reinforces the value of those exemplary practices and acknowledges the participant's contribution to the learning community (DuFour & Eaker, 1998).

Sometimes participants bring to the conference a clear understanding of their areas of strength and those areas needing further development. Other times, participants perceive discrepancies between current performance and established standards only with the help of the school leader's questioning, paraphrasing, and clarifying during the conference. School leaders may need these same cognitive coaching skills to help participants understand the link between certain practices and student achievement.

Once participants identify and articulate these discrepancies, the participants work with the school leader to determine whether a lack of knowledge or understanding, a lack of skills, an issue of beliefs or attitudes, or perhaps a combination of all these factors has created the discrepancy (Costa & Garmston, 2006). When participants make this determination, they meet the primary goal of the needs-assessment conference: identification of areas for professional growth and topics for growth plan development.

The role the school leader plays in the needs-assessment conference influences its success. The school leader helps participants identify, understand, and accept a need to change (Costa & Garmston, 2006). The skills of cognitive coaching—such as questioning, probing, paraphrasing, establishing cause and effect relationships, and summarizing—are essential to this task. Often, the skilled school leader can help participants mesh perceptions of their performance with reality. The more proficient a school leader's cognitive coaching skills, the more productive a needs-assessment conference is. The school leader's nonjudgmental posture is fundamental to the success of the conference.

While benefiting participants, the needs-assessment conference presents equally valuable opportunities to the skilled school leader. Explaining and clarifying the performance standards and best practices that the learning community values helps the school leader build and strengthen a common vision of teaching and learning.

An Opportunity to Build Trust

The needs-assessment conference affords a most critical opportunity for the school leader to create or enhance a climate of trust. Any information participants share with the school leader as part of their needs assessment can never be used for an evaluative purpose. (Information that may serve as exemplary practice or may in some way benefit others in the learning community should be shared only with the participant's permission.) Trust garnered at this stage of the process manifests in participants' greater risk-taking behaviors in later stages of growth plan development and implementation. This trust building further manifests in future growth plans as well as in positive interactions within the learning community. Trust betrayed or compromised at this point of the process significantly compromises the future of the Professional Growth Plan Process.

An Opportunity to Model Professional Behaviors

The integrity and professional behavior the school leader demonstrates throughout the needs-assessment component and the entire Professional Growth Plan Process establishes and models standards for professional relationships for the participants. These standards transfer to the learning community as participants replicate and foster the standards in their practices and in their professional relationships within the learning community.

An Opportunity to Promote Reflective Thinking

The development and refinement of reflective thinking is part of every phase of the Professional Growth Plan Process. Beginning with the needs assessment and continuing through the conference and the entire growth plan process, the school leader's role is to help participants become aware of, develop, and enhance their internal thought processes relating to reflective practices. By asking participants to think about, evaluate, and articulate what they do, why they do it, and the consequences of their actions, the needs assessment engages them in the practice of reflective thinking. Through modeling and coaching in the needs-assessment conference, the school leader can encourage participants' reflective skills.

An Opportunity to Understand Participants as Learners

Teachers must know and understand each student to direct learning purposefully and successfully. To facilitate and maximize learning opportunities for participants, the school leader must also know and understand each individual he or she is leading through the Professional Growth Plan Process. The needs-assessment conference can yield information vital to effective plan development. Through active listening and cognitive coaching, school leaders can discern from the needs-assessment conference any one or all of the following (see also Figure 3.4): participants' understanding of teaching and learning, their level of reflective thinking, their values and goals, their belief systems, their learning styles, and their personality types (Costa & Garmston, 2006).

Figure 3.4   Needs-Assessment Conference and the School Leader

The needs-assessment conference gives school leaders an opportunity to

- establish standards for professional relationships
- articulate performance standards and best practices
- model reflective practices
- discern participants
  - understanding of teaching and learning,
  - level of reflective thinking,
  - values and goals,
  - belief systems,
  - learning styles, and
  - personality types

It is important that the school leader discern participants' understanding of teaching and learning, their belief system about education, and their values and goals. Facilitating the growth plan process with educators who believe teaching means presenting information differs greatly from facilitating educators who believe teaching means helping students construct new knowledge from their past experiences and knowledge. Those who believe teaching is a job that ends with the school day need different guidance than those who believe it is a profession that requires lifelong learning.

Learning styles and personality types impact both the activities participants choose to complete their plan and the organization of those activities for learning. For those who need to see a concept in action, video may be more effective than books and articles. For the auditory learner, audio resources may be more effective than video or books. Knowing that an individual has a checklist-type personality and derives a sense of accomplishment from the completion of tasks, the school leader may help structure an Action Plan that carefully sequences specific tasks. A personality type that thrives on recognition may identify a Method of Sharing with the learning community that provides that positive recognition. The person who loves social interaction may benefit from Action Plan activities that involve other people, such as study groups, site visits, or peer coaching.

Growth plan design should stretch individuals but also allow them to remain to some degree within their comfort zone. To help individuals develop to their potential, the school leader needs to understand where the individuals are and the characteristics that help or hinder movement toward their potential (see Figure 3.5).

Figure 3.5   Needs-Assessment Conference and Participants

The needs-assessment conference offers participants an opportunity to

- discuss and compare practices and beliefs with standards and best practices
- discuss and analyze student achievement data in relation to practices and beliefs
- determine if discrepancies are due to lack of
  - knowledge or understanding;
  - skill(s); or
  - beliefs to support a specified standard or best practice

COMMON NEEDS-ASSESSMENT CONFERENCE PROBLEMS

Not all participants are comfortable with the needs-assessment process, and this discomfort becomes most obvious during the needs-assessment conference. Four different behaviors emerge that can make the conference difficult at best and almost impossible at worst (see Figure 3.6).

Figure 3.6   Common Needs-Assessment Conference Problems

A participant may exhibit the following behaviors during the self-assessment conference:

- Unwillingness to participate—does not offer elaboration
- Self-deprecation—underestimates performance
- Overconfidence—overrates performance
- Diversionary—does not stay on topic

The first behavior is unwillingness to participate or minimal participation in the conference. Participants exhibiting this behavior usually respond with brief yes or no answers or just the rating or ranking itself, offering no elaboration. Unfortunately, these individuals usually do not respond to coaching prompts. It is important to the integrity of the process that these individuals complete the conference regardless of how short or ineffective the conference becomes. To press for more information or to use authority to get a response usually serves no purpose. The school leader needs to accept what participants offer and use the occasion to analyze the situation fully and prepare for the next stage of the development process with these individuals. To prepare for the next stage, the school leader must attempt to understand the motivation behind the behavior, and then devise a strategy to develop a professional growth plan based on the individual's needs and behaviors. Unfortunately, it may be necessary for the school leader to assign a topic arbitrarily to the unwilling participant. If a participant remains totally uncooperative, it may be necessary to take disciplinary measures tied to the school's supervision model.

The next two behaviors, while opposite in presentation, represent the same problem—a vast difference between participants' perceptions and reality. In one instance, participants grossly underestimate their performance, and in the other instance, participants grossly overestimate their performance. Sometimes through skillful cognitive coaching, the school leader can help participants bridge their perception and reality, asking questions such as the following:

- Tell me, how did you do that?
- How would you describe what this standard looks like in your classroom? In your practice?
- What are your thoughts about the effectiveness of ___?
- Help me understand—how do you make that work? Apply that in your practice?
- What examples would you like to share to help me understand?
- How do you feel about that?
- Why do you think that might be?
- What percentage of the time do you feel you do this?
- How regularly are you able to do this?
- Is this what you put in your lesson plans/unit designs?
- Can you help me understand the evidence you use to evaluate your effectiveness?

If this questioning technique does not work, the school leader needs to determine if, in fact, the posture the participant assumes is sincere. If it is, then the school leader has a very clear understanding of the participant's reality and must use this as a beginning point from which to facilitate this individual's growth plan design. If it is not sincere, the school leader needs to try to discern the reasons for the behavior and resolve (if possible) whatever issues are at the source of the behavior. If the school leader cannot discern reasons for the behavior or resolve the problem, he or she must accept this as a beginning point. It may mean the school leader provides more specific direction, sets more realistic tasks, or presses for more challenging activities that match the individual's abilities. Whether the participant is sincere or insincere, the plan must still fit the needs of the individual.

The final behavior that sometimes appears in the needs-assessment conference is diversionary. The participant, while compliant and cooperative, continually digresses from the topic. This behavior may be unintentional and just a mannerism of the participant. In this situation, the school leader should be diplomatic and supportive to keep the participant on task and the conference moving along.

If the diversion appears intentional, the school leader should try discerning the reason for the diversion—perhaps the participant has feelings of incompetence, anxiety, or suspicion about the process or even the school leader. Again, cognitive coaching techniques can help the participant become more directed and on task. If feelings of incompetence appear to be the reason for the diversion, the school leader might offer examples of the individual's competence as a beginning point: "You are always so effective with ___. Why do you think you are so effective?" If anxiety is obvious through body language, voice quality, or content of the discussion, the school leader might ask, "You are doing just fine, but you seem anxious. Are you uncomfortable with this process? Is there something I can do differently to make you more comfortable?" Continually offering reassurances that the individual is doing just fine may solve the problem.

If the school leader cannot discern the intent, but the diversion remains obvious, the school leader must persevere and complete the conference to preserve the integrity of the process. The school leader should convey to the participants that they will complete the conference regardless of the amount of time it takes. Sometimes just this understanding moves the reluctant participant back on task.

None of the behaviors are pleasant or make the role of school leader easy. These behaviors appear most frequently in the early stages of Professional Growth Plan Process implementation. An overabundance of these behaviors may reflect the climate of trust existing within the organization. Each behavior represents a reality the school leader must address, both individually and as it impacts the learning community. These behaviors are a very real reminder of the challenge virtually all educators face: the reluctant learner. Just as teachers confront reluctant learners daily in classrooms, the school leader must also accept reluctant adult learners at their level. Then using his or her knowledge of the learners, the school leader must create an environment and conditions that promote learning. Though not desired, this challenge can produce a more empathic and more credible school leader.

THE NEEDS-ASSESSMENT CONFERENCE RECORD

A brief summary of the needs-assessment conference can serve multiple purposes. First, for the purpose of record keeping and accountability, a conference summary documents that a conference occurred. More importantly, a conference summary helps the school leader develop the participant's growth plan. The content of the summary can be as simple or as detailed as the school leader deems necessary. Generally, a record of the participants, the date of the conference, the areas targeted for growth, and the topic chosen for growth plan development are included. Any comments that might assist in growth plan development are also appropriate. A sample Needs-Assessment Conference Record, Blackline SL-3, appears on page 62. The school leader keeps the form in the participant's growth plan file, where he or she can access it during plan design to recall ideas and items discussed during the needs-assessment conference. Participants may also choose to keep a copy for their reference.

IF NEEDS ASSESSMENT IS NOT FEASIBLE

A formal needs assessment based on established professional performance standards and student performance data strengthens the growth plan process. It ensures that the professional learning and growth that participants target as the focus of their growth plan is grounded in established professional performance standards and student performance data. Yet, while important to the growth plan process, formal needs assessment is not essential to its success. Schools lacking adopted professional performance standards or school leaders lacking time to conduct the needs-assessment process may choose to skip or modify this component.

The needs-assessment component is time-consuming. The start-up stages of the first Professional Growth Plan Process, when many participants need to complete the needs assessment at virtually the same time, can seem quite overwhelming to the school leader. And in reality, this period can be overwhelming! It requires time for completion of the needs assessment and even more time for a conference about the

NEEDS-ASSESSMENT CONFERENCE RECORD

Participant: John K.

School Leader: J. McCormick

Date(s) of Conference: 4/3/07

Areas of Strength:

Knowledge of students and their families—does a lot with newsletter and has families involved in classroom activities.

Engaging students in learning—feels he uses lots of different strategies, and kids are active participants.

Believes he contributes to the school and district because he volunteers to help with all the activities.

Good rapport with kids—they treat others respectfully—creates a safe, risk-taking environment.

Areas Targeted for Growth:

Assessing student learning—believes he does well with traditional methods but is not doing any real performance assessment; doesn't think his assessment matches the activities he has kids do

Organizing his classroom for instruction—feels something is always lost or in a pile

Does adequate job of keeping grades but doesn't feel they reflect student growth or lack of growth

Possible Growth Plan Topics:

Probably authentic assessment—understanding performance tasks, rubrics, when to use it, when traditional is okay

General Comments:

Seems to understand and can articulate strengths and weaknesses completed assessment tool. If done properly, the needs-assessment component, even spread over a period of days, can take time—about thirty minutes to complete the assessment and up to an hour to discuss it. To be effective, a conference session of thirty to sixty minutes is ideal. Less time does not allow for the necessary depth of discussion and more time is often too exhausting. This is a significant commitment and investment of time on everyone's part. However, this investment in reflection and relationship building reaps dividends for not only participants and the school leader but also the entire learning community. School leaders should make great efforts to include needs assessment in the Professional Growth Plan Process. If needs assessment is not included as part of the growth plan process, the first step of the sequence becomes topic selection.

CHOOSING A TOPIC: FOCUSING THE PROFESSIONAL GROWTH PLAN

Participants should take great care when selecting a topic for a Professional Growth Plan. Because implementation of a growth plan may take from one to three years, the topic must have enough substance to support and sustain a depth of study, yet be narrow enough to be manageable. When selecting a topic, participants and the school leader must consider the five questions in Figure 3.7. (See also School Leader Checklists, Blackline SL-1, in Resource A.) For the most part, participants who target professional growth through the needs-assessment process find these questions affirm their topic selection.

Figure 3.7   School Leader Checklist: Topic Selection

- Is the topic relevant to the participant's assignment?
- Do professional performance standards and best practices research support the topic?
- Are resources readily available to support study and practice?
- Can it affect student achievement?
- Does the participant have the background knowledge and skills necessary to pursue this topic successfully?

Is the Topic Relevant?

The topic should be relevant to the participant's assignment. The learning promoted through the Professional Growth Plan Process is purposefully job embedded. Unnecessary obstacles to learning are created if the participant's job assignment does not allow for any investigation, application, or practice of the desired new knowledge and skills acquired through the Professional Growth Plan Process. However, this is not a hard and fast rule. Exceptions may be necessary, but any exceptions require extra work and effort on the part of the participant. The participant needs to understand and accept from the beginning the possible difficulties to be encountered if the topic is not a part of his or her assignment. For example, a high school chemistry teacher wishes to pursue a degree in secondary school administration. The course of study offers little that relates to his role as a chemistry teacher, yet he wants to use his graduate program as the focus of his growth plan. He identifies his need through the district's professional performance standards in the area of professional responsibilities and professional growth, and he can tie his professional goals or targeted learning to these standards. In another example, a fifth-grade teacher may aspire to teach kindergarten but does not have an understanding of phonemic awareness or its role in literacy learning. Before the teacher can apply for a kindergarten opening within her district, she needs to acquire this knowledge. If a participant is truly committed to a topic not related to his or her job assignment and accepts and perseveres through the obstacles, he or she may experience professional growth as much as or more than those choosing a topic related to their assignment.

Do Standards and Research Support the Topic?

A second consideration when choosing a topic is the existence of a research base that supports the topic. Investing time and energy into acquiring knowledge and skills that are not substantiated by research as effective in improving student achievement is a waste of everyone's time. A topic supported by professional performance standards or best practices research focuses growth plan development, and the research-supported standards and best practices provide a target and benchmark for professional growth.

Are Resources Available to Support the Topic?

A third consideration when selecting a topic is the availability of resources. To facilitate the investigation of a topic, it is necessary to have ample resources to support the study. A topic that requires limited or obscure, hard-to-acquire resources creates unnecessary obstacles and problems for participants. If participants cannot find enough information on a topic, they may have chosen a topic that requires more time and effort than they have. A participant choosing a topic with limited resources needs to articulate to the school leader that the lack of resources will not impede work on the growth plan or limit the amount of professional growth experienced.

Can the Topic Affect Student Achievement?

A topic's ability to improve student achievement is perhaps the most important consideration in choosing a topic. Improved student achievement is the purpose of all professional growth activities. Most topics that participants select connect easily to improved student achievement, even if the improvement is not immediate. However, a few topics will not have a direct or obvious connection to improved student achievement. A link to student achievement that is not direct or immediate does not mean the topic is not suitable. For example, a speech pathologist may choose to investigate play-based assessment to enhance her diagnostic skills with her early childhood students. The speech pathologist's evaluations may become more accurate due to the use of play-based assessment. The more accurate evaluations should lead to better goals for her individual education plans, which should lead to more directed teaching by both the speech pathologist and the early childhood teacher, ultimately producing better student performance. The connection between play-based assessment and student achievement is not direct, but the topic does support improved student achievement.

If a link between student achievement and a topic, and the knowledge and skills one hopes to acquire, is not obvious, the participant must articulate how the topic will ultimately impact student achievement. If the participant cannot state the impact, the topic is not suitable for a growth plan. Based on knowledge of the participant and the needs of students within the school, the school leader must decide the appropriateness of a questionable topic.

Are Necessary Knowledge and Skills Present?

The final consideration to be made in topic selection relates to the ability of the participant to pursue the topic successfully. The school leader needs to understand the background knowledge and skills of the participant and determine whether the topic is appropriate. Choosing a topic that requires background knowledge or skills the participant does not possess sets the participant up for frustration at best, but more often failure. This is not a common occurrence but one that does need to be considered before finalizing topic selection.

Other Factors to Consider

In addition to the five primary considerations, other factors that impact topic selection are school improvement efforts and the participants' interests. Ideally, a topic selected for a Professional Growth Plan supports school improvement efforts directly, but this may not happen for a variety of reasons. The professional growth needs a participant identifies may not match targeted school improvement efforts. The participant may already be making a substantial contribution to targeted school improvement efforts. The participant may have more pressing needs than those targeted in a school improvement plan. The individual's job assignment may not significantly impact the goals associated with school improvement efforts. For example, in a school that has targeted improved writing skills (composition) as the school improvement goal, the school counselor may have a greater need to understand and use conflict resolution than to acquire the knowledge and skills to improve student writing. If one accepts the position that all professional growth impacts school improvement, then any topic selected that promotes the professional growth of the individual educator supports school improvement.

It is a well-established fact that the interest of the learner significantly impacts learning. Therefore, it is important that the topic selected for growth plan development be one of significant interest to the participant. Under normal circumstances, it is not appropriate for a school leader to dictate a topic to a participant. This would be acceptable only when the growth plan is part of an assistance or remediation process. A participant soliciting the school leader's input on topic selection is very appropriate, however, the school leader should not encourage this practice.

Finally, a participant's need for specific professional growth may play a prominent role in topic selection. Conducting a needs assessment based on professional performance standards and relevant student performance data allows participants to identify professional performance areas of strength and weakness. Recognizing a weakness or deficiency and a need to learn or improve may enhance a topic's appeal to a participant and may provide motivation for learning.

Topic Selection Without the Needs-Assessment Component

Ideally, every participant should conduct a needs-assessment process before selecting a topic or beginning the Professional Growth Plan Process. For a number of reasons, this may not be a possibility for all learning communities. For those not using the needs-assessment component as a first step of the growth plan process, topic selection usually becomes a matter of participant choice, school improvement initiative, administrator directive, or some combination of these and other factors. Growth Plan Topics, Blackline P-6, on page 67 can provide a starting point for discussion for those who may have difficulty finding a topic of interest. (A blackline master also appears in Resource B.) Participants and school leaders can generate similar topic lists easily by using programs from professional conferences, the titles of articles in professional journals, and the titles of books in catalogs of educational publishers. (Use the topics only, not the actual titles, of course!)

Rationale for Topic Selection

When they select a topic, participants should be able to answer the following questions briefly and simply: Why did I select this topic? What significance and relevance does the topic have to my job assignment and student achievement?

In answering these questions the participant composes the Rationale for Topic Selection, a format component of the Professional Growth Plan Format (see Blackline P-4 in Resource B). In creating a simple rationale, the participant explains why the topic is personally meaningful and relevant, two factors important to learning (Brandt, 1998). These two factors are also fundamental to creating and sustaining interest, motivation, and task commitment throughout the Professional Growth Plan Process.

A COLLABORATIVE GROWTH PLAN

Research continually validates the positive effects of collaboration on the learning process (Brandt, 1998). The design of the Professional Growth Plan Process encourages this characteristic of powerful learning by accommodating group professional growth plans. Whether an individual should be part of a group growth plan is a matter of personal preference.

Finding Participants With Common Needs

Having completed multiple needs-assessment conferences and functioning in a school leadership role, school leaders possess a rather comprehensive and valuable understanding of the strengths, weaknesses, and needs of the entire school staff. They can use this insight to direct schoolwide improvement efforts and to develop individual growth plans. Equally important, school leaders can use this information to assist participants seeking colleagues to create a collaborative growth plan experience.

GROWTH PLAN TOPICS

The list of topics below can serve as a starting point for a Professional Growth Plan. This list represents the topics available for study. Each general topic heading has numerous subtopics that can provide a more defined and specific focus for a growth plan.

ADHD/ADD	Internet in the Classroom
Assessment Literacy	Interpreting and Using Data
Authentic Assessment	Involving Families
Autism/Asperger Syndrome in the Classroom	Looping
Balanced Reading	Mathematics Problem Solving
Block Scheduling	Multiple Intelligences
Brain-Based Learning	Nonfiction Reading
Building Vocabulary	Performance-Based Assessment
Bully Prevention	Phonemic Awareness
Classroom Management	Problem-Based Instruction
Concept-Based Instruction	Questioning Strategies
Conflict Resolution	Reading in the Content Areas
Developmental Spelling	Reading Comprehension
Differentiated Instruction	Reporting Student Progress
Diversity	Running Records
Emergent Literacy	School to Work
English Language Learners	Service Learning
Grading for Learning	Specific Learning Disabilities
Guided Reading and Writing	Student-Led Conferences
Inclusion	Student Physical Fitness
Inquiry-Based Instruction	Teaming
Interactive Instructional Strategies	Writing Process

Participants can also identify colleagues with common needs and interests who want to pursue a collaborative plan. Usually, in this scenario, the common interests, needs, and the working relationships already exist; as an advantage for the school leader, participants have already addressed many of the concerns regarding group work.

The most challenging matches to make, but ones that may be most fruitful, are those matches between individuals with common needs or interests but different job assignments or job assignments that cross grade levels, disciplines, or specialty areas. If the topic is appropriate and the logistical considerations are resolved, such a match has the potential to create a group synergy that extends beyond the life and scope of the Professional Growth Plan (see Logistics of a Group Plan in this chapter). An example of such a match is a high school math teacher and a high school English teacher collaborating on a Professional Growth Plan promoting reflective thinking practices in students. After the growth plan experience, the two teachers continue their working relationship, bringing together their departments for the purpose of identifying opportunities to integrate and interrelate learning opportunities. Through work on their growth plan, a group representing different grade levels or subject areas might identify other initiatives of interest and pursue those interests outside of the growth plan process. For example, working on developing an understanding of how to create and integrate writing prompts into the science and social studies curriculum, a group of teachers decides to develop a student writing portfolio format for use at each grade level. Advantages of a group growth plan appear in Figure 3.8.

Figure 3.8   Advantages of a Group Professional Growth Plan

- Encourages discussion, analysis, and reflections related to instruction and student achievement
- Develops a common understanding of an instructional practice, strategy, program, curriculum, or other area
- Facilitates development and consistent implementation of a strategy, practice, program, or other area across a grade level, discipline, or school
- Develops a common vision for the learning organization through common experiences and common learning
- Provides social interactions that enhance learning
- Builds professional relationships, which strengthens the learning community by increasing the level of trust, support, and risk taking throughout the community

Group Dynamics

The school leader must consider several areas before accepting a group plan. For example, the participants' past experiences with group work should help the school leader determine whether group work is advisable for these participants. Personalities of group members is an area to consider as well. With an understanding of personalities, the school leader can bring to participants' attention potential problems that may arise because of the different personality types of group members. The school leader's skillful questioning might even discourage a group plan or cause individual participants to choose not to participate in the group plan. Questions might include the following:

- You are sensitive to the feelings of others. Will you feel comfortable speaking up and questioning an action, opinion, or observation of another if it conflicts with yours?
- Will you compromise because you do not want conflict?
- How willing are you to compromise your positions, beliefs, or understandings to accommodate the group?
- As a group, how will you ensure that everyone's thoughts are considered and valued?
- How will you ensure that everyone contributes equally?

The school leader should consider the following questions before approving a collaborative growth plan:

- Does each participant work better alone or as part of a group?
- Do any of the participants have a history of problems working in a group?
- Have groups with these participants been productive?
- What are the personality types of the individuals wanting to create the group plan?
- Is one group member a dominating force who will control and limit the potential learning opportunities of others or stifle risk-taking behaviors?
- Will the skills, experience, and knowledge of each member contribute to the group effort?
- Is there a possibility of a synergistic interaction of the group as a result of the collaboration? (This is certainly an ideal outcome.)

The preceding are not the only items to consider. Unfortunately, the school leader must also look at a group's composition to determine if any hidden agendas on the part of individuals within the group or the group itself might undermine school improvement efforts, the Professional Growth Plan Process, or the learning community. One such example would be a group composed of individuals all opposed to the implementation of a program, particular curriculum, or practice. A group whose members oppose the implementation of performance assessment in the middle school mathematics curriculum may want to use the growth plan process to demonstrate that because performance assessment is more time-consuming than traditional testing, it takes time away from important instruction. This group may have chosen to work together to "prove" performance assessment in the math curriculum does not work. While rare, this possibility is one the school leader should consider.

LOGISTICS OF A GROUP PLAN

Pragmatically, the school leader must consider circumstances that might make group work difficult. For example, will members have a common time to meet, plan, and work? Even if common planning times and workshop days exist to support group work, extracurricular activities, district or school committees, family obligations, and even second jobs can significantly limit a group's opportunity to meet and work. If group members do not have sufficient opportunity to work and learn together, their growth plan cannot deliver its potential for their professional growth. The portion of the school leader checklist for group growth plans appears in Figure 3.9; see Blackline SL-1 in Resource A for the complete checklist.

Figure 3.9   School Leader Checklist: Participants in a Group Growth Plan

- Do the personalities of the group members mesh?
- Is one member a dominating force who will control or limit the potential learning of others?
- Do the experience, skills, and knowledge of the participants contribute to the functioning of the group?
- Will group members have an opportunity to meet and work together?
- Do group members have any hidden agendas?
- Are there too many in the group to allow full participation of all members?

Group size can also impact the effectiveness of the group and the Professional Growth Plan Process. Generally speaking, groups of two, three, or even four work best for group plans. In groups larger than four, some of the problems normally associated with group work become more evident, impeding progress for the entire group. For example, in larger groups it becomes difficult to track personal accountability for specified tasks. Communication between members becomes more cumbersome and time-consuming. Finding common group meeting times is more difficult. A single topic often cannot support a large group with an equitable distribution of work and responsibility. As a result, working through components of the growth plan such as the Action Plan, Documentation, and Methods of Evaluation can become a nightmare of logistics for both the group members and the school leader.

The school leader should not prohibit but should strongly discourage a large group growth plan. Good reasons always exist for exceptions. A unique learning opportunity involving a larger group may present itself, and the opportunity should be accepted. However, if an exception is made, the school leader and group members need to understand, accept, and be prepared to resolve potential problems a large group plan creates and also be prepared to expend the additional time required to resolve those unique problems.

A school leader who does not take into consideration all the factors that can impact and impede the functioning of a group is setting the stage for problems that will require solving later during the implementation and summary phases of the process. An additional caution regarding group plans: There might be an inclination or desire, from either administration or staff, to turn a schoolwide improvement effort into one common Professional Growth Plan for all staff members. While this action would kill two birds with one stone and be far easier for the school leader to manage, the result would be a school improvement plan based on the common needs of the entire school, not a Professional Growth Plan based on an individual's need for professional growth. It is important to recognize the difference.

Despite these cautions, school leaders should encourage collaborative growth plans because of their significant potential contributions to individual learning and to the growth of the learning community.

4

Designing the Professional Growth Plan

True professional development is a deliberate process, guided by a clear vision of purpose and planned goals. These goals form the criteria by which content and materials are selected, processes and procedures developed, and assessments and evaluations prepared.

—Guskey, 2000, p. 17

THE SECOND PHASE: PLAN DESIGN

Once participants identify their professional growth needs and select a topic to use as the focus of the growth plan, activity shifts to the second phase and the heart of the Professional Growth Plan Process, designing a Professional Growth Plan. In this phase, participants define a very specific plan of study and action that ensures they acquire the new knowledge, skills, behaviors, and attitudes they identified in the first phase of the process. Figure 4.1 highlights the steps from the Professional Growth Plan Process Participant Checklist that take place in the plan design phase. (See Blackline P-3 in Resource B for the complete checklist.)

Figure 4.1   Professional Growth Plan Process Participant Checklist

---

Phase 2: Plan Design

- Establish Professional and Learner-Centered Goals.
- Create Essential and Related Questions.
- Design Action Plan.
- Determine Modes of Documentation.
- Identify Baseline Data.
- Define Methods of Evaluation.
- Identify Resource Needs.
- Choose Method of Sharing Results With the Learning Community.

WHAT'S IN STORE

Plan design can be a lengthy, time-consuming, and exacting process, particularly the first time through. (The length of the chapter reflects the nature of the process.) It requires conferencing between the school leader and plan participants and between plan participants and colleagues. Of course, those involved in group plans find conferencing essential to the development of a group plan; however, even those working on an individual plan benefit from discussing their proposed plan with colleagues. Informal discussions with colleagues, particularly those who have experience with or knowledge of the proposed topic, often offer participants insights and suggestions that lead to a better plan.

During first generation plan development, it is common to draft multiple plans until a workable, manageable, clearly articulated Professional Growth Plan results. Rarely is a plan developed and finalized in one plan design session. The first session usually results in the identification of all major components and some fine-tuning of details, but questions surface that participants need to investigate or think about before they make final decisions. The number of drafts (and plan design meetings) required depends on the complexity of the plan, whether it has any unique challenges associated with it, and the level of confidence and understanding the participant possesses in plan development.

Each step in growth plan design has its own procedures to help direct and focus the activity. It is important to note the time and energy participants invest initially to ensure that they construct a solid, well-designed plan that maximizes opportunities for professional growth to occur and minimizes conferencing needed to revise, modify, and problem-solve during a plan's implementation. Much like a well-constructed lesson plan, a well-constructed growth plan effectively and efficiently directs and focuses learning.

GUIDING THE DESIGN PROCESS

Though this book presents Professional Growth Plan components individually and sequentially as arranged in the format model (see Blackline P-4 in Resource B), the actual development of the plan is not as clear-cut as the format suggests. As stated earlier, the various components interact dynamically: One component usually contributes in some fashion to the development of other components. For that reason, it may be necessary to go back and forth between components, refining and revising, as the intent and possible execution of the growth plan becomes clearer. Again, flexibility and fluidity are key to successful plan design.

A sample Professional Growth Plan, Figure 4.2, appears below. It is not a perfect plan, but it represents what a typical growth plan should look like. (A "perfect plan" with each component precisely worded and formatted indicates too much time spent on presentation, usually at the expense of action.) No two growth plans will look alike. Each growth plan reflects the individual who designs it. The depth of study, complexity, and degree of detail the plan represents should reflect the ability and the needs of its owner. Having selected a topic, participants move to establishing professional goals.

Figure 4.2   Professional Growth Plan

Name: Becky D.   Date Submitted: 5/18/06

Topic Selected: Interactive Instructional Strategies

Rationale for Selecting Topic:

It is difficult to get high school students to participate in class discussions and to engage them in the topics under study. Including more interactive strategies might raise the level of engagement and understanding and as a result increase student achievement.

Participants: Becky D., social studies teacher

Professional Goals:

Identify and understand interactive instructional strategies that can be used in the social studies classroom.

Use interactive strategies to deliver instruction.

Learner-Centered Goals:

Increase participation in classroom discussions and activities.

Improve student achievement on classroom, district, and state assessments.

Essential Question: How can interactive strategies be incorporated into my classroom to increase student participation and engagement in activities and improve performance on assessments?

Related Questions:

What are interactive strategies?

Where do I find out about these strategies?

How are they different from what I do now?

Is there anything I am currently doing that I can still use?

Do I have to rewrite my entire curriculum?

Do I need different instructional materials?

What skills, experiences, and knowledge do my students need to participate?

Does anyone else on staff use these strategies?

(Continued)

Figure 4.2 (Continued)

Professional Growth Plan

Action Plan/Time Line

Topic Selected: Interactive Instructional Strategies

By October 15	Conduct a survey of students' feelings about the class and their level of involvement. Do a search to see what is available on the topic. Someone will visit my classroom (5-8 visits) and collect data on student participation in my U.S. history class.
By October 30	Identify all the resources available to provide me with information about interactive strategies.
By November 15	Visit Michelle's classroom and watch her use strategies; meet with Michelle and do follow-up to visit.
By December 30	Review resources.

2007

By February 15	Develop plan for implementation of strategies in Civil War unit.
By March 15	Introduce unit and begin strategies.
By March 30	Run informal survey and see what kids think.
By April 15	Someone will visit my classroom (5-8 visits) and collect data on student participation in my U.S. history class.
By May 1	Review implementation; collect initial implementation data.
By May 30	Revise Civil War unit and identify other class units for revision to include interactive instructional strategies.
By September 15	Collect new student baseline data.
By September 30	Implement revised implementation plan.
By December 15	Review student data.

2008

| By February 15 | Collect, interpret, and summarize final data. Summarize growth plan. |
| By March 15 | Complete growth plan. |

Documentation:

Summary of readings

Reflections on readings, observations, and activities

Revised Civil War unit

Lesson plans

Instructional materials

Video of class lessons

Student surveys

Work day reflections

Work day plan sheets

Work log

Baseline Data:

Student attitude survey

Chart of student participation

Videotape of class during a typical lesson

Civil War unit plan

Lesson plans

Student work samples

Methods of Evaluation:

The revised Civil War unit will incorporate interactive strategies.

Student work samples

I will videotape the same class at least four times: at the beginning, two middle sessions, and a final session to demonstrate student participation.

Student participation rates data will show an increase from beginning to end.

Student pre- and post-surveys will show an increase in interest in the class.

Students' scores will begin to show improvement.

Work log

Reflections—at least 6

Resource Needs:

I'll share my videotapes at a staff meeting or within the department, then place a copy in the professional library.

I'm not sure right now. I know I'll need some books and a videotape recorder as well as someone to record the class.

Someone to come in and tally student participation at least 4 times

Method of Sharing With the Learning Community:

I'll share my videotapes at a staff meeting or within the department, then place a copy in the professional library.

Project Completion Date: 3/15/08

(Continued)

Figure 4.2 (Continued)

Progress Meeting Dates:

11/01/06

02/01/07

05/01/07

10/01/07

01/15/08

Plan Approved Date: 05/20/06

Plan Administrator's Signature: Jodi Peine

Participant's Signature: Becky Daniels

ESTABLISHING PROFESSIONAL GOALS

Much has been written recently regarding the importance of goal setting. Whether the forum is education, business, or self-improvement, books, periodicals, and conferences promote the value and success associated with goal-driven behaviors and efforts (Schmoker, 1999). The experts tell us to begin with the end in mind for good reason. Goal setting provides a clear vision of what participants wish to accomplish. Participants can begin goal setting with the following question: What will I know and be able to do when I complete my plan that I cannot do and do not know now? If participants define what they want to know and be able to do when they finish their efforts, all their energies can be directed toward reaching that end. Equally important, through assessment and evaluation, participants can know clearly whether goals are reached.

One of the real strengths of the Professional Growth Plan Process is that it is driven by goals. Once participants establish Professional Goals, the remaining growth plan components evolve from them, either directly or indirectly. Therefore, the single most important task in designing a Professional Growth Plan is defining Professional Goals. In defining their Professional Goals, participants describe the learning to occur as a result of their growth plan activities. Their goal statements define the knowledge and skills they will acquire through the growth plan process. Without Professional Goals, there is no Professional Growth Plan Process or professional growth.

WHERE DO GOALS COME FROM?

Through the process of selecting a topic—whether a result of needs assessment, individual choice, or school improvement activities—participants define an area of interest or need. From this topic, goals defining the desired professional growth emerge.

Participants unsure of their goals can compose a list of questions they have about the selected topic. Reviewing each question on the list, they look for common content. These questions often reveal the specific knowledge and skills participants need or want. Once they identify the knowledge and skills, they can turn their questions into goal statements.

WHAT MAKES A GOOD GOAL?

If Professional Goals drive the Professional Growth Process, it is easy to infer that the quality of professional goals impacts the quality of the process. Similarly, the quality of the goal statement reflects the quality of the goals.

A well-constructed goal statement answers the important question previously stated: What will I know and what will I be able to do when I complete the growth plan that I do not know and cannot do now? Clarity and succinctness are two key characteristics of good goal statements. With clarity and succinctness should also come focus. The more clearly defined the parameters of the desired professional growth, the more manageable the growth plan is. Use of educational jargon should be minimal. The learning to occur must be explicit within the goal statement. The following sections discuss the characteristics of good quality goals. Figure 4.3 contains the portion of the school leader checklist that addresses Professional Goals. (See Blackline SL-1 in Resource A for the complete checklist.)

Figure 4.3   School Leader Checklist: Professional Goals

- Does the participant already have this knowledge or this skill?
- Are the goals attainable?
- Are the goals assessable?
- Do the goals support school improvement directly?
- Do the goals link to improved student achievement?
- Will achieving the goals result in professional growth?
- Is the number of goals appropriate?

Participants Acquire New Knowledge and Skills

The school leader must determine whether the participant already possesses the knowledge or skills the goals describe. If the participant already has the knowledge or skill, he or she may have misunderstood the purpose of the goal. Or, the participant may wish to increase his or her depth of knowledge or proficiency at a skill. The school leader, in an open and honest discussion with the participant, must determine whether the degree of new knowledge or skill to be acquired is sufficient to sustain a growth plan and warrant the time allocated to its implementation.

Goals Are Realistic

Most any goal can be attained given enough time, resources, effort, and talent. The point of consideration is whether the effort and resources required to reach them are realistic. Broadly stated goals, for example, quickly become unmanageable and overwhelm the participant, creating a paralyzing frustration and sense of defeat.

This discouraging experience can destroy for participants the potential of experiencing professional growth through the growth plan process.

The professional goal, "To establish an authentic assessment program for a fifth-grade classroom," is an example of a goal that is too broad in scope. If the participant does not understand authentic assessment, acquiring that understanding is a major undertaking in itself. Even if the participant understands authentic assessment thoroughly, the task of developing authentic assessment tools for the entire fifth-grade curriculum is an unrealistic expectation.

Though the goal is too broad, the intended learning of the goal may be good and worthwhile to use in a redefined goal. The school leader can help the participant narrow the goal's scope, while keeping the intended learning intact. If the participant's intent in the broadly stated goal above is to understand the principles of authentic assessment and apply those principles in the classroom setting, it is possible to rewrite the goal successfully. Turning the goal into two goals and adding parameters provide a narrower and more manageable focus:

- Goal 1—Understand the basic principles of authentic assessment
- Goal 2—Develop and use at least one authentic assessment tool in each of the following curricular areas: language arts, science, social studies, and math

Setting goals that are too broad is the most common problem and one the school leader must anticipate and monitor.

Goals Are Assessable

A well-constructed goal statement lends itself to assessment. When participants know what they wish to learn, they must also understand what documentation will exist and how it will confirm that the targeted learning has occurred. If documentation will be difficult to acquire or interpret, then assessment will be difficult. Goals that are inappropriate, or poorly stated, must be redefined to support assessment.

Goals Support School and Student Improvement

Other considerations important to good goal setting include the effect of the goals on school improvement efforts and student achievement. Generally speaking, if goals cannot be linked either to school improvement efforts or to student achievement, they are not appropriate for a Professional Growth Plan. Professional Goals may not connect directly to school and student improvement, but they should at least link indirectly. Professional Goals unrelated to school improvement, or unrelated to increased student achievement, need to be redefined to provide a link. When the link is in question, the school leader must decide on the appropriateness of the goal.

Goals Promote Professional Growth

Sometimes more challenging to the school leader is determining whether professional growth will result if participants achieve the stated goals or if the goals are, in reality, just activities or projects. Some goal statements look good on the surface. For instance, to revise and update an American government course may seem like a worthwhile goal. The participant could, however, achieve this goal without experiencing any professional growth or without improving student achievement! To make the learning and application of this goal clearer, the participant might restate the goal as two goals, each more explicit than the original goal statement:

- Goal 1—Understand concept-based curriculum and instruction
- Goal 2—Revise a unit of instruction in the American government class using a concept-based curriculum format

This delineation between project and learning is sometimes difficult for participants to understand. If it is unclear whether the goal represents learning or a project, participants need to articulate to the school leader what they will know and be able to do on reaching the goal that they do not know or cannot do now. Sometimes this articulation leads to goal restatement that makes the intended learning clearer.

How Many Goals Should Participants Target?

A final consideration when establishing Professional Goals for a growth plan is the number of goals. Either too many or too few can affect the success of the entire plan negatively. The more common of the two problems is the identification of too many goals. Particularly on a first or second growth plan, it is important to err on the side of too few goals to ensure the goals are manageable within a realistic time frame. Too many goals can be just as unmanageable and overwhelming as having goals with too broad a scope. Two or three goals are ideal; four goals should be a maximum. Sometimes, however, even three goals may prove too many.

Unfortunately, a problem resulting from too few or too many goal statements may not become evident until the creation of an Action Plan. Remember, goals provide a direction for assessment, but they also provide direction for the selection and development of learning tasks and activities, along with the corresponding timeline that leads to the goal achievement. Therefore, the realization that a plan has too many goals may not become obvious until identification of activities and timelines during creation of the Action Plan. If it becomes apparent that the participant has too many goals to manage reasonably, he or she should prioritize the goals, then eliminate the least important goal(s) and save the eliminated goal(s) for use in a future growth plan.

Having too few goals is no less of a problem. A single goal may not provide the depth of study and application to sustain a Professional Growth Plan. Two options exist to address this concern. First, the participant might redefine the goal to broaden its scope, adding breadth and depth. For example, if the original goal was "Understand how to administer and score a running record," the participant could revise the goal:

- Goal 1—Administer, score, and interpret a running record for diagnostic and prescriptive purposes

Another option that accomplishes the same end is to add an additional goal or goals to the growth plan. The revised goal might be the following:

- Goal 1—Administer and score a running record
- Goal 2—Interpret score result for the purpose of prescribing instruction
- Goal 3—Develop lessons based on diagnostic interpretation of running record data

Do note that a single goal may be appropriate. One challenging goal may provide an adequate depth of study to sustain the growth plan process.

The time invested in defining Professional Goals is some of the most valuable time in the process. Quality goals greatly facilitate the remaining plan development and implementation. Once Professional Goals are established, a foundation exists from which to make more informed decisions. With every decision participants make, they can ask themselves, "Will this bring me closer to my goal?" The Professional Growth Plan Process is truly a goal-driven process.

ESTABLISHING LEARNER-CENTERED GOALS

The purpose of all professional growth is improved student achievement, so it is important that participants include Learner-Centered Goals in their growth plan. In other words, participants must state in the form of Learner-Centered Goals how their acquisition of new knowledge or skills will improve student achievement and performance.

Defining Learner-Centered Goals holds some of the same challenges as defining Professional Goals. They need to be narrow, clearly defined, manageable, realistic, and reasonable in number. The portion of the school leader checklist (Blackline SL-1, Resource A) related to Learner-Centered Goals appears in Figure 4.4.

Figure 4.4 School Leader Checklist: Learner-Centered Goals

- Does a clear link exist between the Professional Goals and the Learner-Centered Goals?
- Can these goals impact student achievement?
- Do the goals support school improvement efforts?
- Can participants document these goals fairly easily?

Documenting and assessing the attainment of Learner-Centered Goals is a more elusive task. The cause-and-effect relationship between professional growth and student achievement is not always immediate or direct. Because so many variables can influence student achievement, it may be difficult to generate quality data to substantiate the link between professional growth and student achievement (Guskey, 2000). The time it takes to become proficient in the delivery of some instructional strategies may span more than a school year and a specific group of students, so student achievement is represented by a variety of students with different abilities and needs over a period of years. Trend data—collected and interpreted over time—may be the only data. Sometimes establishing the cause-effect relationship requires data collection or statistical skills beyond the ability of the participant. If a link exists, either a direct or indirect link, the school leader should accept the Learner-Centered Goals with the understanding that the participant will make all attempts to provide documentation of student achievement and performance. When the link between professional growth and student achievement is direct and obvious, however, goal assessment and documentation should be easy, valid, and reliable.

CAN GOALS CHANGE?

This book presents growth plan design in a linear, sequential fashion. In reality, a greater interaction occurs among growth plan components. It may be necessary to revisit Professional and Learner-Centered Goals and make minor or even major adjustments. The Essential and Related Questions, even the Action Plan itself, may indicate a need to go back and adjust goal statements. New information and experiences while implementing the Action Plan may indicate a need to redefine goals. As long as it does not compromise the targeted learning or the integrity of the process, goal modification is quite appropriate; it strengthens the cohesiveness and integrity of the entire growth plan. To modify a goal, however, the school leader and participant must agree a need exists; otherwise, the modification cannot be made.

The Professional and Learner-Centered Goals serve as the compass of the Professional Growth Plan Process. They provide both direction and a destination.

ESTABLISHING THE QUESTIONS

Sometimes more important than answers, questions play an important role in the design and implementation of the growth plan. The most important is the Essential Question, followed by the Related Questions. The Essential Question is the big question that helps direct all the learning activities of the growth plan. The Essential Question helps further define the scope and context of study identified in the professional goals.

CREATING THE ESSENTIAL QUESTION

An Essential Question often arises from a series of questions practitioners pose about a topic during the topic selection process. The kinds of questions that emerge during conversations and activities related to topic selection follow:

What is _____?

How do you _____?

Why _____?

Can _____?

What happens when _____?

What if _____?

Participants and the school leader should record these questions because they can serve a number of purposes facilitating growth plan development. The fact that the participant has many questions about a topic indicates the topic can support a Professional Growth Plan. If the participant selects that topic, then a careful analysis of the content and pattern of the questions may reveal the specific knowledge and skills that need to be targeted for professional growth and turned into professional goal statements.

These initial questions can also assist in the formulation of the Essential Question. Combining these questions into one big question, or umbrella statement of inquiry, forms an Essential Question that defines the scope and context of the Professional Growth Plan. Just like the Professional and Learner-Centered Goals, the Essential Question serves to provide a clear and directed focus for the selection and implementation of growth plan activities. Professional Goals identify what participants wish to learn. The Essential Question provides a contextual setting for that learning. It is the Essential Question, along with the Related Questions, that help tie the Professional Goals to the individual's practice. Figure 4.5 provides two examples of the relationship between topic, topic rationale, goals, and the Essential and Related Questions.

Figure 4.5 The Questioning Path From Topic Selection to Related Questions

Example One	Example Two
Topic: Concept-Based Curriculum	Topic: Play-Based Assessment
Rationale: Kids don't seem to see any importance in my American government class in its current structure. They don't seem to make connections with the big ideas about government. Their performance on state tests seems average at best.	Rationale: Standardized tests are difficult to administer to young children, particularly those with limited language ability. The tests often don't accurately assess a child's development. An alternative to standardized assessment is necessary to provide the most accurate diagnostic information. This information can help me write appropriate goals for students' Individual Education Plans (IEPs).
Professional Goals:	**Professional Goals:**
1. Understand the principles of concept-based curriculum and instruction.	1. Understand the principles of play-based assessment.
2. Identify the concepts that relate best to my American government course.	2. Understand the various models of play-based assessment.
3. Revise at least one unit in my American government class to follow a concept-based format.	3. Administer and interpret play-based assessment as a tool for early childhood evaluations.
Learner-Centered:	**Learner-Centered:**
1. Recognize and understand the big concepts that span disciplines and have real-life application.	1. More accurate student IEPs will provide more directed instruction.
2. Make connections between disciplines.	
Essential Question:	**Essential Question:**
How can I use a concept-based curriculum and instruction format to promote more meaningful learning in my American government class?	How can I use play-based assessment in my early-childhood program to provide useful diagnostic information regarding a student's level of development?
Related Questions:	**Related Questions:**
What is concept-based curriculum?	What is play-based assessment?
What kind of instruction supports concept-based curriculum?	What kind of information does play-based assessment generate?
Where do I find the concepts?	What models of play-based assessment are used most often?
What must I consider when designing a class curriculum?	How do the models differ?
What kind of assessment do I need?	What skills do I need to administer and interpret play-based assessment?
How do I tie this class to other classes and departments?	How do I receive training in administering play-based assessment?
Who uses a concept-based curriculum?	What drawbacks does play-based assessment have?
What are the problems associated with concept-based curriculum?	How does the information from play-based assessment compare with information produced in traditional assessments?

THE PURSUIT OF ANSWERS

Unlike most questions, the answer to the Essential Question is far less important than the question itself. Ironically, professional growth and successful completion of a growth plan do not depend on reaching a correct answer to the Essential Question. It is in the pursuit of the answer to the Essential Question that professional growth occurs.

Some answers that result will not be ones participants anticipated or intended at the beginning of the growth plan. However, the possibility of answering the question must exist. To pursue a question that does not appear to have an answer implies a wild goose chase and is not acceptable. A question with an obvious or known answer is also a poor choice, for a question with a known answer is not really a question at all. Its use as an Essential Question limits the opportunity to design a growth plan that promotes professional growth.

While some questions are unacceptable initially, the addition, deletion, or rearrangement of words can make them acceptable. "Can cooperative learning improve student performance and engage students more effectively?" is a poor Essential Question. Research tells us the answer is yes. Rephrasing the question to ask, "How can cooperative learning improve my students' performance and engage my students more effectively?" turns the question into a very substantial Essential Question. Cooperative learning remains the center of the content and knowledge to be acquired. Once the participant understands cooperative learning, he or she will apply it in the classroom for the purpose of improving student performance and keeping students engaged in learning.

The Essential Question should at least infer the learning that is to occur and the context in which learning is to be applied. Questions that can be answered with a simple yes or no, requiring little investment of effort, are poor choices. Questions too narrowly focused can provide a very limited scope of investigation and equally limited opportunities for learning. Questions too broadly defined cannot provide the focus necessary to direct learning. Questions that are too narrow or too broad, then, should be rejected or rephrased. As you can see, in the sample Essential Questions in Figure 4.6,

Figure 4.6   Essential Questions: The Good, the Bad, the Impossible!

Original Question	Revised Question
Will student participation in study groups enhance student performance and improve class participation?	How can student participation in study groups enhance students' performance and improve class participation?
Will the development of a tool to assess group interaction help improve the quality of group work?	What strategies and practices can improve the quality of group work?
Will integrated thematic units provide opportunities for long-term learning?	This question must be totally rewritten; the statement is too vague.
Will the implementation of a personal fitness program improve levels of student fitness and improve their attitudes about physical education?	The question is acceptable as written.
Will changing the science curriculum increase student achievement and motivate students to enroll in additional science classes?	This needs to be totally rewritten. It is too vague and does not indicate the targeted professional growth.
Will revising the vocational curriculum increase student enrollment in my vocation classes?	What changes will make my vocational program meaningful and engaging to students?

the use of personal and possessive pronouns in an Essential Question or any other component of the growth plan is quite appropriate. The personal reference fosters a greater sense of ownership in the Professional Growth Plan Process. It can also reassure participants of the user-friendly character of the process.

CREATING RELATED QUESTIONS

From the big Essential Question comes the Related Questions. Related Questions are more focused and specific questions whose answers help answer the Essential Question. The resources and activities that provide answers to these questions are vehicles of the learning associated with professional growth. Participants can find many of the Related Questions on the list of questions they generated during topic selection. While there is just one Essential Question, there are many Related Questions. The Related Questions define the true scope of study.

Participants can also use Related Questions as a screening device when selecting the resources and activities to promote professional growth. A measure of the worth of a particular resource or activity is its ability to answer a Related Question. The school leader should therefore review the Essential Question and the Related Questions to ensure the questions facilitate the Professional Growth Plan Process. Figure 4.7 contains the portion of the school leader checklist regarding Essential and Related Questions. (See Blackline SL-1 in Resource A for the combined checklists.)

Figure 4.7   School Leader Checklist: Essential and Related Questions

- Does the Essential Question have a known answer?
- Is it possible to answer the Essential Question?
- Do the questions require more than a yes or no answer?
- Does the Essential Question support the Professional Goals?
- Do the Related Questions support the Professional Goals?
- Will answering the Related Questions help answer the Essential Question?
- Will professional growth result from pursuing answers to the Essential and Related Questions?
- Does the Essential Question define a manageable scope of study?

DESIGNING AN ACTION PLAN

The Action Plan is the growth plan's blueprint for learning. Simply put, creating the Action Plan involves deciding what to do and when to do it. A well-constructed Action Plan that outlines tasks and activities, and establishes a realistic time frame to complete them, optimizes learning opportunities for the participant. The tasks and activities participants select for the Action Plan lead them to explore the chosen topic, then practice and use the new knowledge and skills in a meaningful context. Next, the plan directs participants to evaluate and reflect on their experiences.

Selecting Action Plan Learning Tasks and Activities

Before constructing an Action Plan, participants should consider the following:

- their background experiences and skills
- their learning style preferences
- their personal characteristics, including those related to group dynamics
- any recertification requirements they may need to address
- the availability of resources necessary to implement the plan

For example, a participant with little to no Internet experience should not make the primary learning activities dependent on Internet use, unless he or she is willing to invest the additional time to develop that competence. The individual who has difficulty accepting or offering constructive criticism from or to colleagues may not be well suited for a peer coaching experience. An individual with a demanding personal or professional schedule may not want to commit to participation in a study group. Besides promoting professional growth, growth plan activities may also meet a participant's state or district professional recertification requirements—an important consideration. Lastly, the school leader should feel confident the participant has the skills and resources necessary to complete the identified tasks and activities successfully.

The most important consideration, however, is connecting the Action Plan to the Professional and Learner-Centered Goals. The Action Plan outlines the means participants will use to achieve their Professional and Learner-Centered Goals. The learning activities participants select should facilitate and sustain the learning necessary to achieve the established goals. Regardless of the learning activities they select, participants must define clearly, step-by-step, in the Action Plan what will be done, who will do it, and when it will be completed.

Figure 4.8   Action Plan Learning

Exploration
- Gathering data and information
- Assimilating information
- Understanding the vocabulary and concepts

Application
- Getting the idea
- Connecting new knowledge and skills with other ideas that relate to it
- Using the new knowledge and skills in meaningful contexts

Evaluation
- Judging effectiveness

Reflection
- Relating and comparing current experiences with past experience and knowledge

Refinement
- Making adjustments in application and practice

ACTION PLAN LEARNING

With professional goals established, the process of identifying specific Action Plan tasks and activities and setting corresponding completion dates can begin. Figure 4.8 on page 85 outlines the phases of activity the Action Plan covers. The first six months of activities should be as detailed as possible, yet not burdensome. Ideally, the school leader knows each participant's need for structure and direction well enough to know the exact degree of detail necessary to support the participant.

It is important to remember that the choices participants make when designing the Action Plan direct their efforts and activities at least until the first Progress Meeting, which usually occurs two to three months into the implementation process. The time they spend anticipating problems and resource needs, and thinking through the logistics of specific activities, before beginning the plan can eliminate or at least minimize problems that could later cause unnecessary delays in progress, frustration, and an impediment to learning. With each task or activity statement, participants must analyze the logistics of accomplishing the task in terms of time, place, and materials. Doing so helps anticipate and address such logistical issues as scheduling site visit days early so substitutes can be obtained well in advance. If participants need particular supplies for a specific activity, they should order early so the supplies are available when participants need them. Workshop registration and making hotel and airline reservations are also tasks participants should anticipate and act on well in advance of the actual workshop. Attending to the logistical details of the activities helps sustain movement on the time line.

Most Action Plans begin by outlining activities that provide participants with opportunities to explore and investigate their topic. Workshops, conferences, study groups, readings, interviews, and site visits are just a few of the activities that expand and deepen participants' knowledge and understanding of their topic. It is not uncommon for the exploration phase to consume a disproportionately large percentage of the time allocated to complete the entire Action Plan. So the first portion of an Action Plan might look like the following:

- By October 15, assemble and prioritize a list of potential readings
- By November 30, interview Joe L. about his use of interactive strategies
- By January 15, complete designated readings and reflections
- By January 30, observe Joe L.'s classroom when he is using interactive strategies
- By February 15, conduct follow-up interview with Joe L.

Once participants acquire a knowledge base, their activities then focus on application and practice of the new knowledge. The speech teacher investigating play-based assessment uses it to evaluate her preschool students. The teacher learning to use a running record uses it in his students' reading evaluations. The evaluation phase follows, with activities that focus on evaluating participants' new experiences. During the reflection phase, participants summarize those experiences, then determine what sorts of activities will help them make adjustments to their application of the new knowledge in the refinement phase. Action Plan Learning Experiences, Blackline P-7 on page 87, offers ideas for activities for each phase of the Action Plan.

It is also very appropriate for an Action Plan to include an initial brief and cursory investigation followed by initial trials or applications, with additional and more intensive investigations later. Each Action Plan is unique to the participant and must reflect his or her needs in pursuing the established Professional and Learner-Centered Goals.

ACTION PLAN LEARNING EXPERIENCES

A SAMPLING OF CHOICES

Attend

- a university class
- conferences
- workshops

Collect

- work samples
- specified data

Conduct

- action research
- interviews
- observations
- site visits
- student case study
- surveys

Construct

- lesson plans
- specific assessments
- units of instruction
- worksheets
- instructional materials

Interpret

- specified data

Listen To

- audio recordings

Participate In

- a chat room
- a discussion group
- a study group
- peer coaching
- team teaching
- on-line tutorials/classes

Read

- books
- articles

Reflect On

- readings
- activities
- observations
- instruction

View

- multimedia
- Web sites

Blackline P-7

Many Action Plans require two or even three years to complete. Typically in a multiyear Action Plan, participants describe year one in detail, then target a general outline of activities and tentative time frames for the succeeding years. Participants revise and clarify the content of multiyear plans during Progress Meetings as the work progresses (see Chapter 5).

CAN AN ACTION PLAN CHANGE?

It is important for participants and the school leader to understand that the approved Action Plan is not cast in stone. The Action Plan is a very dynamic component of the Professional Growth Plan Process and can change, when justified, to accommodate the developing needs of the participant. As participants' knowledge and understandings grow and change with their experiences, the Action Plan, too, may need to change to reflect and accommodate those new understandings. Activities or even time frames that seemed appropriate when they first designed the Action Plan may no longer serve to advance the learning associated with the goals of the Professional Growth Plan. Participants can make these modifications in an Action Plan during regularly scheduled Progress Meetings. Participants may also request a special meeting to make changes when they recognize a need to make changes in the Action Plan. Changes in the Action Plan can be used to document a participant's professional growth; therefore, each Action Plan revision should be included in the participant's documentation or portfolio.

DESIGNING GROUP ACTION PLANS

Structuring an Action Plan for a group growth plan can be more challenging than structuring a plan for an individual. The Action Plans of group members may be similar or even exactly alike, but each participant in a group plan must have his or her own Action Plan. While the unique talents and skills of individual group members can contribute significantly to the success of a growth plan, the success or failure of a growth plan cannot be tied solely to any particular group member. It is critical to successful plan completion that group members clearly define responsibilities and time frames, and responsibilities for each phase are balanced among group members. Should the group dynamics not work out or should other changes occur that affect the composition of group participants, the Action Plan should be able, with modifications, to continue to direct the efforts of the remaining participants to successful completion of their Professional Growth Plan.

Some of the questions group members should consider in structuring a group Action Plan follow:

- Who will do what?
- How will we collect information?
- How will we share information? In writing? Orally? In a study group?
- Will group members share reflections? How?
- When will meetings of the group occur?
- How frequently will the group meet?
- How will intergroup communication occur?

As long as group members have anticipated, considered, and provided for problems, the plans should work.

EVALUATING THE PROPOSED ACTION PLAN

Before approving an Action Plan, the school leader evaluates it based on the following five criteria:

1. the activities promote learning
2. the activities address the Professional and Learner-Centered Goals
3. the resources to support the plan are available
4. the participant is capable of completing the tasks and activities
5. the time frame is realistic

The portion of the school leader checklist for an Action Plans appears in Figure 4.9. (See Blackline SL-1 in Resource A for the complete checklist.)

Figure 4.9 School Leader Checklist: Action Plan

- Do the activities outlined in the Action Plan address Professional Goals and Learner-Centered Goals?
- Do the activities cover each phase of the learning cycle: exploration, application, evaluation, reflection, and refinement?
- Are resources available to support the plan?
- Is the participant capable of completing the task and activities?
- Is the time frame realistic?

ALTERNATIVES TO AN ACTION PLAN

The Professional Growth Plan Process can be easily modified to accommodate participant participation in a formal degree program, or participation in the National Board for Professional Teaching Standards Certification process. The school leader and/or district administration must first determine whether these activities are appropriate professional growth activities for the participants involved. Then modification is a simple formatting task.

Formal Degree Program

Enrollment in an accredited master's or doctoral program for the purpose of attaining a degree may serve as a growth plan Action Plan. Depending on the program and the participant's needs, a course of study within a program may also serve as a Professional Growth Plan. A thesis or action research pursued as part of a course of study may serve as a Professional Growth Plan, too. To receive approval to undertake a program or course of study within a degree program as a Professional Growth Plan, participants must follow the format of the Professional Growth Plan and identify goals, establish an Essential Question, and clearly define documentation of growth and Methods of Evaluation.

National Board for Professional Teaching Standards Certification

Successful completion of this formal process, offered through the National Board for Professional Teaching Standards, leads to National Board Certification, valid for ten years. The process requires teachers to measure their practices against rigorous performance standards established for their field and the developmental level of their students by the National Board for Professional Teaching Standards. The year-long process consists of portfolio entries and a written examination designed to determine what a teacher knows and can do in comparison with the established standards. Again by identifying Professional Goals, and an Essential Question, the remaining tasks, timelines, and evaluations established by the National Board easily match with the components of the growth plan. For specific details, contact the National Board for Professional Teaching Standards.

IDENTIFYING MODES OF DOCUMENTATION

After formulating an Action Plan, the next step in development of the Professional Growth Plan is deciding how to document professional growth. Many educators are quite wary of the documentation process because of negative experiences with documentation or a lack of understanding of its purpose. To them, documentation conjures up images of large three-ring binders filled with plastic-covered pages of publishable quality artwork and graphics. These bring-and-brag portfolios, where the content of the portfolio is lost in the presentation, intimidate and turn off many educators to the concept of documentation.

Another vision, quite the opposite of the first, is also intimidating and off-putting. This consists of a collection of boxes, file folders, notebooks, and other paraphernalia that hold all the "stuff" participants feel is in any way related to what they are supposed to be collecting. Either scenario might suggest that documentation is just another task done for administrative compliance, and documentation has little personal or professional worth.

This book does not attempt an in-depth discussion of documentation as it relates to learning, metacognition, reflection, and critical thinking; neither does it discuss the development of professional portfolios. Within these pages, *portfolio* refers to a collection of artifacts that document professional growth. Participants can choose the organization, content, format, and presentation of these artifacts.

WHAT IS AN ARTIFACT?

In its general application, *artifact* is a term most educators understand. However, its application in a learning environment may be less clear. For the purpose of this discussion and its application to the Professional Growth Plan Process, an artifact is a product of an effort or action by an individual or group in pursuit of a professional growth goal. An artifact can be the product of an activity or experience, or it can be the product of the documentation of the activity or experience.

A graph of spelling assessment data is an artifact. The written interpretation of the graph is also an artifact. A portion of Blackline P-8, Artifacts for Documentation, which lists examples of artifacts, appears on pages 91 and 92. (The complete blackline master is in Resource B.)

ARTIFACTS FOR DOCUMENTATION

Documentation serves two purposes. First, it provides evidence of professional growth. Professional growth means you have acquired new knowledge and skills and you are actually using the new knowledge and skills.

Second, documentation promotes learning by encouraging the development of reflective thinking.

When deciding whether to include an artifact as evidence of growth, it is important to ask yourself the following questions.

WHAT DOES THIS SHOW?

- Is it evidence of your work and effort?
- Does it show your professional growth as related to your goals?
- Does it show growth in your ability to use the reflective process?
- Does it show an increase in student achievement?
- Does it show changes you have made in your instructional practices or content?
- Does it show a contribution you have made to the learning community?

If you cannot answer yes to any of the questions, do not include the artifact. Quantity is not necessarily quality!

Authentic artifacts are of most value even though they may not have eye appeal for they verify actual use. Sticky notes, handwritten notes, lesson plans, and student work samples are authentic artifacts. Incomplete or rambling sentences, cryptic notes, no punctuation, and messy handwriting all indicate real evidence.

Polished artifacts can be of value but not always. Plastic-covered pages of perfectly typed entries sometimes represent merely excessive and unnecessary work. They might even suggest manufactured evidence.

The following items can be artifacts for the purpose of documentation. This lengthy list is not all-inclusive; many other options exist.

ARTIFACTS FOR DOCUMENTATION (Continued)

DOCUMENTATION ARTIFACTS

Activity Plans

Activity Reflections

Anecdotal Records

Assessments

Awards

CDs

Checklists

Classroom Observations

Conference Summaries

Curriculum Materials

Grade Sheets/Evaluation Reports

Homework Assignments

Instructional Materials

Instructional Planning Calendars

Learning Logs

Lesson Plans

Likert Scales

Management Plans

Mentoring Activities

Multimedia

New Certification/Degree

Newsletters

Newspaper Articles

Observation Reflections

Observational Instruments

Parent Contact Data

Parent Contact Log

Parent Correspondence

Peer Reviews

Performance Assessments

Photographs

Pre/Post Self-Assessments

Professional Presentations

Rating Scales

Reading Logs

Reading Reflections

Revised Professional Growth Plans

Standardized Test Scores

Student Projects

Student Work Samples

Surveys

   Student

   Parent

   Colleague

Tally Sheets

Teacher Journal

Transcripts

Unit Plans

Visual Maps

Work Logs

Workshop Logs

Several items in the list of artifacts are forms that help participants keep track of and organize their growth plan activities for potential use as documentation later. Blackline masters of these forms—Anecdotal Record, Blackline P-9; Work Log, Blackline P-10; Reading Reflection Guide, Blackline P-11; Activity Reflection Guide, P-12; and Observation Reflection Guide, P-13—appear in Resource B. A sample completed Work Log appears on page 94.

ORGANIZING ARTIFACTS

Participants can organize artifacts to suit their personal preference and working style, using binders, crates, file boxes, banker's boxes, and multimedia resources. The portfolio of artifacts submitted as part of the growth plan evaluation process can take any form the participant wishes. The school leader's major contribution to this effort is to ensure that participants understand documentation and what they will need at the conclusion of the plan.

DOCUMENTATION: A PRODUCT AND A PROCESS

The purpose of this discussion is to give school leaders an overview of the role documentation plays in the Professional Growth Plan Process and also explain how to support participants in their documentation efforts.

The documentation of the Professional Growth Plan Process has a traditional definition as a noun. Documentation is evidence. It is proof. It is validation. It is verification. But it has a second definition as a verb—documenting is the act of producing the evidence, the proof, the validation, the verification.

Documentation also serves two functions in the Professional Growth Plan Process. First and foremost, documentation promotes learning. Second, documentation verifies that growth and change have occurred to participants (the learners) as well as to the school leader (the facilitator) and to an administrator (the evaluator) if the process is used for evaluation or supervision (see also Figure 4.10).

Figure 4.10   The Purpose of Documentation

1. Promotes learning by encouraging the development of reflective thinking
2. Provides information for decision making
3. Provides evidence of professional growth

Through the activities that generate documentation, learning occurs. Participants plan for some of this learning, but they also experience learning they do not anticipate. For example, to learn to administer and interpret a developmental spelling assessment is an intended learning a participant defines within a growth plan goal. The documentation he generates as evidence of that learning might be the assessment data. He generates another form of documentation, a visual presentation, when he creates a graph of the assessment data. Creating a graph on a computer for the first time is

WORK LOG

DATE	LOCATION	PARTICIPANTS	ACTIVITY SUMMARY	TIME
9/3	School	Jenny/Mike	Searched Internet for information Found and printed out articles and other references	2.5 hrs.
9/15	School	Jenny/Mike	Sorted articles—decided which to keep and which to pitch Copied articles then decided the order we would read them and how to respond to them	1 hr.
10/3	Edison Junior High	Jenny/Mike	Visited Ted Brown's 7th– and 8th-grade social studies classrooms; observed cooperative learning groups, then talked with Ted	4 hrs.
10/10	Home	Jenny	Read and took notes on article 3	45 min.

Name: _Jenny Franklin_   Page _1_ of _1_

Blackline P-10

incidental learning he did not anticipate; it occurred as a result of the intended learning. The generation of the graph (documentation) required the participant to learn new skills (using a computer to create a graph) unrelated to the targeted learning. This is an example of the incidental or unanticipated learning documentation promotes.

The processing of an activity or experience required for documentation also encourages learning. During this processing—describing, analyzing, and reflecting on the activity—participants realize deeper understandings and insights (Costa & Garmston, 2006).

Those educators who have used authentic student work to document growth or who have used growth portfolios successfully will need little guidance or support in this area. They understand the real value of documentation. Those who have hesitated to embrace authentic assessment fully may develop a new and different understanding of its value as a powerful tool of learning for both the teacher and the learner after working through the Professional Growth Plan Process.

Educators experienced and comfortable with identification, collection, and evaluation of artifacts to document growth may not need the following activities. For those lacking the background and knowledge, however, the following procedures and accompanying blackline masters can help the school leader introduce them to the basic concepts and steps involved in documentation and reflective practice.

The Professional Growth Plan Process can change participants' beliefs about and attitudes toward documentation from something they do for others to a tool of learning they can use for themselves. The school leader's role is to help them come to understand documentation as a tool of learning and decision making by educating uninformed participants about what constitutes documentation, why documentation is important and useful, how to recognize it, and, finally, how to assemble and manage it. To maximize the potential of documentation, participants must understand the following:

1. Documentation is any artifact or product of an experience or activity.

2. Documentation provides evidence of an experience or activity, and analysis of this evidence provides a basis for making informed decisions regarding their practice.

3. By analyzing artifacts and asking the following questions for each one, participants can quickly recognize artifacts that provide useful information. (These questions also appear on the first page of Blackline P-8, Artifacts for Documentation, in the section What Does This Show? See Resource B for this blackline.)
   – Is it evidence of your work and effort?
   – Does it show your professional growth as related to your goals?
   – Does it show growth in your ability to use the reflective process?
   – Does it show an increase in student achievement?
   – Does it show changes you have made in your instructional practices or content?
   – Does it show a contribution you have made to the learning community?

4. Organizing documentation is a personal choice, but the school leader can provide ideas for helping with organization such as using files, notebooks, boxes, or other electronic means or filing by goals, by evaluation criteria, or by Action Plan activity.

This initial introduction and overview of documentation becomes more meaningful to participants through their participation in the entire Professional Growth Plan Process.

The blackline masters related to documentation (P-8 through P-21, Resource B) help participants see that documentation is a natural product of learning. They can help the school leader assure participants that their activities produce artifacts needed for documentation naturally; participants do not need to manufacture them. Another important understanding is that authentic work does not necessarily have "eye appeal." Artifacts with coffee stains, phone numbers on scraps of paper, even a "To Do" list can supply valuable evidence of professional growth!

Everyone enjoys viewing the perfectly typed page with clear and descriptive graphics enclosed in a protective covering. The polished artifact is user-friendly and certainly reflects the pride of ownership. At times this type of documentation is quite appropriate, very necessary, and should be encouraged. For some, typing is far easier than writing by hand, while others find the management of files much easier on the computer than in a drawer. Neat and printed is fine; however, many artifacts are working documents and sometimes only transitional documents. Participants must balance the time required to produce polished artifacts with the time production takes away from other professional responsibilities, including other growth plan activities. They must ask themselves whether the purpose of the artifact warrants the investment of time. Leaving this decision with participants, as a matter of personal preference, enables participants to continue to assume total responsibility and accountability for their learning.

WHERE WILL ARTIFACTS COME FROM?

To assist those individuals who need additional help identifying artifacts that will result from their work, a graphic organizer, Documentation Artifacts Map, Blackline P-14, appears in Resource B; a completed sample is on the next page. Having established Professional and Learner-Centered Goals and an Action Plan, participants have all the tools necessary to generate a list of artifacts that their growth plan efforts can produce. (Using the list of possible artifacts from Artifacts for Documentation, Blackline P-8, makes the task even easier. See Resource B for blackline.)

Working with the school leader or independently, participants place a goal at the center of the Documentation Artifacts Map. Referring to the Action Plan, they list an activity that is tied to that goal on the line extending from the center circle. Using the list of artifacts as a prompt, participants then list the artifacts the activity will produce, adding spokes and lines to the organizer to accommodate all the activities supporting a particular goal. By completing a sheet for each Professional and Learner-Centered Goal, participants create a comprehensive list of potential artifacts. They can use the lists to identify Baseline Data as well as which artifacts they will use specifically to demonstrate professional growth. A discussion of these artifacts appears in the Identifying Baseline Data and Defining Methods of Evaluation sections in this chapter.

ARTIFACTS: WHAT TO KEEP?

Artifacts begin to accumulate quickly once the Action Plan activities begin. Some participants choose to keep each and every piece of paper they use during the growth

DOCUMENTATION ARTIFACTS MAP

Artifacts:

reading reflections

summaries

notes

Artifacts:

summary notes

reading reflections

Activity
Review instructional
support materials

Activity
View videotapes

GOAL

Understand the
characteristics
and use of
interactive
instructional
strategies

Activity
Readings

Activity
Visit Cathy D.'s classroom

Artifacts:

observation reflection

summary notes

Artifacts:

notes

audio recording

Cathy's lesson plan

student work samples

plan process. Others soon create a screening process to minimize the accumulation of unnecessary items growth plan activity generates. Either way, all participants eventually need to be able to determine an artifact's usefulness.

Participants should choose to keep an artifact for at least three reasons, and they can use these three reasons as an initial screening tool:

1. The artifact may document professional growth.

2. The artifact may provide the information necessary for making a future decision, or it may serve as the basis for future documentation.

3. The artifact may serve participants in a different area of their practice that is totally unrelated to the growth plan process.

Most artifacts can document professional growth, sometimes by providing a benchmark by which participants note change in their practices. Lesson plans created before a growth plan was initiated that do not include use of cooperative learning strategies may serve as a benchmark to compare with lesson plans created at the conclusion of a growth plan that do include cooperative learning. By examining each artifact in relation to the criteria established for professional growth, the participant can further classify or sort the artifacts. Again, participants should ask themselves the following question: Does the artifact demonstrate

- the acquisition of skill or knowledge?
- growth in the ability to use the reflective process?
- increased student achievement?
- changes in practice?
- a contribution to the learning community?

For example, a participant whose Professional Goal is "Use study groups to deliver instruction" collects lesson plans, student work samples, a videotape of students working in study groups, a photograph of groups, and audiotape interviews of students. After reviewing the five artifacts, the participant decides that the photograph does not really demonstrate anything but students sitting in groups and she eliminates it.

Learning From Documentation

An artifact's real value can lie in its ability to encourage and support the reflection that promotes deeper thinking, learning, and change (Taggart & Wilson, 2005). Because artifacts represent an activity or experience, they can help participants by facilitating the processing of the activity or experience. Such processing often allows participants to construct new meaning or gain new insights from the activity or experience. This new knowledge and insight often initiates changes in professional practices. Before accepting or believing in a new or different practice, educators often need to see "proof" that the intervention is, in fact, effective with their students. If one accepts the notion that belief follows practice, educators need to see evidence of the effectiveness of a change (Guskey, 2000), and it is important for school leaders to direct participants' attention to artifacts that may document

Figure 4.11   School Leader Checklist: Documentation

- Does the practitioner understand what artifacts are and the purpose of documentation?
- Does the targeted documentation represent the growth plan?
- Does an adequate amount of documentation exist from which to select Baseline Data and evaluation data?
- Are the resources and supplies needed to support the documentation available?
- Has the participant targeted enough artifacts to document each professional growth criterion adequately?
- Does the practitioner have a plan for organizing the artifacts?

those positive changes. The portion of the school leader checklist for documentation appears in Figure 4.11; see Blackline SL-1 in Resource A for the complete checklist.

THE ROLE OF ARTIFACTS AND REFLECTION

Asking participants to look critically for the learning an artifact does or does not represent is a step toward enhanced reflective practice and toward changing participants' practices. Reflective thinking, at its simplest, is thinking about what has happened, why it happened, and the significance of what happened (Costa & Garmston, 2006). It is about identifying causal relationships and making comparisons. It is important to encourage educators to look critically at artifacts that evidence change to determine what brought about the change. Examining artifacts for diagnostic purposes can produce more prescriptive practices in participants as participants look for, understand, and predict causal relationships.

As in all other aspects of the Professional Growth Plan Process, documentation of reflective practices must adapt to meet the needs and abilities of participants. The reticent participant, less motivated or skilled in reflective practices, will need more support from the school leader than the participant who is articulate, thorough, and well developed in reflective thinking.

Reflection and reflective practice are not necessarily familiar terms to many educators, although they use reflection intuitively in the execution of their jobs and in activities of daily living. They may think of reflective practices as "just more jargon." Because this response sometimes masks a fear of the unknown that can create barriers to learning and to progress in the Professional Growth Plan Process, the school leader must present reflection in the simplest, user-friendly terms. The school leader's use of simple prompts and questions to encourage reflection also models questioning patterns that participants can easily make a regular part of their own routine. Resource B contains reflection guides for various activities and purposes (P-11, P-12, and P-13). These guides offer specific and general questions to help participants recognize causal relationships and to promote comparisons between the participant's beliefs and practices and what they experienced. Two other forms, Reflection Basics, Blackline P-15 (see page 101), and When You Document, You . . . , Blackline P-16 (see page 102), provide a quick and simple set of questions participants can ask themselves to promote reflection. (Both appear as blackline masters in Resource B.)

Blackline P-15, Reflection Basics, lists questions the reflective educator should get into the habit of asking. Educators reflect on action as they go back and analyze what happened during a lesson or activity, looking for cause and effect relationships, patterns of behaviors or responses, and indicators of the effectiveness of the lesson. Educators reflect in action while they are delivering instruction, and based on these reflections, they make decisions and predictions about what will happen next. Again they are looking for cause and effect relationships and patterns of behavior or response to direct their next decision or response. Both types of reflection—in action and on action—are important to learning. Blackline P-16, When You Document, You . . . , reminds participants what they need to reflect on in their classroom practice.

Understanding what happened and why it happened makes for informed and better decisions relating both to participants' practice and to their growth plan. Throughout the Professional Growth Plan Process, participants must decide what to do next. Through documentation, participants come to realize that a thorough analysis of artifacts can provide the information necessary to make the "best" next decision. One hopes that as a result of their experiences with documentation, any misconceptions participants have will be resolved, and they will find value in the documentation process far beyond any accountability purposes it serves. Transferring this concept of artifact analysis for prescriptive purposes to the instructional setting helps facilitate changes in participants' professional practice.

DOCUMENTING GROWTH

The determination of successful completion of a growth plan is whether the participant has met Professional and Learner-Centered Goals. For that determination, documentation must exist to confirm that goals have been met. Once potential artifacts that will document all the learning associated with a growth plan are identified, they need to be carefully examined and evaluated to determine which have the greatest potential for documenting growth. Following that examination, participants can complete the Baseline Data and Methods of Evaluation components of the growth plan.

To make the best artifact selections for Baseline Data and Methods of Evaluation, the participant must be familiar with the criteria used to evaluate successful growth plan completion. The school leader should review these thoroughly with participants when first introducing the growth plan process and again during plan development. Two forms can help with this review. Blackline P-17, Growth Plan Evaluation Criteria, on page 106, identifies professional growth and student achievement as the two basic criteria. Within professional growth, four more specific criteria are defined. Growth Plan Evaluation—Documenting Professional Growth, Blackline P-18, on pages 107 and 108, lists under each criterion the types of artifacts that can provide the documentation necessary to verify growth. (Both blacklines appear in Resource B.)

IDENTIFYING BASELINE DATA

Baseline Data are the data participants use as a starting point to measure growth that occurs during the Professional Growth Plan Process. The data should reflect

REFLECTION BASICS

**What Do You Do? Why Do You Do It?
Should You Do It Again?**

ON ACTION What has happened?	IN ACTION What is happening?
What did I do?	What am I doing?
Why did I do it?	Why am I doing it?
What happened as a result of what I did?	What is happening as a result of what I am doing?
What will I do next time?	What should I do next?
Why?	Why?

THINK!

What have I just experienced?

How does that compare with what I know and believe?

So what does that mean?

Blackline P-15

WHEN YOU DOCUMENT, YOU . . .

DESCRIBE

Who? What? Where?
What was the setting?
Who was involved?
What happened?
What was the specific sequence of events?
Who did what?

ANALYZE

Why? How?
Why did it happen?
How did it happen?

REFLECT

So What?
What does it mean?

participants' beginning knowledge and skill level and provide a basis for comparing them with knowledge and skill levels at the plan's completion. The Baseline Data may also represent student data as they relate to Learner-Centered Goals.

Baseline Data provide a benchmark from which to measure growth or change. The benchmarked growth or change may relate to any aspect of the instructional practice, or it may relate to student performance or achievement data. These data, which can be quite informal, can serve a formative as well as a summative purpose for participants and the school leader. As participants progress through their Action Plan, they can compare the data produced with the Baseline Data to determine what modifications they need to make for the next step in the Action Plan.

The school leader may review some of the data during Progress Meetings (see Chapter 5) to make sure participants are on track, and do not need help interpreting data to ensure they consider all variables. For example, data may indicate an intervention is not effective or only minimally effective. But the school leader helps the participant identify an inordinate number of absences due to a flu epidemic, proving the data are not reliable. The school leader may suggest extending the Action Plan timeline to extend the intervention period and the data collection so they reflect regular attendance patterns. Or perhaps the school leader recognizes the participant does not understand an intervention well enough to implement it effectively. The school leader can suggest modifying the Action Plan timeline to allow the participant to acquire more background knowledge before assessing the effectiveness of the intervention.

In some plans, however, the data necessary to make a comparison may not exist until the conclusion of the Action Plan. For example, if part of a Professional Goal is to acquire new knowledge or skills, it may be difficult to document the absence of the knowledge or skills. A PE teacher who does not have an articulated curriculum that spells out what students should know and be able to do at each grade level has no Baseline Data. In this instance, the lack of any data may serve as a baseline or beginning point.

Multiple measures can be used for Baseline Data, or only one measure can be used. Preintervention tests or surveys are some common measures. Sample lesson plans, unit designs, or instructional materials used before the growth plan are just a few examples of Baseline Data. Student performance data and nontest data such as discipline referrals, graduation rates, and attendance figures provide Baseline Data also. Participants must understand the variety of information that can serve as Baseline Data. It is essential that participants understand that qualitative data such as observational checklists, surveys, and work samples of students and the participant are as valuable as quantitative data. Of course, those quantifiable measures such as standardized tests, grades, discipline referrals, and the rate of absence provide the data for valuable statistical analysis. But the form the data take is less important than the information provided. The primary recommendation is that the data provide a rich base of information from which participants can draw valid and reliable conclusions about the impact of their new knowledge and skills on their practice.

The amount and content of the Baseline Data vary with each plan. A plan focusing on a developmental spelling program may include a parent survey, student survey, writing samples, and spelling tests as Baseline Data. Participants might use the same artifacts for the summative evaluation. Baseline Data for a growth plan whose focus is learning to use running records to diagnose student reading levels may not exist at all because the teacher knows nothing about the running record assessment tool. Regardless of the data selected, it should reflect a direct connection to established Professional or Learner-Centered Goals. The portion of the school leader checklist for Baseline Data appears in Figure 4.12; the complete checklist, Blackline SL-1, is in Resource A.

Figure 4.12   School Leader Checklist: Baseline Data

- Do Baseline Data exist to show a beginning point?
- Can the data selected provide a basis for comparison and analysis of comparable data collected after the intervention?
- Can the data document professional growth: new knowledge or skill, change in practice, ability to reflect, contribution to the learning community, or improvement in student achievement?
- Are the data and the data collection and interpretation processes simple enough for participants to manage?

DEFINING METHODS OF EVALUATION

The Methods of Evaluation component of the Professional Growth Plan describes the documentation that will show that the growth defined in the goal statements has occurred. If that documentation does indeed exist when the plan is complete, it confirms the desired growth has occurred. Defining the Methods of Evaluation at the beginning of the plan provides a very clear ending point for the growth plan and a clear target for data collection and evaluation.

For first-time plans particularly, defining Methods of Evaluation is quite challenging, but participants can alter the Methods of Evaluation during plan implementation. Ideally, a clearly defined Method of Evaluation statement has the following four descriptors:

1. A brief description of the artifact

2. A reference to the growth indicator (how a later artifact will differ from an earlier one)

3. A target number of artifacts to be included

4. The time frame for collection

The specific content of the descriptors varies from plan to plan, participant to participant, and school to school because descriptors are always tied to the goals and the criteria they support. However, factors unrelated to the actual learning may also dictate the detail of description. Union agreements, evaluation or supervision guidelines, and a building's general climate of trust all contribute to the degree of specificity required in this component. More specificity minimizes the subjectivity in the evaluation process, and the degree of subjectivity of the growth plan evaluation process may be an issue with unions, evaluators, and buildings where trust is also an issue. However, whatever form the descriptors take, they must demonstrate the participant's acquisition and application of new knowledge and skills. The ability to accommodate the unique needs and abilities of the individual is compromised when administrative directive or contract language demands excessive uniformity and consistency in defining this and other growth plan components.

With luck, the learning environment is supportive enough to allow modifications to the descriptors as the documentation process becomes clearer to participants. These changes occur typically during a Progress Meeting (see Chapter 5) when it becomes apparent that the Methods of Evaluation do not document what they were originally intended to document. Once agreed on by the school leader and participant, however, the Methods of Evaluation should not be changed unless both agree to the changes. Mutually agreeing on changes means all parties involved acknowledge and understand the problem that has arisen and accept the proposed solution. Mutual agreement prevents frequent, unnecessary, or nuisance changes in a plan, maintaining the integrity of the plan and the process. Guidelines for making changes may need to be more specific in schools and districts with strong labor agreements, where the level of trust is low, or where the need for consistency and precision is high. As in the need for specificity in an evaluation descriptor, specificity of guidelines for changing Methods of Evaluation minimizes the opportunity for subjectivity to come into play.

In keeping with the principles of learning on which the Professional Growth Plan Process is built, the Methods of Evaluation component should reflect the abilities of participants and the content of the growth plan. Those with greater abilities may have more sophisticated and complex Methods of Evaluation. Those with more limited ability may use simpler, less complex Methods of Evaluation.

HELPING THOSE WITH DATA PHOBIA

Any reference to data, data collection, or data analysis creates great anxiety in many educators. Participant visions of formulas, graphs, numbers, and graduate classes in statistics can present immediate roadblocks to the implementation of the growth plan process. One of the greatest challenges for the school leader is changing these participants' perception of the value and importance of data collection and interpretation to their practice.

Those confident in data collection and interpretation can quickly complete the Baseline Data and Methods of Evaluation components of their growth plan, either independently or with minimal support. Those more hesitant must receive more support. With great caution and care, the school leader must introduce those who are wary to a step-by-step, fail-safe, how-to of data collection and interpretation.

As with many participant beliefs, attitudes, and practices that change through the Professional Growth Plan Process, negative perception of data collection can change to positive when participants, required to use data collection, come to understand its value through that use (Guskey, 2000). To verify successful completion of a growth plan, participants must provide documentation that professional growth has occurred, and documentation requires the collection and interpretation of their own data. By collecting and interpreting data for their own purposes, participants can experience the potential for data collection and interpretation to inform and improve their practice when they transfer and apply their new knowledge about data collection and analysis to other areas of their instructional program. For example, finding the data collected from a student survey about study groups useful, a teacher may use student surveys to collect information about other aspects of her instructional program such as grading policies or relevance of homework assignments. This understanding can have a

GROWTH PLAN EVALUATION CRITERIA

DOCUMENTATION SHOWS

1. Professional Growth

Acquisition of new knowledge and skills

Application of new knowledge and skills
(changes in instructional practices)

Enhanced reflective practices

Contributions to learning community

2. Improved Student Achievement

Blackline P-17

GROWTH PLAN EVALUATION

DOCUMENTING PROFESSIONAL GROWTH

The artifacts listed below may help you document your professional growth. The artifacts are grouped by the criteria for evaluating professional growth but are not limited to just one criterion. This list is not all-inclusive; several other artifact possibilities exist.

ACQUISITION OF NEW KNOWLEDGE AND SKILLS

What artifacts demonstrate that you have acquired new knowledge and skills as a result of your Professional Growth Plan work?

Teacher Work Samples

Activity Plans	Homework Assignments	Parent Contact Log	Tally Sheets
Anecdotal Records	Instructional Materials	Peer Reviews	Teacher Journal
Assessments	Instructional Planning Calendars	Pre/Post Self-Assessments	Transcripts
Awards		Rating Scales	Unit Plans
CDs	Lesson Plans	Reflection Guides	Video/Audio Recordings
Checklists	Likert Scales	Revised Professional Growth Plans	Visual Maps
Classroom Observations	Management Plans	Surveys	Work Logs
Conference Summaries	New Certification/ Degree	Student	Workshop Log
Contact Log	Newspaper Articles	Parent	
Curriculum Materials	Observation Instruments	Colleague	
Grade Sheets/Evaluation Reports			

APPLICATION OF KNOWLEDGE AND SKILLS: CHANGES IN INSTRUCTIONAL PRACTICES

What artifacts demonstrate that you have incorporated permanently in your instructional practice the newly acquired knowledge and skills? What artifacts link new knowledge and skills with classroom practice?

Anecdotal Records	**Lesson Plans**	**Newsletters**	**Student Work Samples**
Curriculum Materials	**Management Plans**	**Parent Correspondence**	**Unit Plans**
Instructional Materials	**Multimedia**	**Photographs**	

WHAT ARTIFACTS DEMONSTRATE THE TIME AND EFFORT YOU INVESTED?

Teacher Work Samples
(see Acquisition of New Knowledge and Skills)

GROWTH PLAN EVALUATION (Continued)

Student Work Samples

Homework Assignments	Products
• Projects	• Multimedia Formats • Portfolios • Work/Reading Logs • Writing

ENHANCED REFLECTIVE PRACTICES

What artifacts demonstrate that you have done any of the following:

- Analyzed the principles that underlie new or different instructional practices
- Used these principles in making choices regarding your instructional practices
- Assessed the effectiveness of the instructional practices
- Employed critical thinking to evaluate the instructional practices fully
  Reflection Guides
  Teacher Journal
  Learning Logs
  Reflections on Student Work Samples

CONTRIBUTIONS TO LEARNING COMMUNITY

What artifacts demonstrate contributions resulting from your Professional Growth Plan efforts?

Submission of Articles for Publication
Presentations at Professional Forums
Awards/Recognition
Mentoring Activities
Coaching Activities

IMPROVED STUDENT ACHIEVEMENT

What artifacts demonstrate that student achievement has improved as a result of your Professional Growth Plan work?

Anecdotal Records
Grade Sheets/Evaluation Reports
Multimedia
Performance Assessments
Publisher Tests
Revised Student Work
Standardized Test Scores
Student Work Samples (over time or pre/post intervention)

great impact not only on the area addressed by a participant's Professional Growth Plan but also on the participant's entire practice.

Also at this point, participants should understand the criteria used to evaluate successful completion of a growth plan. With this knowledge (see Blackline P-1 or Blackline P-17 in Resource B), the Methods of Evaluation Plan Sheet, Blackline P-19, and the Artifact Organizer, Blackline P-20, participants can take the next step, selecting the Methods of Evaluation. The plan sheet (pictured on pages 110 and 111) offers prompts for participants to think about as they review their list of artifacts. (A complete blackline master appears in Resource B.) Participants can use the Artifact Organizer to sort artifacts by goal and see whether they can serve as Baseline Data, growth data, or both. A sample completed Artifact Organizer appears on page 112; a blackline master is in Resource B. Sorting through the artifacts and completing these blacklines force participants to think through and articulate the value of each artifact.

Another graphic organizer, Evaluation Artifact Organizer, Blackline P-21, can help sort artifacts by growth plan evaluation criteria. A completed portion of the Evaluation Artifact Organizer appears on pages 113 and 114. (The blackline master is in Resource B.) Participants sort artifacts by the evaluation criteria they support. Many artifacts can serve more than one criterion. Without question, artifacts should exist for each criterion, but an equitable distribution among the criteria is unrealistic and should not be expected. If a goal does not have any artifacts, then participants need to reexamine and, if necessary, redesign the Action Plan to ensure that all goals have learning activities that generate artifacts. Variations in quantity and quality of artifacts from criterion to criterion and plan to plan reflect the growth plan goals, the activities of the Action Plan, and the participant's abilities.

It is most important that participants and the school leader have a clear and common understanding of the Methods of Evaluation they will use to determine a successful growth plan. They should not sign a plan until they have this understanding. The portion of the school leader checklist for Methods of Evaluation appears in Figure 4.13; the complete checklist, Blackline SL-1, appears in Resource A.

Figure 4.13   School Leader Checklist: Methods of Evaluation

- Does the participant address each Professional and Learner-Centered Goal?
- Can the artifacts in the growth plan document growth?
- Are the evaluation methods reasonable and doable?
- Does everyone understand and agree with what professional growth in this plan will look like?
- Is a Method of Evaluation present for each of the criteria that characterize professional growth?

IDENTIFYING RESOURCE NEEDS

If the Action Plan is the blueprint of the Professional Growth Plan, resources are the construction tools and materials from which participants build new knowledge and skills. Identification and acquisition of quality resources to support learning are vital to the Professional Growth Process.

(Text continues on page 115)

METHODS OF EVALUATION PLAN SHEET

Analyze each artifact in your documentation list and project which one(s) might best represent your growth. It is important that you understand and can explain why or how it can represent growth.

ACQUISITION OF NEW KNOWLEDGE/SKILLS

What new knowledge/skills will you acquire?

What artifact(s) will exist to prove it?

How does each artifact selected show growth?

How many of each artifact will you need to show growth?

Over what period of time will you collect each artifact?

What characteristic of the artifact or change in the artifact will reflect your acquisition of new knowledge/skills?

APPLICATION OF NEW KNOWLEDGE/SKILLS

What new knowledge/skills will you use?

What artifact(s) will exist to demonstrate that you are using the new knowledge/skills?

How will each prove that you are using your new knowledge/skills?

How representative is the artifact?

What period of time will the artifact reflect?

What evidence exists of the time and effort you have invested in your learning?

Blackline P-19 (Page 1 of 2)

ENHANCED REFLECTIVE PRACTICES

Educators need to reflect "on action," going back and analyzing what happened in a lesson or activity and "in action," during instruction. What artifacts demonstrate that your on-action and in-action reflections

- show greater depth?
- use more descriptive words?
- provide more explanation and reasoning why?
- question what you did or what happened?
- examine and try to explain the consequences of instructional decisions?
- are tied to theory or principles?
- are tied to the context of the situation?

CONTRIBUTIONS TO LEARNING COMMUNITY

What will you do to share your new knowledge/skills with the learning community?

What artifact(s) will show that you have acquired or improved a collaborative skill, making you a better member of the learning community?

IMPROVED STUDENT ACHIEVEMENT

When should evidence of improved student achievement exist?

What artifact(s) will show that student achievement has improved as a result of your new knowledge and skills?

Can you use this artifact as Baseline Data?

How will this artifact show the impact of your new knowledge and skills on student achievement?

_____ TENTATIVE PLAN   _____ FINAL PLAN   Date: _____

ARTIFACT ORGANIZER

GOAL: Understand the characteristics and use of interactive instructional strategies

BASELINE DATA *(Artifacts)*	**GROWTH DATA** *(Artifacts)*
Lesson plans	Summaries
Student surveys	Reflections
Video of classroom session	Lesson plans
Student work samples	Student work samples
	Video
	Work log
	Work day reflections

GOAL: Use study groups to deliver instruction

BASELINE DATA *(Artifacts)*	**GROWTH DATA** *(Artifacts)*
Lesson plans	Lesson plans
Video	Video
Student work samples	Student work samples
Instructional materials	Instructional materials
Student surveys	Student surveys

EVALUATION ARTIFACT ORGANIZER

New Knowledge/Skills:

BASELINE DATA *(Artifacts)*	GROWTH DATA *(Artifacts)*
None—I don't know anything about it!	Summaries of readings Reflections of readings, observations, activities

Application of New Knowledge/Skills:

BASELINE DATA *(Artifacts)*	GROWTH DATA *(Artifacts)*
Lesson plans Student work samples Videotape of class sessions	Lesson plans Student work samples Videotape of class sessions

Enhanced Reflective Practice:

BASELINE DATA *(Artifacts)*	GROWTH DATA *(Artifacts)*

Blackline P-21 (Page 1 of 2)

EVALUATION ARTIFACT ORGANIZER (Continued)

Contributions to the Learning Community:

BASELINE DATA (Artifacts)	GROWTH DATA (Artifacts)

Improved Student Achievement:

BASELINE DATA (Artifacts)	GROWTH DATA (Artifacts)

(Text continued from page 109)

Resources cover a rather broad category of items, people, and events that can contribute to an individual's professional growth. Resource needs within one plan may be as diverse as CDs for documentation purposes, attendance at a workshop or conference, books, college courses on videotape or online, and a particular software package. The Resource Needs of any growth plan are as unique as the plan itself.

Because the Professional Growth Plan Process is a staff development tool, the school or district should assume primary responsibility for funding acquisition of resources to support Professional Growth Plans. (See the detailed discussion of allocation of resources in Chapter 2.) The school leader must understand the total support available to make resource allocation decisions on an individual plan basis.

From the first stages of plan development, Resource Needs are a consideration. Early discussions about possible growth plan topics should address the issue of essential resources. It is the school leader's responsibility to anticipate Resource Needs and understand the school's capacity to support those needs, both of individual plans and of all plans collectively. To allow a participant to go through the entire growth plan design process only to find out that the resources necessary to support the plan are not available, making the growth plan unacceptable, is an irresponsible act on the part of the school leader. While the school leader should know how much money can be spent and where participants might find resources, it is primarily the participant's responsibility to determine the availability of resources to support the plan before settling on a topic.

If resources to support a plan topic are not readily available, particularly research materials, the participant must select a different topic. If the success of a growth plan depends on access to a particular resource, the participant must ensure the resource is available before work on plan development proceeds. Once participants identify a resource, the school leader must determine whether the school can financially support the resource request. If the school cannot support the resource request and alternative funding is not available, the school leader and participant must determine the importance of the resource to the successful completion of the growth plan. If the resource is essential to success, the participant must modify or redefine the plan topic to eliminate the need for the resource. If essential resources are not available to support a growth plan, the school leader should not approve the plan.

Most resources necessary to support growth plans are readily available and within most staff development budgets. It is only the isolated topic that requires expensive or obscure resources. A more common challenge is the organization of resources to facilitate their acquisition.

Some topics have an overwhelming amount of information and instructional materials available, and culling through the materials and resources to select those that address the needs of the participant can be a monumental task. Those participants who need help identifying or organizing possible resources can use the Resource Survey, Blackline P-22, on page 116. (A blackline master is also included in Resource B.) This list represents a starting point from which the individual can conduct a more critical review of resources. The most important factor in selecting a resource is its ability to help participants reach their goals. An initial list of resources may be much shorter than a list submitted after work begins.

Unfortunately, most school districts have limited financial resources. To ensure adequate planning and fair allocation of available resources, the school leader needs the estimated annual costs of each plan. Participants can assist the school leader by projecting a budget for their plan. With the Resource Request Budget Form, Blackline

RESOURCE SURVEY

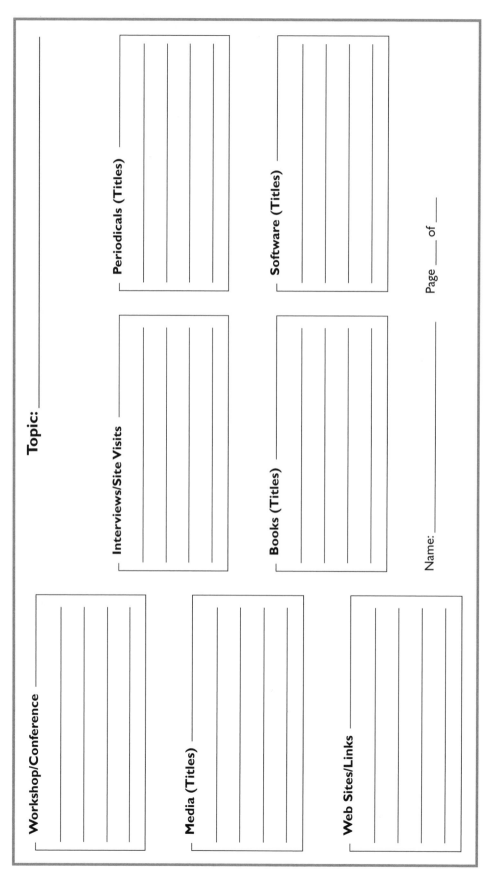

Topic: _____

Workshop/Conference

Media (Titles)

Web Sites/Links

Interviews/Site Visits

Periodicals (Titles)

Books (Titles)

Software (Titles)

Name: _____

Page ____ of ____

Blackline P-22

RESOURCE REQUEST BUDGET FORM

Projected Expenses for Fiscal Year 20_____ –20_____

Professional Growth Plan:

Participants:

Projected Completion Date:

TOTAL $_____

Workshop/Conference/Site Visit:

Title/Sponsor	Date	Fee	Expenses
			Travel: Food: Hotel:
			Travel: Food: Hotel:

Total Workshop/Conference: $_____

Print Materials:

Title/Author	Amount

Total Print: $_____

Supplies:

Item	Amount

Total Supplies: $_____

RESOURCE REQUEST BUDGET FORM (Continued)

Media/Software:

Title/Publisher	Amount

Total Software: $ _____

Substitutes:

# of Days	Projected Date(s)	Amount

Total Substitutes: $ _____

Miscellaneous:

Item	Amount

Total Miscellaneous: $_____

Grand Total*: $ _____

Comments:

*Please remember to include shipping and handling costs in your figures.

P-23 (see pages 117 and 118), participants prioritize the items as essential or desired so the school leader can approve a plan that meets the essential needs, and monies not available for the desired items will not compromise the growth plan process. (See Chapter 2, pages 22 and 23, for a sample completed Resource Request Budget Form; see Resource B for a blackline master.) If monies are or become available for the desired items, it will enhance the learning opportunities. While it is understood that participants can only project some figures, the more accurate the figures, the better decisions a school leader can make regarding budget allocations.

In growth plans with multiple participants, the group must decide what resources they can share and what resources each group member needs. Workshops and conferences can present unique problems for the group and school leader. To send a group to a workshop or conference is an expensive proposition. If there is more than one conference or workshop, the issue becomes even more difficult. Does the entire group or a representative go? The potential members of a group should discuss this eventuality when deciding to function as a group.

Resource Needs change throughout the life span of a growth plan. Once a plan is initiated, participants may discover the need for resources they were not aware of during the design phase. They may also discover that what they initially thought was a valuable resource may not be useful at all. Before purchasing materials, participants should make every attempt to ensure that the resource does, in fact, meet the needs of the learner. See Figure 4.14 for the portion of the school leader checklist that covers resources. (See Resource A, Blackline SL-1, for the complete checklist.)

Figure 4.14   School Leader Checklist: Resources

- Will the resources help the participant reach his or her goals?
- Are the resources readily available?
- Does the success of the plan depend on access to a particular resource?
- Can the school provide the resources?
- If not, are there other sources to acquire the resources?

Progress Meetings (see Chapter 5) offer an opportunity to discuss resource issues, although requests for resources and changes can occur at any time. Ideally, these requests can be accommodated quickly. The size of a school or even political considerations may require the use of specific guidelines regarding resource requests. The school or school district must define the policy and procedures for resource requests and changes.

Quality resources support quality learning opportunities. The school leader and participants must work together to ensure that quality resources are part of the Professional Growth Plan Process.

CHOOSING A METHOD FOR SHARING RESULTS WITH THE LEARNING COMMUNITY

As part of designing the Professional Growth Plan, participants must identify what aspects of their growth plan experience they will share, how they will share it, and with whom they will share it. The initial plan for sharing may be vague and poorly defined. A more clear description will evolve after implementation of the plan. It is not uncommon for this component to change as participants acquire new information, knowledge, and skills, and collaborative experiences within the learning community occur. Progress Meetings (see Chapter 5) provide opportunities to make and document changes in the Method of Sharing with the Learning Community component.

This section addresses the information participants need to consider to complete the sharing component. (For a detailed discussion of sharing guidelines, see Chapter 6.) To guide participants successfully in this component of development, the school leader must thoroughly understand the component, its role in the growth plan process, and its impact on the learning community.

WHY SHARE PROFESSIONAL GROWTH PLANS?

Continuous school improvement is the goal of the Professional Growth Plan Process. By promoting individual professional growth and growth of the learning community, the Professional Growth Plan Process aggressively promotes and supports the change necessary to advance school improvement efforts (Fullan & Hargreaves, 1998).

As designed, the growth plan process capitalizes on the dynamic relationship that exists between individual professional growth and growth of the learning community. Each type of growth nourishes and supports the other (Fullan, 1993). Initially, the growth plan process promotes individual professional growth; then, because all participants have an opportunity and an obligation to share their newly acquired knowledge and skills with the learning community, the individual professional growth fuels growth within the learning community. This requirement to share growth plan information with the learning community fosters continuous growth by establishing and cultivating a climate and culture that promotes and encourages inquiry, examination, review, and discussion (Costa & Garmston, 2006).

The learning community also fuels individual professional growth by providing an open forum for the free and constant flow of new and relevant information to members both formally, in staff meetings and other gatherings designed for the specific purpose of sharing, and informally, around the lunch table or at the copy machine (DuFour & Eaker, 1998). The forum provides members of the learning community quick and easy access to important new information and to new skills relating to their practice. In more traditional professional development models, this information and these skills would not be so readily available for use by its members.

Visions cannot be mandated, but shared experiences and joint effort build common visions within a learning community (Fullan, 1993). So it is in the Professional Growth Plan Process. Through discussions, questioning, and communications that result from sharing growth plan experiences, the learning community defines and clarifies a common vocabulary, common understandings, and, ultimately, a common vision of education. Once the learning community establishes a shared vision, a vision that all members of the learning community feel ownership of and commitment to, school improvement efforts become more focused, more directed, and more effective (Fullan, 1993).

The various forums and formats the learning community uses to share professional information and skills model and establish for all members of the learning community high standards of professional behavior and performance (DuFour &

Eaker, 1998). Through the act of sharing, the learning community models, practices, and refines exemplary professional behaviors for conducting professional dialogues, resolving conflicts, and overcoming obstacles (Bereens, 2000). This sharing provides an opportunity for the learning community to discuss and establish supportive strategies for handling conflicts or disagreements in a professional manner. Just one excellent presentation sets a standard and model for others to imitate or modify. Even poor presentations, if offered in a supportive environment, can present opportunities to learn what is not effective as well as reinforce the value and comfort of a supportive environment.

The sharing of a growth plan experience should include more than describing new information and skills. Sharing particular activities, processes, and procedures used, and discussing failures and setbacks is as important as sharing the successes—new knowledge and skills. Sharing failures and setbacks helps the learning community define failure as an opportunity for learning, not as a demonstration of inadequacy or incompetence (Fullan, 1993). A learning community that defines failure as an opportunity for learning builds a climate and culture that values and promotes risk taking and candor.

METHODS OF SHARING

A number of factors determine how participants share growth plan information. The content of the growth plan, the climate and culture of the learning community, the individual skills and preferences of the participant doing the sharing, and the background knowledge of the audience determine how participants share their growth plan experience. A variety of formats and forums for sharing growth plans exist. Forums and Formats for Sharing with the Learning Community, Blackline P-24 shown on page 123, lists some of those possibilities, although the list is certainly not all-inclusive. (See Resource B for the blackline master.) The selected format and forum for growth plan sharing should facilitate the sharing process and address the needs of the presenter(s), the content, and the audience.

THE EFFECT OF SCHOOL CLIMATE ON SHARING

The climate of the learning community influences the format and forum for sharing. A climate lacking in trust encourages participants to choose formats and forums that require less exposure to colleague scrutiny and criticism. Written summaries, portfolios, and videos placed in professional libraries for review represent safer methods of sharing than face-to-face encounters. In climates that encourage and celebrate professional growth, participants choose more open, inclusive, and interactive forums and formats. Panel discussions, formal oral presentations, and actual demonstrations of new skills, perhaps even in authentic contexts, reflect more secure learning environments. School leaders should be sensitive to the comfort level expressed by participants and reflected in their choice of a method of sharing. Regardless of the forum and format selected, if participants feel safe in their sharing and believe their sharing contributes to the learning community, the growth plan process is successful and is laying a foundation for a more trusting climate.

Whatever forum and format participants select for sharing growth plan products, it is the school leader's role to ensure that the sharing is a positive, supportive, and edifying experience for everyone. Chapter 6 offers presentation guidelines to help the school leader ensure that sharing with the learning community reinforces the integrity of the Professional Growth Plan Process.

WHO IS THE LEARNING COMMUNITY?

The learning community comprises a variety of constituencies. From parents, the board of education, and administration to instructional staff, students, and support staff, each constituency has a valued role within the community (DuFour & Eaker, 1998). Identifying the appropriate constituency with whom to share a growth plan experience requires some consideration. Three factors contribute most to the selection of an audience:

- the content of the growth plan
- the purpose of the sharing
- the climate for sharing

Sharing with more than one constituency can strengthen the bonds of the entire community, but rarely does the entire learning community participate in the sharing of growth plan experiences. While this would certainly be an ideal to pursue, just the logistics to accomplish such an endeavor in most schools and districts would be overwhelming. Most growth plan sharing occurs among the instructional staff. This audience usually benefits most from the content of the growth plan. If the content of a growth plan has a particular application to a developmental level or discipline, it may be appropriate to limit the audience to specific grade levels or disciplines.

MATCHING PURPOSE WITH AUDIENCE

Sharing growth plan experiences with different audiences can serve many purposes. Sharing with school board members and school administration can validate the effectiveness of the growth plan process by verifying the participant's acquisition and application of new knowledge and skills. This verification can serve to increase board and administrative support for the Professional Growth Plan Process, support critical to the success and institutionalization of the process.

Besides garnering support for the growth plan process itself, sharing growth plan experiences with board members, administrators, and parent groups may help gain their support for particular programs, instructional strategies, and practices. By sharing results of growth plan activities, particularly those that clearly document increased student achievement, participants can make a strong case for the effectiveness of a program, strategy, or practice. Each constituency may feel more comfortable and confident supporting a formal adoption of a proposed intervention with the additional documentation the growth plan activity provides.

Sharing growth plans in some fashion with the student population demonstrates to students that adults are learners, too, and learning is a lifelong process. Such sharing helps students understand that the learning community extends beyond themselves. It can also demonstrate to students and to parents the professionalism of participants sharing their growth plans. Students and parents can take pride and confidence in the professionalism the sharing of growth plan experiences evidences.

FORUMS AND FORMATS FOR SHARING
WITH THE LEARNING COMMUNITY

◆ Staff Meetings

◆ Team Meetings

◆ Grade-Level Meetings

◆ Staff Exhibitions

◆ Presentations at Professional Conferences (local, state, regional, national)

◆ Multimedia Presentations

◆ Written Summaries Distributed to Staff

◆ Professional Newsletters

◆ Professional Journals

◆ Conducting a Workshop/Training for Staff

◆ Presentation to Board of Education

◆ Presentation to Parent Organization

(One caution: Participants should exercise care to ensure that they do not share any confidential information that is part of growth plan documentation in more public forums.)

Sharing with constituencies other than colleagues can help build a climate of trust and professionalism among the instructional staff. Those who do not feel safe sharing with colleagues, often the most intimidating group, may feel less threatened sharing their results with administrators, board of education members, or parents, particularly if the particular audience requests that they share. These forums can build confidence in participants. If the sharing is done with other colleagues, presenting before the mixed audience including colleagues can help open doors to colleague presentations, making the experience less threatening to those lacking confidence when presenting to peers. The school leader must work to ensure that these sharing experiences are positive for all parties involved because they offer another opportunity to enhance the learning environment.

A final consideration in choosing an audience is one of logistics. Depending on the format and forum chosen for sharing, the number of growth plans to be shared can dictate who the audience will be. The time required to share a large number of plans with an audience may necessitate that one large audience be divided into smaller audiences. The smaller audience would be targeted by growth plan content.

The portion of the school leader checklist for sharing with the learning community appears in Figure 4.15. (See Resource A, Blackline SL-1, for the complete checklist.)

THE SCHOOL LEADER AS ARCHITECT OF THE LEARNING COMMUNITY

Building relationships builds learning communities (Costa & Garmston, 2006). Sharing growth plan experiences contributes to the building of those relationships so important to the health of a learning community. Providing direction and support during the design process, then monitoring and sometimes controlling what participants share, how they share it, and with whom they share it during the implementation and completion stages, defines the school leader's role as architect of the learning community.

Figure 4.15   School Leader Checklist: Sharing With the Learning Community

- Does the format selected facilitate sharing of the growth plan information?
- Is the purpose for sharing clear?
- Is the forum/audience appropriate?
- Does the format or presentation encourage "bring and brag"?
- Is the content of the growth plan experience and its significance (not the step-by-step procedures) the focus of sharing?
- Do the skills, abilities, and talents of the participant complement the forum and format?

FINALIZING THE GROWTH PLAN

At this point in the design process, finalizing the Professional Growth Plan becomes a simple process of setting dates and signing the document. A Projected Completion Date appears after the Method of Sharing component on the Professional Growth Plan Format.

Because participants and the school leader should have discussed all the considerations concerning the pacing of growth plan activities and the target completion date during development of the Action Plan, they can place a fair degree of confidence in the Projected Completion Date. Of course, this date may change as work on the growth plan progresses.

Participants set Progress Meeting Dates after a quick review of the Action Plan. Examining the tasks, activities, and time frames helps determine when participants might need Progress Meetings most. Typically, over the course of a school year, three Progress Meetings are quite adequate to support growth plan implementation. Obviously, the participant or school leader can set more meetings if either has concerns regarding obstacles or problems affecting plan progress. The Progress Meeting Dates are target dates and may need to be rescheduled within a specified time frame as calendars become full with other school commitments.

The Plan Approval Date is the date both the participant and school leader accept the plan as ready for implementation. Efforts relating to implementation of the growth plan officially begin on or after this date. It is not uncommon, however, for participants to initiate some growth plan efforts before this official date.

Finally, signing off on a growth plan by participants and the school leader can be an insurance policy that everyone understands and agrees on what is to happen and when it is to happen. Depending on the contractual responsibilities or trust levels within a school or district, the formality of signatures may or may not be needed. A signature does add a sense of importance to the document.

When the school leader and participant have reviewed and revised the plan, the third phase of the Professional Growth Plan Process, implementation, begins. Sometimes sharing the finalized growth plans with all of the volunteer participants before implementation helps create a sense of camaraderie and collaboration. It can also strengthen the commitment to the process.

As the process moves from design to implementation, the school leader's role remains the same: facilitator, problem solver, mediator, coach, resource allocator, and cheerleader.

5

Professional Growth Plans in Progress

The challenge is to improve education in the only way it can be—through the day-to-day actions of empowered individuals.

—Fullan, 1997, p. 47

IMPLEMENTATION AND MONITORING

The activities associated with the implementation phase occur as participants follow their Action Plans and assume primary responsibility for implementing their Professional Growth Plan. This phase is unique to each plan, and plan timelines determine the pacing.

The monitoring phase, primarily an administrative function, runs concurrently with the implementation phase. In this phase, the school leader assumes responsibility for ensuring that participants, particularly those new to the process or those needing guidance, make progress toward their established goals. If progress is not occurring or if other problems impede progress, such as an extended illness or difficulty acquiring support materials, it is the school leader's responsibility to help participants solve the problem. Doing so may include modifying the original Professional Growth Plan to accommodate changing or unanticipated needs. A dynamic process, the Professional Growth Plan Process adapts continually to the needs of its participants.

Figure 5.1 shows the steps from the Professional Growth Plan Process Participant Checklist that take place during the implementation and monitoring phases (the complete checklist is in Resource B, Blackline P-3). Each of the first two phases

Figure 5.1   Professional Growth Plan Process Participant Checklist

---

Phase 3: Plan Implementation and Monitoring

- Implement Action Plan.
- Conduct Progress Meetings.
- Participate in interim sharing of growth plan.

---

of the Professional Growth Plan—identification of need and plan design—requires a significant and intensive investment of time, reflection, and energy from both participants and the school leader. If a Professional Growth Plan is well constructed initially, however, the remaining phases of implementation, monitoring, and evaluation are less arduous.

MONITORING THE PROCESS

Participants' enthusiasm for and commitment to the Professional Growth Plan Process are tied closely to their ability to make continuous progress toward their plan's successful completion. The school leader's role during the implementation phase is to facilitate the process, monitor progress, and offer support and encouragement. Facilitating and cheerleading cannot be effective if monitoring is superficial or sporadic. Attentively monitoring participants' progress, particularly during initial implementation of the growth plan process, is critical to their successful completion of the plans and to the institutionalization of the Professional Growth Plan Process.

The primary purpose of monitoring is to ensure that participants progress toward successful completion of their growth plan. Monitoring can be formal, conducted during regularly scheduled Progress Meetings, and informal, occurring as a result of normal daily interactions. In either mode, the monitoring process provides the school leader with valuable information relating to growth plan progress and the need for administrative intervention. Sometimes an administrative intervention may be simply offering words of encouragement and recognizing the difficulty of a particular task or activity. An intervention may provide logistical assistance such as covering a class period for a participant to allow him or her to finish a special task or activity. Such an intervention may help the participant initiate or maintain momentum.

FORMS ASSIST IN MONITORING

Chapter 2 explains the use of forms to track the growth process, facilitate communication, and provide documentation—all aspects of monitoring. Using the blacklines in Resource B, participants can provide the school leader with information about their progress easily and efficiently. For example, status forms such as Request for Assistance, Blackline P-25, provide school leaders with insights needed to make informed monitoring decisions. Primarily, a school leader can use the information submitted on these forms to determine whether participants need intervention to continue progressing toward their goals. (Chapter 2, page 34, includes a sample completed Request for Assistance.)

Other forms provide direct information about participant activities. When participants use workshop or inservice days to work on their growth plans, they can file a Work Day Plan, Blackline P-26, in advance of the workshop day to help focus their efforts and help the school leader monitor activities. A sample completed plan sheet appears on page 130. (A blackline master appears in Resource B.) On this form, participants identify their goals for the day, where the work will take place, and who will be involved. After the work day, they can reflect on progress made that day by completing a Work Day Summary Reflection Guide, Blackline P-27, on page 131, and share the completed form with the school leader. (A blackline master appears in Resource B.)

In environments where trust is lacking, use of these forms is a good way to build a more trusting relationship. As an initial trust-building tool and an intermediate step in transferring responsibility for professional growth from the school leader to participants, these forms document to the school leader that participants are self-directed and do not need direct supervision on a workshop day. They are capable of planning activities, then implementing those activities. For participants, the forms validate that the administration is giving them control, trusts them to choose the activities they think are most important for them, and will not monitor them closely during this work session.

FORMAL MONITORING: PROGRESS MEETINGS

Participants set tentative dates for formal Progress Meetings in the original Action Plan timeline. These dates are simply targets—reminders to participants and the school leader that it is time to touch base and review what has been going on. The Progress Meeting is an opportunity to discuss and address problems or obstacles participants have encountered. It is also a time to share new insights and understandings, surprises, and disappointments. Critically reviewing what has happened to date in the process not only provides an opportunity for reflection and deeper learning, it also helps the participant and school leader anticipate and plan for the upcoming tasks and activities specified on the Action Plan before the next scheduled meeting. It is important for the school leader to use cognitive coaching skills to help participants understand the significance of what they have done and determine if they are making adequate progress or if adjustments to the growth plan are necessary.

A key indicator of progress is the status of the Action Plan. Is the participant on schedule? If behind, how far, and why? Depending on the answers to these questions and the documentation shared with the school leader, the school leader determines the degree of progress. The school leader might ask questions similar to the following:

- Are you up-to-date on your timeline?
- Have you been able to complete each activity on your timeline satisfactorily?
- Have you been able to accomplish with each activity what you intended?

If participants are up-to-date on their Action Plan timelines, this indicates progress. If the timeline is not up-to-date, and participants have not attempted or completed activities, the school leader may be more specific in the questioning:

- What has caused the delay in completing your Action Plan timeline?
- Why do you think this is a problem?
- How are you addressing this problem?
- What impact is this delay going to have on your plan?
- Do you feel you need to make any changes on your plan?

WORK DAY PLAN

Please submit three days before workshop day.

Date of Work Day: 1-12-07

Work Site: My home office

Participants: Joyce K.

Goals:
1. Receive comments and suggestions from consultant regarding Spelling Competency Scale I have been working on.
2. Review Dr. Gentry's suggestion for improving the scale.
3. Reread the pages Dr. Gentry suggested I consider in his book.
4. Revise the Competency Scale.

Planned Activities: I've arranged a time to connect finally with Jean M. by phone. She has indicated that she has some suggestions I should consider for my Spelling Competency Scale and some other questions about classroom management of my spelling program. Depending on the length of our phone conversation, I would anticipate carrying out the activities that will allow me to complete the above goals.

Resource Needs: I'm about out of space in my binder. Do you happen to have an extra one?

Miscellaneous/ Comments: When I finish this work, I was wondering if we might meet? I have a few things I need to run by you. Thanks.

WORK DAY SUMMARY REFLECTION GUIDE

This form helps you document your work and reflect and process your experiences. A summary is what happened. A summary documents effort. A reflection is an analysis of what happened, why it happened, and the significance of what happened. A reflection can document the acquisition of new knowledge and skills. It can also document the depth of reflective thinking. Remember complete sentences, perfect grammar, and neatness are not as important as your thoughts. Using the format below, provide the following information on a separate sheet of paper.

Date of Work Day: **Worksite:**

Participants:

Activities (briefly summarize what you did):

Answer the questions most appropriate to your experience.

Did you meet the goals you set for the day? Why or why not?

What new insights or surprises did you gain from your activities?

What problems/difficulties/frustrations did you experience? Could you resolve them? Why? How?

How will your activities impact your future work?

Will you make any changes or try something different as a result of what you learned? Briefly explain.

What do you need to do next as a result of these activities?

What help or assistance do you need that you had not anticipated?

Blackline P-27

To help participants clarify their progress and to provide the school leader some background before the Progress Meeting, participants can complete and submit a brief synopsis of their activity. They can use the list of questions in Progress Meeting Questions, Blackline Master P-28, on page 133 to prompt reflection on their growth plan work to date. (A blackline master appears in Resource B. Participants do not have to use the form; free response serves the same purpose.) The school leader can also use these questions to direct the Progress Meeting discussion. In addition to providing background for discussion, this formative summary can maximize efficient use of the meeting time allotted. If problems, obstacles, or special needs require attention, the school leader can also begin addressing the issues before the meeting.

Until participants and school leaders are comfortable with the growth plan process, face-to-face Progress Meetings should take place. Once a comfort level is established, participants can submit written or recorded progress summaries to the school leader. Some Progress Meetings can be eliminated if the submitted progress summary indicates progress toward goals, and no obstacles exist that require the school leader's assistance.

In general, Progress Meetings are energizing for both participants and the school leader. The Progress Meeting can validate and encourage participants in growth plan efforts and validate the school leader's efforts to implement the Professional Growth Plan Process as he or she witnesses evidence of professional growth and change among staff. The Progress Meeting validates professionalism as the school leader and participants recognize accomplishments and solve problems. Blackline SL-7, Progress Meeting Record, documents and summarizes the Progress Meeting. (A sample appears on page 134 and a blackline master is included in Resource A.) See Figure 5.2 for the portion of the school leader checklist for Progress Meetings; a complete checklist is in Resource A, Blackline SL-1.

Figure 5.2   School Leader Checklist: Progress Meetings

- Is the participant making adequate progress?
- If it is a group plan, are all participants contributing actively?
- Is documentation adequate?
- Does the plan require modification?
- Is the reason for modification reasonable?
  - New knowledge or understandings
  - Insurmountable obstacles
  - Lack of resources or information
- Do all parties agree that the modification is necessary?

INFORMAL MONITORING: LISTENING, WATCHING, VISITING

While formal monitoring through scheduled Progress Meetings is very important, so is informal monitoring. Informal monitoring is truly casual and usually not planned. It occurs as part of the daily routine of the school leader and participants. Informal monitoring may include drop-in visits that are part of the school leader's regular

PROGRESS MEETING QUESTIONS

The following prompts can help facilitate discussion at the Progress Meeting. The purpose of these meetings is to ensure that you receive the necessary support and you are making progress toward successful completion of the growth plan. You can write your answers before the meeting, or the questions can act as a conversation guide for the meeting. If problems or concerns have arisen, it may be beneficial to submit your responses to the school leader before the meeting to allow him or her some problem-solving time.

Where are you on your Action Plan? Are you on schedule? Explain.

What have you done to this point?

Do you feel you are making progress toward your established goals? Explain.

What insights or new information have you discovered?

Has anything you have done or read changed what you believed or understood? Explain.

Have you experienced any difficulties, frustrations, or obstacles? Explain what they are/were. Have you resolved them? How?

Has anything surprised you? What? Why?

Do you feel your goals are still appropriate? Do they need to be modified? If so, how? Why?

Do you feel your goals are still attainable? Do they need to be modified? Is so, how? Why?

Does your Action Plan still make sense? Do you need to make changes? What are they? Why?

PROGRESS MEETING RECORD

GROWTH PLAN: <u>Writing Prompts for 5th-Grade Curriculum</u>

PARTICIPANTS: <u>Mary Smith, Milly Kelly, Jeanne Jones</u>

COMPLETION DATE: <u>May 1, 2007</u>

PROGRESS MEETING #: <u>4</u> DATE: <u>2/12/07</u>

THOSE PRESENT: _____

ACTION PLAN: ☒ BEHIND ☐ ON SCHEDULE ☐ AHEAD

COMMENTS: It turns out that writing a quality prompt is taking much longer than anticipated, given the numerous revisions. At this point, they thought they would have most of the prompts done for three social studies units and they have just finished one.

DOCUMENTATION: ☐ NONE ☐ INADEQUATE ☒ ADEQUATE

COMMENTS: They have substantial documentation of all the efforts they have put forth and the revisions they have made as well as reflections.

MODIFICATIONS: ☐ NONE ☒ SEE EXPLANATION

Explanation of Modification (include reason for modification): Because it is taking so long to complete a unit's worth of prompts, we are going to change the methods of evaluation to say that prompts will be completed for two units of social studies and science instead of four.

NEW RESOURCE NEEDS: None

NEXT MEETING DATE: _____

GENERAL CONCERNS/COMMENTS (see back): No concerns

Blackline SL-7

school rounds. Even conversations in the teacher's lounge over coffee and birthday treats provide insight into progress or problems! These informal conversations and observations of some of the participants' activities can provide the school leader with important information needed to determine if participants need a school leader's supportive intervention. Many interventions are logistical in nature: locating supplies, covering class periods, or accessing a resource the participant did not anticipate. Intervention might simply entail asking questions to help the participant think through what is happening and why a problem exists.

Not all participants will ask for help, even when they need it. Depending on the level of trust existing within the learning community, particularly within the administrator-teacher relationship, and his or her degree of self-confidence, a participant experiencing difficulty may be reluctant to ask for help or assistance. He or she may fear a request for assistance will be perceived as a sign of incompetence or inadequacy. Informal monitoring can alert the school leader to a particular need for intervention. A clue to possible problems is when a participant avoids discussion about a growth plan. Most typically, the less confident participant struggles and does not request help. (More self-confident participants are quick to ask for help or advice.)

Early intervention on the part of the school leader can often result in a quick and easy resolution of problems or removal of obstacles. It keeps participants on task and moving forward and can reinforce in them a feeling of personal competence and confidence. Informal monitoring also provides the school leader with opportunities to encourage risk taking and promote desired professional behaviors, such as consulting with or offering support to colleagues. Informal monitoring allows the school leader to acknowledge through a simple spoken or written word specific efforts and accomplishments that can instill confidence in the participant. The school leader might offer more formal acknowledgment at a staff meeting, in a newsletter, or even at a board of education meeting.

DECIDING WHAT IS NOT WORKING AND WHY

If formal or informal monitoring reveals a participant is not making the anticipated progress, it is important that the school leader become proactive in helping the participant address the problems that impede progress. Some obstacles and frustrations are inevitable and even necessary because they cause important learning to occur, such as figuring out how to collect and organize data for easy interpretation. However, ongoing frustration, continuous obstacles, and lack of real progress produce discouragement, lack of commitment, and feelings of failure among participants. Overwhelmed with failure and frustration, participants may fail to complete a plan. Once participants fail, it is difficult for them to regain their commitment to the process. The negative attitude attendant with failure can spread a general lack of support for the Professional Growth Plan Process throughout the learning community.

Reasons for lack of progress are numerous. Some may have little to do with the topic or design of the plan itself but may be more closely related to the process. The school leader must first determine whether participants have put forth adequate effort, and he or she should address the issue of lack of effort with great caution. While it is easy to jump to conclusions that hold the participant totally responsible, lack of participant effort may not be a willful act or even a lack of desire to do the work. A lack of effort may indicate fear of failure or of making mistakes and the need for more intensive involvement and guidance on the part of the school leader to help the participant overcome the hesitation. Because the process is such a dramatic departure from standard staff development programs, participants simply may not fully understand what they are to do or how they are to do it. Just as with students in classrooms, the fear of making a mistake or not getting the "right" answer may cause participants to avoid taking any action or to make minimal efforts to complete their plans. So, just like teachers with their students, the school leader must be supportive, offering ample assistance and guidance until the confidence level or level of understanding increases to a point where work can progress.

If the plan is not on schedule, the school leader needs to determine if procrastination is the cause. Putting off until tomorrow is easy when participants' job demands are so pressing. Unlike term papers, however, growth plans cannot be completed at the last minute. They are structured to be completed over time. The school leader's role is to ensure that participants understand the process and the allocation and use of time. A gentle nudge by the school leader can often provide the impetus to start the process moving.

Sometimes participants become so overwhelmed with the documentation process, thinking they must document everything, that record keeping becomes burdensome and slows or halts all progress. Again, quick intervention by the school leader can dissolve worries and eliminate, or greatly reduce, the impediments to progress. Sitting down with the participant and creating or identifying artifacts, reviewing each quickly and determining which to keep, models what the participant can and should do and gets them moving.

Other times lack of progress may be related directly to the plan itself. Information that participants gain through Action Plan activities may change the understandings and premises on which they designed the plan originally. They may discover, for example, that the focus is too narrow or too broad or the resources needed to support the plan are not as available as originally thought. All components of the Professional Growth Plan are open to revision, including the Essential Question and Professional Goals. The most common changes occur in the Action Plan activities and the timelines associated with them. Sometimes progress is made more quickly, but more often the activities take longer than anticipated, so participants need more time to complete them.

PROTECTING THE INTEGRITY OF THE PROFESSIONAL GROWTH PLAN PROCESS

Adjustments should not be made without reasonable justification. Frequent and/or frivolous changes, such as changing the timeline with each delay or each acceleration of the Action Plan, can weaken the plan and the process significantly. To ensure changes are appropriate, the participants and school leader must agree that the proposed changes are necessary and, if made, will help participants complete their growth plan successfully. Additionally, all parties need to sign off on the changes. If there is not a total agreement on changes, changes cannot be made. Documentation of changes in a growth plan can be used to demonstrate growth and placed in the final portfolio.

Monitoring and supporting implementation of growth plans is an opportunity for the school leader to continue to build a climate of trust and risk taking. The school leader must exercise reasonable flexibility and patience when evaluating a participant's progress. Sometimes life circumstances can interfere with progress. However, the school leader must also protect the integrity of the process by dealing directly and promptly with those who choose willfully not to make progress. The consequences of such behavior should be established and understood by all parties before implementation of the Professional Growth Plan Process. Rarely does this noncompliance occur, but when it does, the entire learning community will watch the school leader's actions. The school leader must be prepared to take the appropriate action to preserve the integrity of the Professional Growth Plan Process and with it the integrity of the learning community. Participants who choose willfully not to complete a growth plan may be required to participate in more structured and administratively prescribed staff development activities, be unable to move on the salary schedule, be unable to attend professional conferences, or be required to have more classroom observations.

INTERIM SHARING: WHAT HAS HAPPENED SO FAR?

The need to share interim growth plan results becomes most obvious during Progress Meetings because they reveal, particularly to the school leader, that many in the learning community are actively involved in some very engaging, challenging, and productive professional activities relating to their growth plans. The school leader is in a unique position to witness all the learning that is occurring within the learning organization. The school leader can promote informal opportunities to facilitate sharing of growth plan experiences and make informal sharing a regular, permanent part of the learning organization's procedures. Asking participants at a staff meeting to share briefly what is happening with their growth plan can infuse interest and enthusiasm into the learning organization. Participants sharing information that will support other participants in their efforts and endeavors encourages communication, builds the learning community, and helps individual participants. This interim sharing can provide a constant and valued flow of information to the learning community. As long as interim sharing is simple and does not require a lot of participant time and preparation, participation will grow as participants feel more comfortable and confident with sharing.

TROUBLESHOOTING: WHAT HAPPENS IF . . .

Problems are inevitable in any process that involves people—the Professional Growth Plan Process is no exception. Most problems result from circumstances beyond anyone's control. Each of the following scenarios represents typical problems that can arise during implementation of the Professional Growth Plan Process and possible responses.

Problem: A member of a group plan leaves a school or district for personal or professional reasons, leaving the remainder of the group to complete the plan. The individual may leave with valuable resources, knowledge, or skills.

Response: Remaining group members should reorganize and determine whether they need to start over with the same plan, extend the timeline because they need to get new materials, or design a totally different plan because the knowledge and skills the departing person had were essential to the plan.

Problem: An individual has a change in position or responsibilities, making the growth plan less meaningful, relevant, or job embedded.

Response: The individual may complete the plan regardless of the change in assignment; the individual may abbreviate the plan, summarizing the learning that has taken place, and then start a new, more relevant plan; or the individual may drop the plan and start a new one.

Problem: An individual experiences an extended, serious illness.

Response: The participant and school leader extend the timeline for the Action Plan.

Problem: An individual within a group fails to contribute to the group's efforts, impeding everyone's progress.

Response: The individual must leave the group and do a separate plan or receive other consequences, such as closer supervision or prescribed staff development activities. Those remaining in the group modify the plan to reflect the loss of the individual and reassign responsibilities.

Unfortunately, these problems have no easy solutions. Each school's or district's solutions depend on how it employs the Professional Growth Plan Process. Is it solely a staff development model or is it also a supervision model? Union contracts, board of education policies and practices, and even state laws all may impact the resolution of these and other problems. Participants and the school leader should try to identify potential problems before implementing the process. Thinking through, in advance, each problem, possible solutions, and the impact of each solution ensures the smoothest implementation. Written and adopted policies and practices specifically addressing potential problems can eliminate confusion and frustration and help avoid conflict. If possible, the learning community should write the policies and recommend them to the board of education for adoption. Involving representatives of the learning community in identifying potential problems and finding professional solutions can be important to the acceptance, effectiveness, and success of adopted policies, practices, and procedures.

In reality, the solution to most problems simply requires the use of common sense. Often additional time will help the situation. Sometimes it may be necessary to drop a plan and just start over. Sometimes the potential of a particular plan may not be realized because of extenuating circumstances. If intent and effort are present, the school leader should exercise the flexibility to make the growth plan work if it can. If the plan cannot be salvaged, both the school leader and participant(s) must be willing to dismiss the plan. The school leader should recognize the efforts of those involved, not penalize anyone, and help everyone start over, while remembering that failure is an opportunity for learning.

No one can anticipate all problems. The school leader must be prepared to address those that are not anticipated, recognizing that not all problems will have solutions or solutions that will please everyone. If the school leader and participants address solutions to problems in a professional manner, they can protect the integrity of the Professional Growth Plan Process.

PREPARING FOR THE FINAL PHASE

If participants have implemented the Professional Growth Plan Process effectively, the final phase of the process, plan evaluation, gives them the opportunity to reflect on, process, recognize, share, and celebrate the professional growth resulting from the growth plan.

6

Completing the Growth Plan Process

One of the distinguishing characteristics of a professional learning community will be the collective attention that is given to analyzing and advancing the highest standards of the profession.

—DuFour and Eaker, 1998, p. 215

PLAN EVALUATION

Evaluation occurs throughout the Professional Growth Plan Process but assumes a more prominent role at plan completion during the final phase—evaluation. Formative evaluation occurs through the artifacts participants collect throughout the growth plan implementation. These activities document the entire process, as participants record their data, findings, reflections, and conclusions about every aspect of their activities and experiences. This ongoing documentation not only promotes the metacognition that enhances learning, it also provides a record of the professional growth participants experience throughout the entire growth plan process. At plan completion, participants assemble and organize the formative evaluation documentation, forming the basis for a summative evaluation of the growth plan by the participant and school leader. Figure 6.1 depicts the steps of the Professional Growth Plan Process Participant Checklist that occur during the evaluation phase. (The complete process checklist, Blackline P-3, is in Resource B.)

Participants and the school leader identify and agree on the artifacts or documentation that will support the evaluation criteria before implementation of the plan,

Figure 6.1   Professional Growth Plan Process Participant Checklist

---

Phase 4: Plan Evaluation

- Summarize growth plan activities.
- Conduct growth plan self-evaluation.
- Participate in growth plan summary conference.
- Share results with the learning community.

---

during the design phase. Activities and experiences occurring during growth plan implementation might suggest that a change in evaluation methods is appropriate and necessary.

GROWTH PLAN SUMMARY ACTIVITIES

Four growth plan summary activities bring the Professional Growth Plan Process to an end: participants compose a growth plan summary; they submit this summary and the portfolio collection of documentation of professional growth to the school leader for review; participants and the school leader hold a conference to discuss the completed Professional Growth Plan; and participants share the completed work with the learning community. See Growth Plan Summary Activities, Blackline P-29, on page 141. (A blackline master appears in Resource B.)

SUMMARIZING THE GROWTH PLAN EXPERIENCE—WHAT HAPPENED?

Growth plan summary activities begin with participants summarizing their growth plan. This summary can be written or developed into some form of media presentation. Within the summary, participants should, at a minimum, address these four key points:

1. the new knowledge, skills, beliefs, and attitudes they acquired

2. the impact this learning has had and will have on student achievement and their practice

3. the documentation that exists as evidence of growth

4. the insight they gained about how they learn

The purpose of the summary is to help participants reflect on their work, their learning, and its impact on student achievement. This capsulation of their work brings a sense of closure and completion to participants and, one hopes, a sense of accomplishment.

Preparing the summary should not be a long or burdensome task. A one-page typed summary is a reasonable length; however, some participants may choose to provide longer summaries. The summary's purpose is not to prove professional growth but to review and sum up the learning that has occurred from the participant's perspective. (Remember, evidence of professional growth appears in the portfolio

GROWTH PLAN SUMMARY ACTIVITIES

1. Summarize your plan in writing or on audiotape. Be sure to answer the following questions:

   - What new knowledge, skills, beliefs, or attitudes did you acquire?
   - How will this acquisition impact your practice?
   - What documentation shows evidence of your growth?
   - What did you learn about the way you learn?

2. Submit summary and portfolio to school leader.

3. Meet with school leader in summary conference.

4. Share completed growth plan with learning community.

documentation.) Having participants complete the Growth Plan Self-Evaluation, Blackline P-30, helps them summarize the extent of their professional growth under each criterion heading. The self-evaluation provides the school leader with some insight into participants' perceptions of their professional growth. By comparing a participant's perception of growth with the school leader's perception, the school leader can develop a deeper understanding of the participant that will help in the development of the next growth plan. A sample completed Growth Plan Self-Evaluation appears on page 143. The Growth Plan Summary Reflection Guide, Blackline P-31 (appears on pages 144 and 145), can assist those who need help with the summarizing process. If need be, the school leader can also use the guide to direct conversation in the summary conference. Both blacklines also appear in Resource B.

THE GROWTH PLAN SUMMARY CONFERENCE

The growth plan summary conference is another occasion to encourage and continue professional dialogue. It is a time for participants to brief the school leader about their Professional Growth Plan experience, reflecting on the learning that has occurred, the significance of that learning to their practice and student achievement, and the impact of the Professional Growth Plan Process on their learning. Through questioning, summarizing, and paraphrasing, the school leader helps participants reflect on and internalize the growth plan experience. The Growth Plan Summary Reflection Guide, Blackline P-31, can facilitate the conference.

In addition to providing a forum to review what has happened, the conference also can set the stage for what may be the next step: the continued application of the new knowledge and perhaps a discussion of what may become the focus of the next growth plan.

To maintain credibility as a facilitator of the process and to conduct the growth plan summary conference effectively, the school leader must spend time before the conference reviewing the contents of the growth plan summary and portfolio documentation. The review should give the school leader enough background knowledge to respond to specific artifacts in the portfolio or comments in the summary. It should also provide enough background to allow the school leader to ask the probing questions that may further the assimilation of new learning. Such questions enable the school leader to determine whether the participant understands causal relationships, deeper concepts, and understandings related to their own learning and to student achievement. Sometimes during these conversations, as participants explain what happened and why they think it happened, they see new relationships or links to new and different understandings. The depth of understanding, then, continues. The review of the growth plan summary and the portfolio should not take a lot of the time. If the school leader has been monitoring plan progress regularly, the plan and its artifacts should be fairly familiar to the school leader.

The summary conference serves another very important purpose. The conference demonstrates to participants that the school leader values their learning, efforts, and contributions. Most professionals welcome such validation, and it builds a commitment to the learning community.

When reviewing the summary and portfolio, it is most appropriate for the school leader to write a commentary of his or her perceptions of the documented growth plan experiences for each participant. See Growth Plan Summary School Leader

GROWTH PLAN SELF-EVALUATION

Please circle the number that correlates to your assessment of your Professional Growth Plan. A 1 represents the least amount of growth, and a 5 represents the greatest. Include any comments you feel are appropriate.

Acquisition of New Knowledge and Skills   1   2   3   4   (5)
I knew nothing about the different kinds of writing prompts!

Application of New Knowledge and Skills   1   2   3   (4)   5
(changes in instructional practices)
My approach to writing instruction has changed dramatically.

Enhanced Reflective Practices   1   2   3   4   (5)
This is so hard for me! But this process forced me to reflect.
I still need to improve on this area.

Effort   1   2   3   4   (5)
Look at the portfolio! It is packed!

Contribution to Learning Community   1   2   (3)   4   5

Improved Student Achievement   1   2   3   4   (5)
Student writing has improved in direct proportion to the
improvement in my instruction.

Name: _Marian C._   Date: _2/14/06_

Plan Topic: Developing and Using Writing Prompts

Comments on back please. They all fit on front.

GROWTH PLAN SUMMARY
REFLECTION GUIDE

Use some or all of the following questions to help you prepare your Professional Growth Plan Summary. Your school leader may also use these questions during your summary conference.

What answer(s) did you find to your Essential Question?

Did you meet your Professional Goals? Explain.

What were the most important understandings you gained from your work?

What obstacles did you encounter? How did you overcome them?

What did you learn about your knowledge, beliefs, or practices as they relate to this topic?

What did you learn about your learning?

What evidence did you gather that helped you develop a deeper understanding of your topic?

What artifacts document your professional growth?

How do these document your professional growth?

How does what you have learned impact your teaching?

How will this inform and improve your teaching in the future?

What evidence will exist two years from now that demonstrates you are using this new knowledge or skill?

Did you impact student achievement? How do you know? What evidence exists? If evidence does not exist currently, when do you expect to see improvement? What will be the evidence?

Did any of your beliefs or attitudes change as a result of your work? Explain.

What will you do differently because of your learning?

Who within our learning community could also benefit from this knowledge or skill?

How could the Professional Growth Plan Process meet your needs better?

Does what you have learned through your growth plan transfer to any other area of your teaching? Explain.

Have you incorporated any features of the Professional Growth Plan Process into your practice? What are they? Why have you chosen the features? How do you use them?

What other comments or insights would you like to share?

What topic would you like to explore next?

Comments, Blackline SL-8, on page 147 and in Resource A for an outline to follow when preparing this commentary. The commentary may address the specific growth the school leader has witnessed, the contributions this plan makes to the learning community, and the obstacles the participant overcame. Each commentary must truly address the individual plan reviewed, and is, therefore, as individual as the plan. Understanding the learning community, the participant, and the growth plan, the school leader must determine what is important for comment. While time-consuming, writing a commentary demonstrates to participants a concern and investment on the part of the school leader in their growth plan and their professional growth.

Talking with a participant in the summary conference is a sure way to determine the degree of learning that occurred. With skillful conferencing techniques, the school leader can gather the information needed to assess the participant's learning (Guskey, 2000). The school leader is looking and listening for confirmation that professional growth has occurred. The participant might have comments similar to the following:

I really didn't know how to _____. I thought if I did _____, I was okay. But now that I know how to _____, I can't believe the difference. It really works just like they described it in the books!

I don't know how good the reflections are. I just didn't know what to put down. It was hard.

Through careful listening, the school leader can make his or her own assessment of the participant's professional growth in each defined criterion area. To know and understand the learning that occurred, under what conditions it occurred, and the level of reflective thinking that developed is important for the school leader, not only to evaluate professional growth but to provide direction and an informed base from which to support development of the participant's next Professional Growth Plan. The portion of the school leader checklist relating to the summary conference appears in Figure 6.2. For the complete checklist, Blackline SL-1, see Resource A.

Figure 6.2 School Leader Checklist: Summary Conference

- Did the participant achieve the Professional Goals?
- Did the professional growth impact student achievement?
- Did the participant address the Essential Question?
- Does evidence exist to document each professional growth criterion?
- Can the participant articulate the growth he or she has experienced?
- Has the participant made a contribution to the learning community?
- Do you agree with the participant about the growth that has occurred?

Also in this nonthreatening discussion, an analysis of any mistakes made and what participants learned from the mistakes can be a very valuable learning activity for participants and the school leader. A safe discussion of mistakes sends the message that learning from mistakes is part of the learning process and reinforces risk-taking behaviors.

GROWTH PLAN SUMMARY
SCHOOL LEADER COMMENTS

Acquisition of new knowledge and skills:

Application of new knowledge and skills:

Enhanced reflective practices:

Contribution to learning community:

Improved student achievement:

Additional comments:

Participant: Date:

Plan Administrator:

Growth Plan Topic:

Blackline SL-8

THE SUMMARY CONFERENCE
AND GROUP GROWTH PLANS

Growth plan summary conferences for group growth plans require special consideration. A summary conference can take place with all participants, but the school leader must ensure that all group members participate in the discussion. The benefit of a group conference is that when all participants contribute their unique and common perceptions, it enriches the meeting. The drawback to a group summary conference is that it is not unusual to have some members of the group let others speak for them or at least allow others to dominate the conversation. For this reason, it is best, generally, to meet with group members individually, particularly if the growth plan is part of the supervision model. Sharing as a group can take place when it is time to share the plan with the learning community. Whether a group has a group summary conference or individual conferences is a decision that really must be made on an individual school, or even district, level.

EVALUATING DOCUMENTATION
OF PROFESSIONAL GROWTH

Examination of documentation is the next step in the Professional Growth Plan Process. During the growth plan design, participants defined successful completion of their growth plan in the Methods of Evaluation component. Because the criteria by which the growth plan is evaluated have been determined previously, the final determination regarding whether the targeted professional growth has occurred should be clear-cut. In most instances, if the documentation described in the Methods of Evaluation component does, in fact, exist, then the plan has been completed successfully. The participant has therefore shown acceptable professional growth.

The portfolio containing all the artifacts generated from the growth plan might not be submitted in its entirety as evidence of professional growth. It is not uncommon that a review of the entire portfolio reveals that significantly more professional growth has occurred than was originally targeted in the Professional Growth Plan!

Most often, participants target particular artifacts for consideration as evidence of professional growth from among the numerous artifacts generated from growth plan activities. The Methods of Evaluation component specifies and explains these particular artifacts.

The specified artifacts document professional growth within one or more of the five criteria for evaluating professional growth:

1. acquisition of new knowledge and skills

2. application of new knowledge and skills

3. enhanced reflective practices

4. contributions to the learning community

5. improved student achievement

The number of artifacts associated with each criterion may vary. While all criteria must be present in the completed growth plan, rarely, if ever, is each criterion represented equally within the professional growth experience. The degree to which each criterion is present reflects the participant's abilities, the topic pursued, and the learning environment. A participant might acquire a variety of new skills or make a significant contribution to the learning community, but the reflections on the learning experiences may be minimal.

For example, a group of fourth-grade teachers developing a comprehensive writing program for their grade level create, as part of their plan, rubrics and writer's checklists for persuasive, expository, and narrative writing to help students evaluate their own writing. Teachers throughout the elementary school can use these rubrics and writer's checklists with minor adaptations. In this instance, by providing a tool for use schoolwide, these plan participants have each made a significant contribution to the learning community.

Individually, however, their reflections on their activities and learning varies— some show minimal reflection, while others show a great depth of reflection. While these participants made a significant contribution to the learning community, the contribution of other participants may be less significant. A high school PE teacher, for example, pursues a growth plan on developing a personal fitness program for students. Through this growth plan, the teacher acquires a deep understanding of what constitutes a quality fitness program for adolescents, then implements a fitness program resulting in an increased enrollment in fitness classes and increased levels of student fitness. The reflections on the learning and experiences are of the highest quality. But because this is a PE program, the immediate contributions this plan makes to the learning community are limited to the students enrolled in the fitness classes. Except for personal applications of some of the fitness principles, the instructional staff and the overall school program gain little from this growth plan. Yet the success of this plan is undeniable, as growth has occurred within each criterion. To try to affix a target value or percentage representation to each criterion as a measure of professional growth would be burdensome to the participant and to the school leader, if not impossible to execute.

As stated before, documentation of some student achievement may be delayed until after the professional growth plan is completed. Trend data over time, years perhaps, may be necessary to evaluate the professional growth's impact on student achievement. While rare, situations may occur in which significant professional growth takes place, but there is no or limited impact on student achievement. The individual pursuing a degree in school administration, for example, gains a deep understanding of the management and functioning of the school organization and probably a better understanding of curriculum and instruction. This is valuable learning. This individual will be a better teacher, if only in terms of understanding and supporting some administrative decisions. This knowledge may or may not manifest itself in student achievement, and that achievement tie would be very difficult to document. But the learning is valuable to the individual and the school.

If the documentation the participant chose as the Method of Evaluation does not exist or is not clearly met, schools and school districts need to determine the consequences for the participant. If the school leader has been monitoring progress and has provided as much supportive intervention as possible, then the professional performance of the participant comes into question. If successful completion of a growth plan is part of an evaluation/supervision model, then the model should prescribe the consequences. The supervision model may place the participant in another supervision strand, or the participant may receive an unsatisfactory performance evaluation. The school leader's documentation of the Progress Meetings and interventions resulting from those meetings become very important at this point. The learning community should address and specify consequences for this issue before implementation of the Professional Growth Plan Process.

If Progress Meetings were not held or the school leader did not monitor progress adequately, fault may be more difficult to assign. Again, the learning community needs to discuss and resolve this scenario before implementing the process.

It is very important to remember that as with student learners, the professional growth experienced by educators using the Professional Growth Plan Process will differ depending on their motivation, time, and ability. To compare the growth of various participants for any purpose other than to help the school leader develop and implement future plans more effectively undermines the integrity of the process. Such action violates one of the basic tenets on which the process is built—all learners receive acceptance for their current learning level and encouragement to develop to their potential.

Comparisons foster a competitive environment that stifles risk taking and collaboration and, therefore, compromise the learning community by altering the learning environment. It follows that comparisons of professional growth are destructive and counterproductive to the goals of the Professional Growth Plan Process. This is an important consideration for the school leader when it is time to share the results of the growth plan with the learning community.

SHARING WITH THE LEARNING COMMUNITY

Once again, if the Professional Growth Plan Process has been implemented effectively, the way participants share the growth plan with the learning community was established in the design phase. Sharing the finished growth plan brings the entire cycle of the Professional Growth Plan Process to a conclusion. School leaders should remind participants that the products of the growth plan are most important to nourishing and strengthening the learning community. It is not necessarily the growth plan itself that is of the greatest value to the learning community.

The school leader should make all efforts to minimize any occasions for making comparisons among growth plans. School- or districtwide exhibits are most susceptible to providing occasion for intimidating comparisons. The school leader and the learning community need to create guidelines for such exhibits to discourage the bring-and-brag displays that can impress but may not reflect the true significance or depth of the work. Occasions for the oral sharing of plans should also have guidelines the learning community designs or at least endorses. The sharing of growth plans should not be burdensome to either the presenters or listeners. Presentations should be succinct and should address the information that is of most significance for or use to the learning community. Sometimes an informal conversation format provides more opportunity for the sharing of information than a formal presentation does. Obviously, anyone interested in obtaining more detailed information about the results of any growth plan can meet with presenters individually.

GUIDELINES FOR THE PRESENTATION TO THE LEARNING COMMUNITY

Participants determine what they share with the learning community from the growth plan experience; however, the school leader should define simple guidelines for sharing, at least initially. These initial guidelines encourage succinctness, brevity, and candor. Later, as its experience with the sharing process increases, the learning community can refine these guidelines to accommodate the evolving needs of the community.

Keep It Brief

In the beginning, the most important guidelines a school leader sets concern the length of a presentation. Whether written or oral, the presentation should be a synopsis of the growth plan experience, not a detailed account. The energy and enthusiasm for learning that sharing growth plan experiences generates can quickly dissipate when presentations become long and drawn out. The length of presentations can always expand later, but the damage done by presentations that are too long is hard to repair. Even growth plans whose content can support more lengthy sharing sessions must be held to the same guidelines. Provision can always be made for additional sharing opportunities for those interested in a more comprehensive presentation of a particular growth plan.

Focus on Content

The content of a professional growth plan should always be the focus of the sharing experience. Participants and the school leader should take care to prevent the presentation from becoming the primary focus of the sharing experience. Formats and forums that promote competition or contrived collegiality are destructive to the growth plan process and to the learning community (Fullan, 1993). Elaborate presentations, displays, and exhibits can introduce a level of competition and expectation that redirects growth plan efforts from their intended purpose. The competition and expectation anxieties resulting from such sharing nurture a bring-and-brag culture, which promotes criticism, faultfinding, and defensiveness. Individually and collectively, these characteristics are very destructive to any learning environment and to the professional growth process. It is the school leader's responsibility to ensure that this kind of sharing does not develop.

On the other hand, presentations that encourage professional dialogues, discussions, inquiries, and discoveries energize the learning community. They provide positive feedback to participants, validating their efforts and the professionalism of the learning community. Participants should focus their sharing on what topic they studied, why they studied it, how they studied it, what new knowledge and skills they acquired, and what significance the topic has to their classroom practice and improved student achievement. To help participants determine what they want to share, they might use Sharing With the Learning Community Prompts, Blackline P-32, which appears on pages 152 and 153. (The full blackline appears in Resource B.) The information should be meaningful and relevant to the learning community. It need not be new to the field of education or even new to the learning community; the information may simply serve to validate beliefs and practices the learning community already embraces.

Know the Audience

The background knowledge and experiences of the audience contribute to the depth and sophistication of the presentation. For example, if the information might be new to the learning community audience, participants should take this into

SHARING WITH THE LEARNING COMMUNITY

Use the questions below to help you develop a plan to share your growth plan experience.

The questions should help you think about what you should share, how you should share, and with whom you should share your growth plan experience. Check with your plan administrator if you have questions or concerns.

What was your topic?

Why did you choose it?

What did you do?

What do you know and can do that you did not know and could not do before?

Why is that important?

How does it impact student achievement?

What do you think is the most important information and/or skills you gained from your growth plan experience?

Why should you share this information with the learning community?

What audience(s) could benefit most from this information?

___ colleagues   ___ grade level(s)   ___ disciplines   ___ everyone

___ administration   ___ board of education   ___ students   ___ parents

How can you best convey this information/skill?

___ Samples of student work   ___ Collected and interpreted data   ___ Demonstration

___ Discussion   ___ Exhibit of materials   ___ Panel discussion

___ Video/audiotape of experiences   ___ Photo journal   ___ Oral presentation

___ Summary

What did not work? Why do you think it did not work?

Of what significance is the failure? What did you learn from it?

What advice would you have for others?

What procedures, processes, or information were important to the success or failure of an individual activity or the growth plan itself?

Is this new information for the learning community?

Does this information validate beliefs the learning community already holds or practices?

account and avoid using a lot of unfamiliar terminology. As the background knowledge and experience of the learning community audience increases, so can the complexity of the presentation. A proactive school leader who understands the audience and the content of a growth plan can help participants ensure the presentation is a quality learning experience for everyone.

Group Members Present Together

While the growth plan summary conference of a group plan is often most productive when the school leader meets with group members individually, the group should share its plan with the learning community together. A group presentation, with its spirit of camaraderie, reinforces to the entire learning community the value and power of the collaborative effort. The group presentation may also benefit group members who are uncomfortable presenting to colleagues. As a result of the experience of sharing with one's group, a hesitant individual may gain confidence to present individually in the future. The climate for learning and the environment for individual and collective risk taking are built through sharing growth plans with the learning community.

WRAPPING UP THE PROFESSIONAL GROWTH PLAN PROCESS

When participants have shared their plan, the Professional Growth Plan Process cycle is complete. Depending on the need for official documentation within a school or district, it may be necessary for all parties to sign off officially on a completed plan. It may also be of value to the school leader to keep a Growth Plan Summary Record, Blackline SL-9. The school leader can use this form to help participants develop their next growth plan. A sample completed form appears on page 155; the blackline master appears in Resource A.

GROWTH PLAN SUMMARY RECORD

Growth Plan Topic: Developmental Spelling

Participants(s): Becky D., Millie P., Marian A.

Summary Conference Date: February 11, 2007

Goals Have Been Met: ☒ Yes ☐ No

Comments: The entire first-grade spelling program was revised to reflect the developmental stages of spelling. Formal diagnostic procedures have also become part of the program to determine on a regular basis the stage of spelling development at which their first-grade students are functioning. Also in place is a process to document student growth.

Method of Evaluation Documentation Provided: ☒ Yes ☐ No

Comments: More than adequate - ample examples of student work demonstrating their new knowledge and skill. Reflections were minimal but adequate.

Date Plan Shared With Learning Community: February 20
Format for Sharing: Presentation to primary staff

Comments: Well-received by primary staff. Excellent discussion of how to pass information on from first- to second-grade teachers.

General Comments:
All expectations met.

Growth Plan Successfully Completed: ☒ Yes ☐ No

Participant Signature(s)/Date: *Becky D.* **Millie P.** *Marian A.*
2/11/07

Plan Administrator Signature/Date: *Jodi McCormick* *2/11/07*

Blackline SL-9

7

The Process Continues

If a system is to be mobilized in the direction of sustainability, leadership at all levels must be the primary engine.

—Fullan, 2005, p. 27

Leading the Professional Growth Plan Process through a successful first cycle is quite an accomplishment for any school leader. As with most anything of value, though, the first cycle takes a great deal of time, energy, and commitment. Hopefully, for those leading the process for the first time, the development of specific growth plans, whether individual plans or group plans, is staggered among staff, so not all begin and end at the same time. The staggering of first cycle growth plans provides more time for the school leader to attend to the important implementation issues that can make or break the process. Staggering at the beginning also helps keep the plans staggered in later cycles. This initial investment in the development and implementation of first cycle plans pays significant dividends in subsequent cycles.

By working to provide a successful first growth plan cycle experience, the school leader builds support for, and some independence into, the process. Good experiences mean participants better understand the purpose, procedures, and benefits of the process. This familiarity and increased confidence in the process provides participants with the skills and knowledge necessary to develop their second growth plan without much direction from the school leader. Often second generation plans are created by the participant(s) in just one draft and require only feedback and affirmation from the school leader, a significantly smaller investment of school leader's time and energy than with the first plan. And not only does plan design become easier for everyone, but implementation and monitoring does too. For example, the most capable participants quickly learn to streamline the process. To save meeting time, participants may provide written summaries to supplant Progress Meetings. Feeling more comfortable with the process, participants are more open and request assistance more freely, not only from the school leader but from other colleagues. This can mean less time spent troubleshooting for the school leader. Problems will continue to arise but participants take more active roles in the solutions. The transfer of responsibility for professional growth has then occurred and is partly evidenced by their participation in problem-solving activities.

SECOND GENERATION PLANS AND BEYOND

While the more capable and confident staff members move with greater independence into their second growth plan cycle, some staff members still need the guidance and support of the school leader. In either case, the second growth plan cycle presents opportunities to target new areas for professional learning or to build on the knowledge and skills developed in the first plan cycle.

A surefire way of targeting new, meaningful, and relevant professional learning is for the participants to repeat the needs-assessment process used in the first growth plan cycle. With a greater familiarity of the performance standards/best practices, with their student performance data, and with the needs-assessment process itself, targeting new learning for the second growth plan cycle becomes an easier task.

Changing growth plan topics in the next plan cycle is not always a given, however. Some participants may wish to remain with the same topic. A few participants may be reluctant to move on to a new topic because a comfort level with the first topic exists. Other participants may choose to remain with the same topic for their next plan because, through work on their current plan, they have discovered new skills, strategies, or knowledge that would complement, enhance, or extend those they have just acquired through their current growth plan. Staying with a topic is certainly an option if (1) there are no other instructional needs more pressing; (2) the targeted learning is truly new and; (3) there is enough new learning to support a growth plan.

When a participant wants to stay with a particular topic, one additional and fairly important factor needs consideration. Depending on the needs and abilities of the individual(s) wanting to stay with a topic while also taking into account the needs of the school, it may be advisable to continue work in a particular area. Doing so begins to build "in-house experts." As staff members, through their growth plan experiences, develop certain proficiencies, they become recognized by other staff members as a valuable resource or in-house experts. They become the "go-to" person when one needs advice or help in their area of expertise. Fullan (2005) refers to this as lateral capacity building. This can happen with one growth plan cycle, but more commonly it takes two focused plans to develop that confidence and skill set. The ability of the professional growth plan process to generate in-house experts increases with each cycle. It can happen incidentally or it can happen purposefully. It can be an individual in-house expert or it can be a group in-house expert representing a grade level, discipline, or specialty area.

The high school social studies teacher who works on reading in the content areas, developing the skills, strategies, and practices to support the marginal and poor reader in his classroom, experiences success with his students and as a result of his success and enthusiasm becomes the in-house expert on the topic. He is an in-house expert not only to those in the social studies department, but he also becomes a resource to those in the sciences, the arts, and even business. Three third-grade teachers choose classroom management as a focus of their growth plan. They want to understand and apply the skills, strategies, and practices that would create community, student ownership in classroom operation, and independence in their students' work habits.

Through the growth plan related learning, these classrooms become models for classroom management throughout the district and among the in-house experts. As such these teachers open their classroom to other teachers within their building and throughout the district. They also offer follow-up "how-to" mini-workshops to help others bring the same changes to their classrooms. For smaller schools and districts that do not have content specialists on staff, or for those who may be more geographically isolated, the development of a resource bank of in-house experts is a valuable by-product of the growth plan process. One cautionary note, recognizing in-house experts also means that the practices being shared and promoted do in fact represent best practice and are not just the participant's interpretation of best practice (Fullan, Hill, & Crevola, 2006). It is the school leader's responsibility to know the difference. Not everyone can be or wants to be an expert. Some staff members have other professional learning needs that are more pressing. Others do not want the attention or the responsibility.

IMPEDIMENTS TO THE PROCESS

With successive growth plan cycles, modifications and adaptations will likely emerge to strengthen and enhance the process to best meet the needs of those using it.

This is a natural and desired progression. Unfortunately, along with process improvements comes challenges that jeopardize not only the integrity of the process but the process itself.

Changes in Personnel

Sustaining the growth plan process, or any program for that matter, through personnel changes may be the greatest challenge. The current turnover of personnel created by the ongoing retirement of the baby boomer generation brings changes at all levels of education. From classroom to superintendent's office, new faces appear everywhere. Changes in instructional staff frequently suggest an influx of novice teachers replacing retiring teachers. For the growth plan process this means a shift in focus from developing and refining more complex advanced teaching skills and strategies associated with experienced staff to a more fundamental focus on the very basics of classroom management and best practice instruction. It is an opportunity to start the novice with data-driven decision making tied to best practice instruction. The veteran staff can continue on with their own professional growth plans. When changes occur in personnel at a building leadership level as with the principal, or at the district level with the superintendent, the commitment to continue the growth plan process may not be there. Unfortunately, new leadership may bring new agendas and initiatives that change program focus and allocation of resources (Fullan, 2005).

Inconsistent Implementation

Inconsistent implementation of the Professional Growth Plan Process, either at the department level or between buildings within a district, threatens both the integrity of the process and staff support too. Holding different groups to different expectations creates huge problems with the process. If a staff or groups within a staff in one district building use time set aside for growth plan work to do whatever they choose or conduct extracurricular activities, while all other district staff work on growth plan activities, word of the inconsistencies quickly spreads. And unfortunately, it is the growth plan process that is called into question rather than the supervision problem it really is. Requiring polished artifacts for documentation purposes in one building (consuming a great deal of staff time), when a draft quality standard exists in all other buildings, represents another example of inconsistent implementation. Again, this action unnecessarily places the process at the center of a controversy. Consistency among departments and buildings is essential to the vitality and longevity of the growth plan process.

Lack of Administrative Support

Inconsistent implementation and changes in personnel relates closely to a third concern—lack of administrative support. Lack of administrative support sets both individuals and the process up for failure. For the Professional Growth Plan Process to improve student achievement and build a robust learning community, active administrative leadership and collaboration are necessary (Fullan, Hill, & Crevola, 2006). The instructional leader must lead!

Demands of Compliance Directives

The final impediment to the growth plan process relates to issues of compliance. The resources used by schools to comply with the laws, procedures, and policies generated by different governmental agencies can limit the resources available for other school uses—energy being the resource in shortest supply (Fullan, 2005)! To counter this, identifying opportunities for professional learning and growth plan development within the compliance obligations promotes both causes. The threat to program sustainability presented by compliance directives is not unique to the Professional Growth Plan Process. Resource consuming compliance requirements can and do compromise programs and initiatives in schools everywhere.

THE PROFESSIONAL GROWTH PLAN PROCESS IS SCHOOL IMPROVEMENT

Know more, do more, be more. . . more quickly! For all too many in education, most particularly for those in the trenches, the teachers and their principals responsible for day-to-day operations, this has become the mantra of school improvement. Just the words "school improvement" bring feelings of overload, burnout, and extreme frustration to many. What has been lost in the morass of mandated school improvement planning efforts, so common to so many, is that which brought many educators to the profession in the first place—kids, teaching, and learning. Thankfully, research is beginning to expose the futility and counterproductive consequences associated with those elaborate resource consuming school improvement initiatives (Schomoker, 2006; Reeves, 2006). Research is also telling us to return to our roots, and to focus on quality classroom instruction. To do this means school improvement efforts must address the needs of individual educators in the context of their practice (Fullan, Hill, & Crevola, 2006).

Anyone who has served as a building principal understands how difficult addressing these needs can be. Generally, the learning needs represented in any teaching staff are numerous and quite diverse. Experience, content areas, and skill sets are first to come to mind, saying nothing about learning styles—novices vs. veteran, primary vs. intermediate, math vs. science, master teacher vs. struggling teacher, and on and on. It is obvious to those responsible for professional learning that educators need differentiated learning much like the students in their classrooms. The Professional Growth Plan Process accommodates these diverse needs, helping to manage and focus school improvement efforts. Through either individual plans or small group growth plans, the process focuses professional learning and growth on quality classroom instruction. The Professional Growth Plan Process is not just one more thing to do, it is not just a model for professional development, it is school improvement.

THE SCHOOL LEADER AS MECHANIC AND CHANGE AGENT

The Professional Growth Plan Process is not a quick fix. To suggest that any quick fix exists to address the complex problems associated with school improvement is, at the very least, naive. It is all too common to expect instant results (Guskey, 2000). The Professional Growth Plan Process has the potential to bring about enduring systematic and systemic changes in instructional practices, changes the educational community has so diligently pursued for so long. However, in its initial implementation stages, the Professional Growth Plan Process is slow, at times arduous and cumbersome, labor intensive, and loaded with logistics and frustrations. Yet we know change that is enduring and meaningful is also slow and sometimes messy (Fullan, 1993). To be successful, everyone involved with the Professional Growth Plan Process must exercise patience, perseverance, and flexibility to realize the desired changes and meet established goals. A three- to five-year commitment to the process is necessary to begin to actualize fully its potential for changing and improving schools.

Implementation of the Professional Growth Plan Process will challenge the school leader. Trying to manage individual growth and the needs of the organization is quite demanding. A staff member once said that trying to bring about meaningful school improvement is much like trying to fix a car while driving it. No statement could describe the task better. However, the school leader who accepts the challenge and effectively and efficiently leads the implementation of the Professional Growth Plan Process can become a powerful and potent change agent for school improvement.

Resource A

School Leader Blacklines

- ❑ SL-1 School Leader Checklists
- ❑ SL-2 Annual Growth Plan Projected Budget
- ❑ SL-3 Self-Assessment Conference Record
- ❑ SL-4 Growth Plan Tracking Chart
- ❑ SL-5 Monthly Tracking Chart
- ❑ SL-6 Annual Tracking Chart
- ❑ SL-7 Progress Meeting Record
- ❑ SL-8 Growth Plan Summary School Leader Comments
- ❑ SL-9 Growth Plan Summary Record

SCHOOL LEADER CHECKLISTS

Topic Selection

- ❑ Is the topic relevant to the participant's assignment?
- ❑ Do professional performance standards and best practices research support the topic?
- ❑ Can it impact student achievement?
- ❑ Are resources readily available to support study and practice?
- ❑ Does the participant have the background knowledge and skills necessary to pursue this topic successfully?

Participants in a Group Growth Plan

- ❑ Do the personalities of each group member mesh?
- ❑ Is one member a dominating force who will control or limit the potential learning of others?
- ❑ Do the experience, skills, and knowledge of the participants contribute to the functioning of the group?
- ❑ Will group members have an opportunity to meet and work together?
- ❑ Do group members have any hidden agendas?
- ❑ Are there too many in the group to allow full participation of all members?

Professional Goals

- ❑ Does the participant already have this knowledge or this skill?
- ❑ Are the goals attainable?
- ❑ Will achieving the goals result in professional growth?
- ❑ Are the goals assessable?
- ❑ Do the goals link to improved student achievement?
- ❑ Do the goals support school improvement directly?
- ❑ Is the number of goals appropriate?

Learner-Centered Goals

- ❑ Does a clear link exist between the Professional Goals and the Learner-Centered Goals?
- ❑ Can these goals impact student achievement?

- ❑ Do the goals support school improvement efforts?
- ❑ Can participants document these goals fairly easily?

Essential and Related Questions

- ❑ Does the Essential Question have a known answer?
- ❑ Is it possible to answer the Essential Question?
- ❑ Do the questions require more than a yes or no answer?
- ❑ Does the Essential Question support the Professional Goals?
- ❑ Do the Related Questions support the Professional Goals?
- ❑ Will answering the Related Questions help answer the Essential Question?
- ❑ Will professional growth result from pursuing answers to the Essential and Related Questions?
- ❑ Does the Essential Question define a manageable scope of study?

Action Plan

- ❑ Do the activities outlined in the Action Plan address Professional Goals and Learner-Centered Goals?
- ❑ Do the activities cover each phase of the learning cycle: exploration, application, evaluation, reflection, and refinement?
- ❑ Are resources available to support the plan?
- ❑ Is the participant capable of completing the task and activities?
- ❑ Is the time frame realistic?

Documentation

- ❑ Does the practitioner understand what artifacts are and the purpose of documentation?
- ❑ Does the targeted documentation represent the growth plan?
- ❑ Does an adequate amount of documentation exist from which to select Baseline Data and evaluation data?

❑ Are the resources and supplies needed to support the documentation available?

❑ Has the participant targeted enough artifacts to document each professional growth criterion adequately?

❑ Does the practitioner have a plan for organizing the artifacts?

Baseline Data

❑ Do Baseline Data exist to show a beginning point?

❑ Can the data selected provide a basis for comparison and analysis of comparable data collected after the intervention?

❑ Can the data document professional growth: new knowledge or skill, change in practice, ability to reflect, contribution to the learning community, or improvement in student achievement?

❑ Are the data, the data collection and interpretation process simple enough for participants to manage?

Methods of Evaluation

❑ Does the participant address each Professional and Learner-Centered Goal?

❑ Can the artifacts in the growth plan document growth?

❑ Are the evaluation methods reasonable and doable?

❑ Does everyone understand and agree on what professional growth in this plan will look like?

❑ Is a Method of Evaluation present for each of the criterion that characterizes professional growth?

Resources

❑ Will the resources help the participant reach his or her goals?

❑ Are the resources readily available?

❑ Does the success of the plan depend on access to a particular resource?

❑ Can the school provide the resources?

❑ If not, are there other sources to acquire the resources?

Sharing With the Learning Community

❑ Does the format selected facilitate sharing of the growth plan information?

❑ Is the purpose for sharing clear?

❑ Is the forum/audience appropriate?

❑ Does the format or presentation encourage "bring and brag"?

❑ Is the content of the growth plan experience and its significance (not the step-by-step procedures) the focus of sharing?

❑ Do the skills, abilities, and talents of the participant complement the forum and format?

Progress Meetings

❑ Is the participant making adequate progress?

❑ If it is a group plan, are all participants contributing actively?

❑ Is documentation adequate?

❑ Does the plan require modification?

❑ Is the reason for modification reasonable?
  • New knowledge or understandings
  • Insurmountable obstacles
  • Lack of resources or information

❑ Do all parties agree that modification is necessary?

Summary Conference

❑ Did the participant achieve the Professional Goals?

❑ Did the participant achieve the Learner-Centered Goals?

❑ Did the participant address the Essential Question?

❑ Does evidence exist to document all five professional growth criteria?

❑ Can the participant articulate the growth he or she has experienced?

❑ Has the participant made a contribution to the learning community?

❑ Do you agree with the participant about the growth that has occurred?

Blackline SL-1 (Page 2 of 2)

Copyright © 2008 by Corwin Press. All rights reserved. Reprinted from *The Educator's Professional Growth Plan: A Process for Developing Staff and Improving Instruction, Second Edition,* by Jodi Peine. Thousand Oaks, CA: Corwin Press, www.corwinpress.com. Reproduction authorized only for the local school site or nonprofit organization that has purchased this book.

ANNUAL GROWTH PLAN PROJECTED BUDGET

Fiscal Year 20_____ –20_____

Topic/Contact Person	# in Plan/Grade	Workshop	Print	Supplies	Media	Substitutes	Misc.
TOTAL							

Page _____ of _____

Blackline SL-2

Copyright © 2008 by Corwin Press. All rights reserved. Reprinted from *The Educator's Professional Growth Plan: A Process for Developing Staff and Improving Instruction, Second Edition*, by Jodi Peine. Thousand Oaks, CA: Corwin Press, www.corwinpress.com. Reproduction authorized only for the local school site or nonprofit organization that has purchased this book.

SELF-ASSESSMENT CONFERENCE RECORD

Participant:

School Leader:

Date(s) of Conference:

Areas of Strength:

Areas Targeted for Growth:

Possible Growth Plan Topics:

General Comments:

Blackline SL-3

Copyright © 2008 by Corwin Press. All rights reserved. Reprinted from *The Educator's Professional Growth Plan: A Process for Developing Staff and Improving Instruction, Second Edition,* by Jodi Peine. Thousand Oaks, CA: Corwin Press, www.corwinpress.com. Reproduction authorized only for the local school site or nonprofit organization that has purchased this book.

GROWTH PLAN TRACKING CHART

Name(s): _____

Plan Topic: _____

Projected Completion Date: _____

	Target Completion Date	**Task Date Completed**
Explanation of Growth Plans/ Components Handout		
Self-Assessment/Handout		
Needs-Assessment Conference		
Growth Plan Draft/Final Draft		
Progress Meetings Year 1—1, 2, 3	1. 2. 3.	1. 2. 3.
Interim Sharing		
Progress Meetings Year 1—1, 2, 3	1. 2. 3.	1. 2. 3.
Interim Sharing		
Progress Meetings Year 1—1, 2, 3	1. 2. 3.	1. 2. 3.
Interim Sharing		
Completion Date		
Growth Plan Summary Due Date		
Growth Plan Summary Conference		
Final Sharing		

Blackline SL-4

Copyright © 2008 by Corwin Press. All rights reserved. Reprinted from *The Educator's Professional Growth Plan: A Process for Developing Staff and Improving Instruction, Second Edition,* by Jodi Peine. Thousand Oaks, CA: Corwin Press, www.corwinpress .com. Reproduction authorized only for the local school site or nonprofit organization that has purchased this book.

MONTHLY TRACKING CHART

NEEDS-ASSESSMENT CONFERENCES Date/Practitioner(s)	PLAN DESIGN MEETINGS Date/Practitioner(s)	PROGRESS MEETINGS Date/Practitioner(s)	SUMMARY CONFERENCE MEETINGS Date/Practitioner(s)

MONTH: _____

Page _____ of _____

Blackline SL-5

Copyright © 2008 by Corwin Press. All rights reserved. Reprinted from *The Educator's Professional Growth Plan: A Process for Developing Staff and Improving Instruction, Second Edition*, by Jodi Peine. Thousand Oaks, CA: Corwin Press, www.corwinpress.com. Reproduction authorized only for the local school site or nonprofit organization that has purchased this book.

ANNUAL TRACKING CHART 20__–20__

NEEDS ASSESSMENT/ PLAN DEVELOPMENT	PLAN DEVELOPMENT ONLY	PLAN IN PROGRESS	PLAN SUMMARY CONFERENCES

Page _____ of _____

Blackline SL-6

Copyright © 2008 by Corwin Press. All rights reserved. Reprinted from *The Educator's Professional Growth Plan: A Process for Developing Staff and Improving Instruction, Second Edition,* by Jodi Peine. Thousand Oaks, CA: Corwin Press, www.corwinpress.com. Reproduction authorized only for the local school site or nonprofit organization that has purchased this book.

PROGRESS MEETING RECORD

GROWTH PLAN: _____

PARTICIPANTS: _____

COMPLETION DATE: _____

PROGRESS MEETING # _____ DATE: _____

THOSE PRESENT: _____

ACTION PLAN: ☐ BEHIND ☐ ON SCHEDULE ☐ AHEAD
COMMENTS:

DOCUMENTATION: ☐ NONE ☐ INADEQUATE ☐ ADEQUATE
COMMENTS:

MODIFICATIONS: ☐ NONE ☐ SEE EXPLANATION
Explanation of Modification (include reason for modification):

NEW RESOURCE NEEDS:

NEXT MEETING DATE: _____

GENERAL CONCERNS/COMMENTS (see back):

Blackline SL-7

Copyright © 2008 by Corwin Press. All rights reserved. Reprinted from *The Educator's Professional Growth Plan: A Process for Developing Staff and Improving Instruction, Second Edition,* by Jodi Peine. Thousand Oaks, CA: Corwin Press, www.corwinpress.com. Reproduction authorized only for the local school site or nonprofit organization that has purchased this book.

GROWTH PLAN SUMMARY SCHOOL LEADER COMMENTS

Acquisition of new knowledge and skills:

Application of new knowledge and skills:

Enhanced reflective practices:

Contribution to learning community:

Improved student achievement:

Additional comments:

Participant: Date:

Plan Administrator:

Growth Plan Topic:

Blackline SL-8

Copyright © 2008 by Corwin Press. All rights reserved. Reprinted from *The Educator's Professional Growth Plan: A Process for Developing Staff and Improving Instruction, Second Edition,* by Jodi Peine. Thousand Oaks, CA: Corwin Press, www.corwinpress.com. Reproduction authorized only for the local school site or nonprofit organization that has purchased this book.

GROWTH PLAN SUMMARY RECORD

Growth Plan Topic:

Participants(s):

Summary Conference Date:

Goals Have Been Met: ❑   Yes   ❑   No
Comments:

Method of Evaluation Documentation Provided: ❑   Yes   ❑   No
Comments:

Date Plan Shared With Learning Community:
Format for Sharing:
Comments:

General Comments:

Growth Plan Successfully Completed: ❑ Yes   ❑ No

Participant Signature(s)/Date:

Plan Administrator Signature/Date:

Blackline SL-9

Copyright © 2008 by Corwin Press. All rights reserved. Reprinted from *The Educator's Professional Growth Plan: A Process for Developing Staff and Improving Instruction, Second Edition,* by Jodi Peine. Thousand Oaks, CA: Corwin Press, www.corwinpress.com. Reproduction authorized only for the local school site or nonprofit organization that has purchased this book.

Resource B

Participant Blacklines

- ❑ P-1   Professional Growth Criteria
- ❑ P-2   Growth Plan Process Benefits
- ❑ P-3   Professional Growth Plan Process Participant Checklist
- ❑ P-4   Professional Growth Plan Format
- ❑ P-5   Explanation of Professional Growth Plan Components
- ❑ P-6   Growth Plan Topics
- ❑ P-7   Action Plan Activities and Tasks
- ❑ P-8   Artifacts for Documentation
- ❑ P-9   Anecdotal Record
- ❑ P-10   Work Log
- ❑ P-11   Reading Reflection Guide
- ❑ P-12   Activity Reflection Guide
- ❑ P-13   Observation Reflection Guide
- ❑ P-14   Documentation Artifacts Map
- ❑ P-15   Reflection Basics
- ❑ P-16   When You Document, You . . .
- ❑ P-17   Growth Plan Evaluation Criteria
- ❑ P-18   Growth Plan Evaluation
- ❑ P-19   Methods of Evaluation Plan Sheet
- ❑ P-20   Artifact Organizer
- ❑ P-21   Evaluation Artifact Organizer
- ❑ P-22   Resource Survey
- ❑ P-23   Resource Request Budget Form
- ❑ P-24   Forums and Formats for Sharing With the Learning Community
- ❑ P-25   Request for Assistance

❏ P-26   Work Day Plan

❏ P-27   Work Day Summary Reflection Guide

❏ P-28   Progress Meeting Questions

❏ P-29   Growth Plan Summary Activities

❏ P-30   Growth Plan Self-Evaluation

❏ P-31   Growth Plan Summary Reflection Guide

❏ P-32   Sharing With the Learning Community

PROFESSIONAL GROWTH PLAN

Participant Blackline Master Guide

The following pages have been designed to guide you through the entire growth plan process. Do not be overwhelmed by the number of blackline masters! You do not need to use or complete each one. Use only those you need to help you identify your needs, design your growth plan, implement your growth plan, and evaluate and summarize your growth plan.

PROCESS OVERVIEW

P-1 Professional Growth Criteria—identifies the school district's definition of professional growth

P-2 Growth Plan Process Benefits—identifies the benefits of the growth plan to you, your school, and your students

P-3 Professional Growth Plan Process Participant Checklist—describes the steps of the growth plan process

P-4 Professional Growth Plan Format—identifies the components of a growth plan

P-5 Explanation of Professional Growth Plan Components—explains each component of the growth plan

Targeting Your Professional Growth

P-6 Growth Plan Topics—lists possible topics for a growth plan

Designing Your Growth Plan

Action Planning

P-7 Action Plan Activities and Tasks—describes different learning activities you may use as part of your Action Plan

Documentation

P-8 Artifacts for Documentation—describes the purpose of documentation and how to determine whether an artifact is documentation

P-9 Anecdotal Record—helps you organize your observations of effective teaching techniques, strategies, lesson plans, behaviors, skills, and attitudes

P-10 Work Log—helps you document the time you spend working on your growth plan

P-11 Reading Reflection Guide—provides reflective thinking prompts to respond to after completing a reading to help you process and learn from the reading

P-12 Activity Reflection Guide—provides reflective thinking prompts to respond to after completing an activity to help you process and learn from the activity

P-13 Observation Reflection Guide—provides reflective thinking prompts to respond to after completing an observation to help you process and learn from the observation

P-14 Documentation Artifacts Map—provides a graphic organizer to help determine what artifacts an activity might generate

P-15 Reflection Basics—describes reflective thinking

P-16 When You Document, You . . . —describes what to do when you document

P-17 Growth Plan Evaluation Criteria—describes the criteria by which professional growth will be evaluated

P-18 Growth Plan Evaluation—documents professional growth—next to each professional growth evaluation criterion are examples of the types of documentation that demonstrate professional growth

Identifying Documentation for Baseline Data and Methods of Evaluation

P-19 Methods of Evaluation Plan Sheet—provides questions to help you think about what artifacts can provide Baseline Data and measure growth and what artifacts can demonstrate that you have met the professional goals

P-20 Artifact Organizer—a graphic organizer to help sort artifacts by goal; you might use these artifacts as baseline data, to document growth, or for both purposes

P-21 Evaluation Artifact Organizer—provides a graphic organizer to help sort artifacts by professional growth criteria and help you identify and define your Methods of Evaluation

Resources and Sharing

P-22 Resource Survey—provides a graphic organizer to help you identify the resources you may need to support your growth plan

P-23 Resource Request Budget Form—provides a form you submit to your supervisor to help project and plan for costs associated with your growth plan

P-24 Forums and Formats for Sharing With the Learning Community—lists possible forums and formats in which you might choose to share your growth plan experience with your colleagues

Implementing Your Growth Plan

P-25 Request for Assistance—provides a form you can use to communicate to your supervisor your need for any particular kind of help

P-26 Work Day Plan Sheet—provides a form that communicates to your supervisor your work plans for a workshop day; you might also use this form as documentation for the Work/Effort professional growth criteria

P-27 Work Day Summary Reflection Guide—provides reflective thinking prompts to help you process and learn from your workday experiences; you can also use this form to document to your supervisor your efforts on your work day as well as provide documentation for the professional growth criteria Enhanced Reflective Practice and/or Work/Effort

P-28 Progress Meeting Questions—lists questions you can use to prepare for your progress meeting with your supervisor and help you reflect on the progress you have made on your growth plan

Evaluating and Summarizing Your Growth Plan

P-29 Growth Plan Summary Activities—lists the steps for summarizing and completing your growth plan

P-30 Growth Plan Self-Evaluation Professional Growth Scale—provides a 5-point scale for you to evaluate the growth you have experienced as a result of your growth plan

P-31 Growth Plan Summary Reflection Guide—provides reflective thinking prompts to help you summarize your growth plan experience

P-32 Sharing With the Learning Community—lists questions to help you prepare to share your information with the learning community

PROFESSIONAL GROWTH CRITERIA

You grow professionally when you

✓ acquire new knowledge/skills,

✓ apply new knowledge/skills,

✓ enhance reflective practices,

✓ improve student achievement, and

✓ contribute to the learning community.

Blackline P-1

Copyright © 2008 by Corwin Press. All rights reserved. Reprinted from *The Educator's Professional Growth Plan: A Process for Developing Staff and Improving Instruction, Second Edition,* by Jodi Peine. Thousand Oaks, CA: Corwin Press, www.corwinpress .com. Reproduction authorized only for the local school site or nonprofit organization that has purchased this book.

GROWTH PLAN PROCESS BENEFITS

The Professional Growth Plan Process Benefits You, Your Students, Your School

✓ You develop the skills, knowledge, attitudes, and behaviors that increase your professional competence.

✓ You assume control and responsibility for your learning.

✓ You choose

- what you learn,
- how you learn it, and
- the time frame for learning.

✓ You improve student achievement.

✓ You support school improvement.

✓ You build collegial relationships and strengthen your learning community.

Blackline P-2

Copyright © 2008 by Corwin Press. All rights reserved. Reprinted from *The Educator's Professional Growth Plan: A Process for Developing Staff and Improving Instruction, Second Edition,* by Jodi Peine. Thousand Oaks, CA: Corwin Press, www.corwinpress.com. Reproduction authorized only for the local school site or nonprofit organization that has purchased this book.

PROFESSIONAL GROWTH PLAN
PROCESS PARTICIPANT CHECKLIST

Phase 1: Targeting Professional Growth

❑ Review and understand professional performance standards and best practices research.

❑ Perform professional performance standards self-assessment.

❑ Analyze available student achievement data.

❑ Look for correlations between practices and student performance.

❑ Participate in Needs-Assessment Conference.

❑ Choose plan Topic.

❑ State Rationale for Topic Selection.

❑ Identify Participants if a group plan.

Phase 2: Plan Design

❑ Establish Professional and Learner-Centered Goals.

❑ Create Essential and Related Questions.

❑ Design Action Plan.

❑ Determine modes of Documentation.

❑ Identify Baseline Data.

❑ Define Methods of Evaluation.

❑ Identify Resource Needs.

❑ Choose Method of Sharing Results With the Learning Community.

Phase 3: Plan Implementation and Monitoring

❑ Implement Action Plan.

❑ Conduct Progress Meetings.

❑ Participate in interim sharing of growth plan.

Phase 4: Plan Evaluation

❑ Summarize growth plan activities.

❑ Participate in growth plan summary conference.

❑ Conduct growth plan self-evaluation.

❑ Complete growth plan summary reflection guide.

❑ Share results with the learning community.

Blackline P-3

Copyright © 2008 by Corwin Press. All rights reserved. Reprinted from *The Educator's Professional Growth Plan: A Process for Developing Staff and Improving Instruction, Second Edition,* by Jodi Peine. Thousand Oaks, CA: Corwin Press, www.corwinpress.com. Reproduction authorized only for the local school site or nonprofit organization that has purchased this book.

PROFESSIONAL GROWTH PLAN FORMAT

Name: Date Submitted:

Topic Selected:

Rationale for Selecting Topic:

Participants:

Professional Goals:

Learner-Centered Goals:

Essential Question:

Related Questions:

Action Plan/Time Line:

Documentation:

Baseline Data:

Methods of Evaluation:

Resource Needs:

Method of Sharing With the Learning Community:

Projected Completion Date:

Progress Meeting Dates:

Plan Approved Date:

Plan Administrator's Signature:

Participant's Signature:

Blackline P-4

Copyright © 2008 by Corwin Press. All rights reserved. Reprinted from *The Educator's Professional Growth Plan: A Process for Developing Staff and Improving Instruction, Second Edition,* by Jodi Peine. Thousand Oaks, CA: Corwin Press, www.corwinpress.com. Reproduction authorized only for the local school site or nonprofit organization that has purchased this book.

EXPLANATION OF PROFESSIONAL GROWTH PLAN COMPONENTS

The following explanation of growth plan components endeavors to help you develop your Professional Growth Plan. This guide helps you define (1) what you want to know or be able to do at the end of the plan, (2) how you will acquire that knowledge and skill, and (3) how you will know that professional growth has occurred.

First, talk through your plan with the plan administrator/school leader or a colleague to help you clarify what you want to do and ensure that the scope of your plan is narrow enough for you to attain without unnecessary frustration. Simplicity is the key to the Professional Growth Plan.

PROFESSIONAL GROWTH PLAN COMPONENTS

NAME: _____   DATE SUBMITTED: _____

TOPIC SELECTED

Identify the focus of your plan.

- What is the general subject, content, focus of your plan (e.g., personal fitness, emergent literacy, play-based assessment, writing prompts)?
- What would you choose as a title for your plan?
- Under what subject would you look for information in the library?

RATIONALE FOR SELECTING TOPIC

Explain your reason for choosing this topic.

- Why have you chosen this area as the focus of your plan?
- Why should you investigate this area?
- What problem or issue would you like to resolve?

PARTICIPANTS

- Identify the plan participants by name and position.
- Is this an individual plan or are you working with a colleague?
- If you are working in a group, who are the participants?

PROFESSIONAL GOALS

These goal statements represent the professional growth you would like to experience on plan completion. It is important to focus the goals and not try to do too much. Keep goals manageable and realistic.

- What do you want to know or be able to do at the completion of this plan that you do not know or cannot do today?
- How will you be a more proficient educator when you have completed this plan?

EXPLANATION OF PROFESSIONAL GROWTH PLAN COMPONENTS (Continued)

LEARNER-CENTERED GOALS

These goal statements represent the growth in student achievement or performance that will occur on completion of the plan. It is understood that not all students attain these goals, but the majority of students should attain them. Again, it is important to keep a narrow, clearly defined focus that produces manageable and realistic goals. Be as specific as possible about how your plan will improve student achievement. This achievement may not be immediate; it may take a year or two to see results. However, if you cannot link your efforts to an improvement in student achievement, you need to rethink your plan.

- What will students know or do better as a result of this plan?

ESSENTIAL QUESTION

Establish a question, which when addressed, helps you meet your established Professional and Learner-Centered Goals. Keep the question as focused as possible.

- What do you want to know?
- Does this question have an answer?
- Is the question too narrow or too broad?
- Can you think of other questions you need to address first to answer this question?
- Do you know the answer to this question?

RELATED QUESTIONS

The answers to these questions help answer the Essential Question. You might want to think of them as subquestions.

- What else do you need to know to answer the Essential Question?

ACTION PLAN/TIME LINE

List the tasks or activities you need to complete and a time line of when you will complete the task or activity. Merely approximations, these times serve as benchmarks to ensure that you are progressing toward plan completion. Use action verbs to write your tasks (e.g., research play-based assessment, read, interview, visit where it is in use; conduct a survey of area schools that have personal fitness plans as part of the curriculum; and create writing prompts that support the curriculum). The more details you provide, the better the direction you will have to begin your plan. Details also help you identify what resources you may need to support your plan.

- What sequential steps will you follow to complete your plan?
- What resources will you review?
- Whom will you interview?
- What will you create?

Blackline P-5 (Page 2 of 5)

Example Action Plan Time Line statements:

By November '06
Identify and clarify for the purpose of instruction the characteristics of narrative, persuasive, and expository writing and writing prompts.

By December '06
Map the third-grade curriculum by topic/unit/activity.

By January '07
Complete a student attitude survey regarding personal fitness plans.

By March '07
Solicit from local high schools personal fitness plans that are part of their curriculum.

DOCUMENTATION

The sum total of your documentation constitutes your Professional Growth Plan portfolio. The documentation demonstrates your work on the plan and the professional growth you have experienced as a result of completing the plan. Each piece of documentation (artifact) should relate closely to your Professional Growth Plan; each piece is unique to you and your plan. Self-reflection and metacognition (evaluating what you know, how you know it, and why you know it) are critical components of the documentation process. Collecting documentation may be one of the most important tasks you do related to your professional growth. It is important to outline at least the basic contents or potential artifacts you will include in your portfolio before you implement your plan. Common artifacts are a reading log and reflections or comments about your readings, samples of student work, lesson plans, units developed, a work log, or any other items that are important in the completion of your plan. Once you get into the process, you may add or delete particular items. You may even include a "Portfolio Rejection Log" containing artifacts you chose not to include and reasons why.

- What data or artifacts are you going to collect and why?
- What artifacts will help demonstrate your work, activities, reflection and metacognition, learning, and application of learning associated with the Professional Growth Plan?

BASELINE DATA

Collected at the beginning of your plan, this information gives you a basis of measurement to determine whether growth has occurred. The data does not necessarily have to include numbers or quantified test results. Baseline data can come from an observational checklist, attitudinal survey, or a combination of quantitative and subjective data. If you cannot measure growth, your plan may not have enough focus or specificity.

- What information can you collect before you begin your plan that reflects your beginning point?
- Can this information provide a basis for comparison of information collected after your action or intervention plan?
- Can this information demonstrate growth or change, should they occur?

EXPLANATION OF PROFESSIONAL GROWTH PLAN COMPONENTS (Continued)

METHODS OF EVALUATION

Explain what you will do to provide evidence that you have addressed your Essential Question and attained your goals at completion of your plan. (You may want to refer back to your baseline data to determine how you will evaluate the plan's effectiveness and the attainment of your established goals.) These methods do not have to be statistically pure, but they need to demonstrate that you have achieved the goals. Your professional development portfolio should demonstrate your professional growth and the attainment of your Professional Goals.

- How will you determine whether growth has occurred (yours and your students')?
- How will you determine whether you implemented your growth plan effectively?
- Did you attain the Professional and Learner-Centered Goals you established?
- What documentation will show new knowledge or skill?
- What documentation will show changes in instructional practices?
- What documentation will demonstrate increased reflection skills?
- What documentation will show your effort?
- What documentation will show a contribution to the learning community?
- What documentation will show improvement in student achievement?

RESOURCE NEEDS

Identify the types of support you need to complete your plan. Be as specific as possible, listing workshop titles, dates, and sponsoring agencies; book titles, authors, and publishers; and so on. If possible, attach anticipated costs associated with each item. Your needs may change once you implement your plan.

- What resources do you need to complete this plan?
- Do you have specific technology needs?
- Do you need particular books, videotapes, or audiotapes?
- Do you need release time to visit other programs or observe other teachers?
- Do you need to attend a specific workshop or training?
- Do you need to find an expert who can provide you with the training?

METHOD OF SHARING WITH THE LEARNING COMMUNITY

Explain how you will share your growth plan experience with your learning community.

- Who might benefit most from your new knowledge and skills?
- What forum and format will you use to share your growth plan experience?
- When do you think you will have something to share?

Blackline P-5 (Page 4 of 5)

PROJECTED COMPLETION DATE

Specify the month and year you anticipate completing your plan. Be as realistic as possible, but also know you can adjust the time frame if necessary.

- How much time will you need to complete your plan?

PROGRESS MEETING DATES

Identify dates to meet with the plan administrator to monitor progress toward goals.

PLAN APPROVED DATE:

PRACTITIONER'S SIGNATURE:

PLAN ADMINISTRATOR'S SIGNATURE:

Blackline P-5 (Page 5 of 5)

Copyright © 2008 by Corwin Press. All rights reserved. Reprinted from *The Educator's Professional Growth Plan: A Process for Developing Staff and Improving Instruction, Second Edition,* by Jodi Peine. Thousand Oaks, CA: Corwin Press, www.corwinpress.com. Reproduction authorized only for the local school site or nonprofit organization that has purchased this book.

GROWTH PLAN TOPICS

The list of topics below can serve as a starting point for a Professional Growth Plan. This list represents the topics available for study. Each general topic heading has numerous subtopics that can provide a more defined and specific focus for a growth plan.

ADHD/ADD	Internet in the Classroom
Assessment Literacy	Interpreting and Using Data
Authentic Assessment	Involving Families
Autism/Asperger Syndrome in the Classroom	Looping
Balanced Reading	Mathematics Problem Solving
Block Scheduling	Multiple Intelligences
Brain-Based Learning	Nonfiction Reading
Building Vocabulary	Performance-Based Assessment
Bully Prevention	Phonemic Awareness
Classroom Management	Problem-Based Instruction
Concept-Based Instruction	Questioning Strategies
Conflict Resolution	Reading Comprehension
Developmental Spelling	Reading in the Content Areas
Differentiated Instruction	Reporting Student Progress
Diversity	Running Records
Emergent Literacy	School to Work
English Language Learners	Service Learning
Grading for Learning	Specific Learning Disabilities
Guided Reading and Writing	Student-Led Conferences
Inclusion	Student Physical Fitness
Inquiry-Based Instruction	Teaming
Interactive Instructional Strategies	Writing Process

Blackline P-6

Copyright © 2008 by Corwin Press. All rights reserved. Reprinted from *The Educator's Professional Growth Plan: A Process for Developing Staff and Improving Instruction, Second Edition,* by Jodi Peine. Thousand Oaks, CA: Corwin Press, www.corwinpress.com. Reproduction authorized only for the local school site or nonprofit organization that has purchased this book.

ACTION PLAN ACTIVITIES AND TASKS

A SAMPLING OF CHOICES

Attend

- a university class
- conferences
- workshops

Collect

- work samples
- specified data

Conduct

- action research
- interviews
- observations
- site visits
- student case study
- surveys

Construct

- lesson plans
- specific assessments
- units of instruction
- worksheets
- instructional materials

Interpret

- specified data

Listen To

- audio recordings

Participate In

- a chat room
- a discussion group
- a study group
- peer coaching
- team teaching
- on-line tutorials/classes

Read

- books
- articles

Reflect On

- readings
- activities
- observations
- instruction

View

- multimedia
- Web sites

Blackline P-7

Copyright © 2008 by Corwin Press. All rights reserved. Reprinted from *The Educator's Professional Growth Plan: A Process for Developing Staff and Improving Instruction, Second Edition,* by Jodi Peine. Thousand Oaks, CA: Corwin Press, www.corwinpress.com. Reproduction authorized only for the local school site or nonprofit organization that has purchased this book.

ARTIFACTS FOR DOCUMENTATION

Documentation serves two purposes. First, it provides evidence of professional growth. Professional growth means you have acquired new knowledge and skills and you are actually using the new knowledge and skills.

Second, documentation promotes learning by encouraging the development of reflective thinking.

When deciding whether to include an artifact as evidence of growth, it is important to ask yourself the following questions.

WHAT DOES THIS SHOW?

- Is it evidence of your work and effort?
- Does it show your professional growth as related to your goals?
- Does it show growth in your ability to use the reflective process?
- Does it show an increase in student achievement?
- Does it show changes you have made in your instructional practices or content?
- Does it show a contribution you have made to the learning community?

If you cannot answer yes to any of the questions, do not include the artifact. Quantity is not necessarily quality!

Authentic artifacts are of most value even though they may not have eye appeal for they verify actual use. Sticky notes, handwritten notes, lesson plans, and student work samples are authentic artifacts. Incomplete or rambling sentences, cryptic notes, no punctuation, and messy handwriting all indicate real evidence.

Polished artifacts can be of value but not always. Plastic-covered pages of perfectly typed entries sometimes represent merely excessive and unnecessary work. They might even suggest manufactured evidence.

The following items can be artifacts for the purpose of documentation. This lengthy list is not all-inclusive; many other options exist.

DOCUMENTATION ARTIFACTS

Activity Plans	Parent Contact Log
Activity Reflections	Parent Correspondence
Anecdotal Records	Peer Reviews
Assessments	Performance Assessments
Awards	Photographs
CDs	Pre/Post Self-Assessments
Checklists	Professional Presentations
Classroom Observations	Rating Scales
Conference Summaries	Reading Logs
Curriculum Materials	Reading Reflections
Grade Sheets/Evaluation Reports	Revised Professional Growth Plans
Homework Assignments	Standardized Test Scores
Instructional Materials	Student Projects
Instructional Planning Calendars	Student Work Samples
Learning Logs	Surveys
Lesson Plans	Student
Likert Scales	Parent
Management Plans	Colleague
Mentoring Activities	Tally Sheets
Multimedia	Teacher Journal
New Certification/Degree	Transcripts
Newsletters	Unit Plans
Newspaper Articles	Visual Maps
Observation Reflections	Work Logs
Observational Instruments	Workshop Logs
Parent Contact Data	

Blackline P-8 (Page 2 of 2)

Copyright © 2008 by Corwin Press. All rights reserved. Reprinted from *The Educator's Professional Growth Plan: A Process for Developing Staff and Improving Instruction, Second Edition,* by Jodi Peine. Thousand Oaks, CA: Corwin Press, www.corwinpress.com. Reproduction authorized only for the local school site or nonprofit organization that has purchased this book.

ANECDOTAL RECORD

Activity Observed Date: _____	COMMENTS
	_____ _____ _____ _____ _____ _____
Activity Observed Date: _____	COMMENTS
	_____ _____ _____ _____ _____ _____
Activity Observed Date: _____	COMMENTS
	_____ _____ _____ _____ _____ _____

Name: _____

Blackline P-9

Copyright © 2008 by Corwin Press. All rights reserved. Reprinted from *The Educator's Professional Growth Plan: A Process for Developing Staff and Improving Instruction, Second Edition,* by Jodi Peine. Thousand Oaks, CA: Corwin Press, www.corwinpress.com. Reproduction authorized only for the local school site or nonprofit organization that has purchased this book.

WORK LOG

DATE	LOCATION	PARTICIPANTS	ACTIVITY SUMMARY	TIME

Name: _____   Page _____ of _____

Blackline P-10

Copyright © 2008 by Corwin Press. All rights reserved. Reprinted from *The Educator's Professional Growth Plan: A Process for Developing Staff and Improving Instruction, Second Edition,* by Jodi Peine. Thousand Oaks, CA: Corwin Press, www.corwinpress.com. Reproduction authorized only for the local school site or nonprofit organization that has purchased this book.

READING REFLECTION GUIDE

Use the following prompts to help you process and document your readings. You do not need to answer each question. Answer questions that are appropriate to your experience.

❑ Book ❑ Article ❑ Other_____

Title:

Author:

Copyright:

Magazine:

Publisher:

Briefly summarize your reading.

What did you hope to gain from this reading? Why?

Did the reading provide the information you were seeking? How?

What new information or insight did you acquire from this reading?

Did the text make sense? What did you find difficult to accept or understand? Why?

What did you totally reject? Why?

How does what you read compare with your past experience or your current beliefs? Explain.

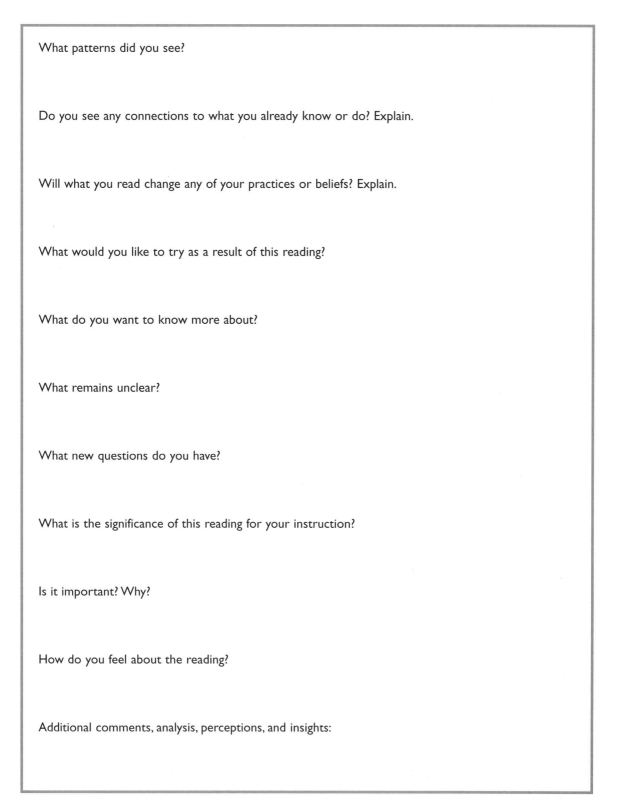

What patterns did you see?

Do you see any connections to what you already know or do? Explain.

Will what you read change any of your practices or beliefs? Explain.

What would you like to try as a result of this reading?

What do you want to know more about?

What remains unclear?

What new questions do you have?

What is the significance of this reading for your instruction?

Is it important? Why?

How do you feel about the reading?

Additional comments, analysis, perceptions, and insights:

Blackline P-11 (Page 2 of 2)

Copyright © 2008 by Corwin Press. All rights reserved. Reprinted from *The Educator's Professional Growth Plan: A Process for Developing Staff and Improving Instruction, Second Edition,* by Jodi Peine. Thousand Oaks, CA: Corwin Press, www.corwinpress.com. Reproduction authorized only for the local school site or nonprofit organization that has purchased this book.

ACTIVITY REFLECTION GUIDE

Use the following prompts to help you process and document your activity. You do not need to answer each question. Answer those questions that are appropriate to your experience.

Briefly describe the activity. Who was involved? When did the activity take place? Where? What happened?

What was the purpose of this activity? Why did you do it?

Why did you choose this particular activity?

What did you want or expect to happen? Did it?

Was the activity successful? Explain why you think it was or was not successful.

What evidence indicates the activity was successful in meetings its purpose?

What problems, difficulties, or frustrations did you experience?

What surprises did you encounter? How did you deal with them?

Did the activity produce any data? What do the data indicate?

Did you see any patterns evolve? What were they? Why did they occur?

Do you see any connections between what happened in this activity and other experiences you have had?

Did you gain any new insights or understandings? What were they?

What, if anything, would you do different? Why?

Did the activity confirm your beliefs and understandings or challenge them? Why?

What new questions do you have?

What do you want to know more about as a result of this activity?

How will you use this experience in your future teaching?

What will you do next? Did that change as a result of this activity? Why?

What is the significance of this activity for your instruction?

Why is it important? Or is it?

Additional comments, analysis, perceptions, and insights:

Blackline P-12 (Page 2 of 2)

Copyright © 2008 by Corwin Press. All rights reserved. Reprinted from *The Educator's Professional Growth Plan: A Process for Developing Staff and Improving Instruction, Second Edition,* by Jodi Peine. Thousand Oaks, CA: Corwin Press, www.corwinpress.com. Reproduction authorized only for the local school site or nonprofit organization that has purchased this book.

OBSERVATION REFLECTION GUIDE

Use the following prompts to help you process and document your observation. You do not need to answer each question. Answer the questions that are appropriate to your experience.

Describe the sequence of events or activity you observed.

Where did the observation occur? Describe the environment.

When did the observation occur? (Time of day and time of year may have significance.)

How long was the observation?

Who was involved?

Were you a participant observer or a nonparticipant observer?

What was the purpose of the observation? What were you looking for? What was the focus of your observation?

What did you observe?

Did you record your observation? How?

Did you record any data? How? What did it indicate?

What caused the events to occur as they did?

What new insights or understandings did you gain?

What surprised you? Why?

What did not make sense? Why?

How does what you observed compare with what you believe, understand, or practice/do?

How will this observation impact what you do?

What would you like to try? Why?

What will you never try? Why?

What changes might occur in your practices and beliefs as a result of your observation?

What new questions do you have?

What conclusions did you reach from this observation?

What is the significance of this observation for your instruction? Why is this important?

How do you feel about the teaching/learning experience?

Additional comments, analysis, perceptions, and insights?

Blackline P-13 (Page 2 of 2)

Copyright © 2008 by Corwin Press. All rights reserved. Reprinted from *The Educator's Professional Growth Plan: A Process for Developing Staff and Improving Instruction, Second Edition,* by Jodi Peine. Thousand Oaks, CA: Corwin Press, www.corwinpress.com. Reproduction authorized only for the local school site or nonprofit organization that has purchased this book.

DOCUMENTATION ARTIFACTS MAP

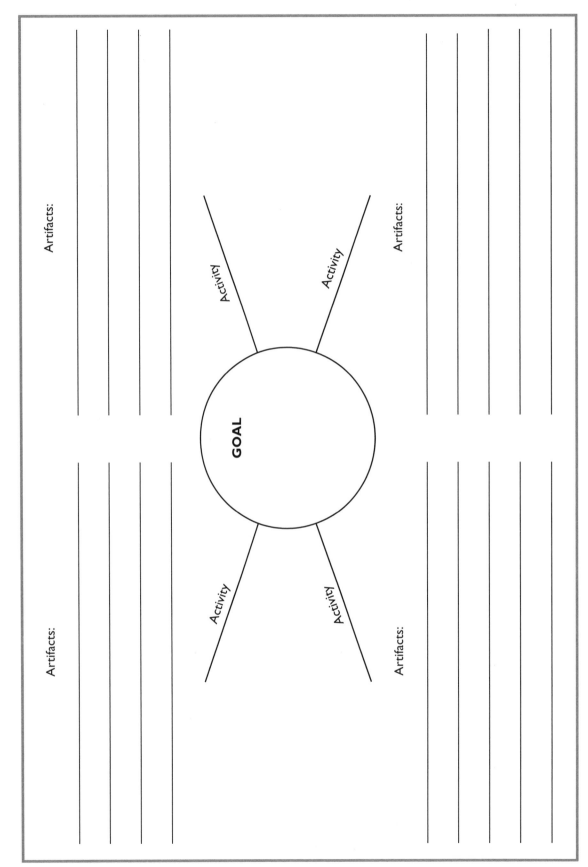

Artifacts:

Artifacts:

GOAL

Activity

Activity

Activity

Activity

Artifacts:

Artifacts:

Copyright © 2008 by Corwin Press. All rights reserved. Reprinted from *The Educator's Professional Growth Plan: A Process for Developing Staff and Improving Instruction, Second Edition*, by Jodi Peine. Thousand Oaks, CA: Corwin Press, www.corwinpress.com. Reproduction authorized only for the local school site or nonprofit organization that has purchased this book.

REFLECTION BASICS

What Do You Do? Why Do You Do It?
Should You Do It Again?

ON ACTION	IN ACTION
What has happened?	What is happening?
What did I do?	What am I doing?
Why did I do it?	Why am I doing it?
What happened as a result of what I did?	What is happening as a result of what I am doing?
What will I do next time?	What should I do next?
Why?	Why?

THINK!

What have I just experienced?

How does that compare with what I know and believe?

So what does that mean?

Blackline P-15

Copyright © 2008 by Corwin Press. All rights reserved. Reprinted from *The Educator's Professional Growth Plan: A Process for Developing Staff and Improving Instruction, Second Edition,* by Jodi Peine. Thousand Oaks, CA: Corwin Press, www.corwinpress.com. Reproduction authorized only for the local school site or nonprofit organization that has purchased this book.

WHEN YOU DOCUMENT, YOU . . .

DESCRIBE

Who? What? Where?

What was the setting?

Who was involved?

What happened?

What was the specific sequence of events?

Who did what?

ANALYZE

Why? How?

Why did it happen?

How did it happen?

REFLECT

So What?

What does it mean?

Blackline P-16

Copyright © 2008 by Corwin Press. All rights reserved. Reprinted from *The Educator's Professional Growth Plan: A Process for Developing Staff and Improving Instruction, Second Edition,* by Jodi Peine. Thousand Oaks, CA: Corwin Press, www.corwinpress.com. Reproduction authorized only for the local school site or nonprofit organization that has purchased this book.

GROWTH PLAN EVALUATION CRITERIA

DOCUMENTATION SHOWS

1. Professional Growth

Acquisition of new knowledge and skills

Application of new knowledge and skills
(changes in instructional practices)

Enhanced reflective practices

Contributions to learning community

2. Improved Student Achievement

Blackline P-17

Copyright © 2008 by Corwin Press. All rights reserved. Reprinted from *The Educator's Professional Growth Plan: A Process for Developing Staff and Improving Instruction, Second Edition,* by Jodi Peine. Thousand Oaks, CA: Corwin Press, www.corwinpress.com. Reproduction authorized only for the local school site or nonprofit organization that has purchased this book.

GROWTH PLAN EVALUATION

DOCUMENTING PROFESSIONAL GROWTH

The artifacts listed below may help you document your professional growth. The artifacts are grouped by the criteria for evaluating professional growth but are not limited to just one criterion. This list is not all-inclusive; several other artifact possibilities exist.

ACQUISITION OF NEW KNOWLEDGE AND SKILLS

What artifacts demonstrate that you have acquired new knowledge and skills as a result of your Professional Growth Plan work?

Teacher Work Samples

Activity Plans	Homework Assignments	Parent Contact Log	Tally Sheets
Anecdotal Records		Peer Reviews	Teacher Journal
Assessments	Instructional Materials	Pre/Post Self- Assessments	Transcripts
Awards	Instructional Planning Calendars	Rating Scales	Unit Plans
CDs	Lesson Plans	Reflection Guides	Video/Audio Recordings
Checklists	Likert Scales	Revised Professional Growth Plans	Visual Maps
Classroom Observations	Management Plans	Surveys	Work Logs
Conference Summaries	New Certification/ Degree	Student	Workshop Log
Contact Log	Newspaper Articles	Parent	
Curriculum Materials	Observation Instruments	Colleague	
Grade Sheets/ Evaluation			
Reports			

APPLICATION OF KNOWLEDGE AND SKILLS: CHANGES IN INSTRUCTIONAL PRACTICES

What artifacts demonstrate that you have incorporated permanently in your instructional practice the newly acquired knowledge and skills? What artifacts link new knowledge and skills with classroom practice?

Anecdotal Records	**Lesson Plans**	**Newsletters**	**Student Work Samples**
Curriculum Materials	**Management Plans**	**Parent Correspondence**	**Unit Plans**
Instructional Materials	**Multimedia**	**Photographs**	

WHAT ARTIFACTS DEMONSTRATE THE TIME AND EFFORT YOU INVESTED?

Teacher Work Samples
(see Acquisition of New Knowledge and Skills)

Blackline P-18 (Page 1 of 2)

Student Work Samples

Homework Assignments	Products
• Projects	• Multimedia Formats
	• Portfolios
	• Work/Reading Logs
	• Writing

ENHANCED REFLECTIVE PRACTICES

What artifacts demonstrate that you have done any of the following:

- Analyzed the principles that underlie new or different instructional practices
- Used these principles in making choices regarding your instructional practices
- Assessed the effectiveness of the instructional practices
- Employed critical thinking to evaluate the instructional practices fully
  Reflection Guides
  Teacher Journal
  Learning Logs
  Reflections on Student Work Samples

CONTRIBUTIONS TO LEARNING COMMUNITY

What artifacts demonstrate contributions resulting from your Professional Growth Plan efforts?

Submission of Articles for Publication
Presentations at Professional Forums
Awards/Recognition
Mentoring Activities
Coaching Activities

IMPROVED STUDENT ACHIEVEMENT

What artifacts demonstrate that student achievement has improved as a result of your Professional Growth Plan work?

Anecdotal Records
Grade Sheets/Evaluation Reports
Multimedia
Performance Assessments
Publisher Tests
Revised Student Work
Standardized Test Scores
Student Work Samples (over time or pre/post intervention)

Blackline P-18 (Page 2 of 2)

Copyright © 2008 by Corwin Press. All rights reserved. Reprinted from *The Educator's Professional Growth Plan: A Process for Developing Staff and Improving Instruction, Second Edition,* by Jodi Peine. Thousand Oaks, CA: Corwin Press, www.corwinpress.com. Reproduction authorized only for the local school site or nonprofit organization that has purchased this book.

METHODS OF EVALUATION PLAN SHEET

Analyze each artifact in your documentation list and project which one(s) might best represent your growth. It is important that you understand and can explain why or how it can represent growth.

ACQUISITION OF NEW KNOWLEDGE/SKILLS

What new knowledge/skills will you acquire?

What artifact(s) will exist to prove it?

How does each artifact selected show growth?

How many of each artifact will you need to show growth?

Over what period of time will you collect each artifact?

What characteristic of the artifact or change in the artifact will reflect your acquisition of new knowledge/skills?

APPLICATION OF NEW KNOWLEDGE/SKILLS

What new knowledge/skills will you use?

What artifact(s) will exist to demonstrate that you are using the new knowledge/skills?

How will each prove that you are using your new knowledge/skills?

How representative is the artifact?

What period of time will the artifact reflect?

What evidence exists of the time and effort you have invested in your learning?

Blackline P-19 (Page 1 of 2)

ENHANCED REFLECTIVE PRACTICES

Educators need to reflect "on action," going back and analyzing what happened in a lesson or activity, and "in action," during instruction. What artifacts demonstrate that your on-action and in-action reflections

- show greater depth?
- use more descriptive words?
- provide more explanation and reasoning why?
- question what you did or what happened?
- examine and try to explain the consequences of instructional decisions?
- are tied to theory or principles?
- are tied to the context of the situation?

CONTRIBUTIONS TO LEARNING COMMUNITY

What will you do to share your new knowledge/skills with the learning community?

What artifact(s) will show that you have acquired or improved a collaborative skill, making you a better member of the learning community?

IMPROVED STUDENT ACHIEVEMENT

When should evidence of improved student achievement exist?

What artifact(s) will show that student achievement has improved as a result of your new knowledge and skills?

Can you use this artifact as Baseline Data?

How will this artifact show the impact of your new knowledge and skills on student achievement?

____TENTATIVE PLAN   _____ FINAL PLAN   Date: _____

Blackline P-19 (Page 2 of 2)

Copyright © 2008 by Corwin Press. All rights reserved. Reprinted from *The Educator's Professional Growth Plan: A Process for Developing Staff and Improving Instruction, Second Edition,* by Jodi Peine. Thousand Oaks, CA: Corwin Press, www.corwinpress.com. Reproduction authorized only for the local school site or nonprofit organization that has purchased this book.

ARTIFACT ORGANIZER

GOAL:

BASELINE DATA (Artifacts)	GROWTH DATA (Artifacts)

GOAL:

BASELINE DATA (Artifacts)	GROWTH DATA (Artifacts)

Page _____ of _____

Blackline P-20

Copyright © 2008 by Corwin Press. All rights reserved. Reprinted from *The Educator's Professional Growth Plan: A Process for Developing Staff and Improving Instruction, Second Edition,* by Jodi Peine. Thousand Oaks, CA: Corwin Press, www.corwinpress.com. Reproduction authorized only for the local school site or nonprofit organization that has purchased this book.

EVALUATION ARTIFACT ORGANIZER

New Knowledge/Skills:

BASELINE DATA *(Artifacts)*	GROWTH DATA *(Artifacts)*

Application of New Knowledge/Skills:

BASELINE DATA *(Artifacts)*	GROWTH DATA *(Artifacts)*

Enhanced Reflective Practice:

BASELINE DATA *(Artifacts)*	GROWTH DATA *(Artifacts)*

Blackline P-21 (Page 1 of 2)

EVALUATION ARTIFACT ORGANIZER (Continued)

Contributions to the Learning Community:

BASELINE DATA *(Artifacts)*	GROWTH DATA *(Artifacts)*

Improved Student Achievement:

BASELINE DATA *(Artifacts)*	GROWTH DATA *(Artifacts)*

Blackline P-21 (Page 2 of 2)

Copyright © 2008 by Corwin Press. All rights reserved. Reprinted from *The Educator's Professional Growth Plan: A Process for Developing Staff and Improving Instruction, Second Edition,* by Jodi Peine. Thousand Oaks, CA: Corwin Press, www.corwinpress.com. Reproduction authorized only for the local school site or nonprofit organization that has purchased this book.

RESOURCE SURVEY

Topic: _____

Workshop/Conference _____

Interviews/Site Visits _____

Periodicals (Titles) _____

Media (Titles) _____

Books (Titles) _____

Software (Titles) _____

Web Sites/Links _____

Name: _____

Page ____ of ____

Blackline P-22

Copyright © 2008 by Corwin Press. All rights reserved. Reprinted from *The Educator's Professional Growth Plan: A Process for Developing Staff and Improving Instruction, Second Edition*, by Jodi Peine. Thousand Oaks, CA: Corwin Press, www.corwinpress.com. Reproduction authorized only for the local school site or nonprofit organization that has purchased this book.

RESOURCE REQUEST BUDGET FORM

Projected Expenses for Fiscal Year 20_____ –20_____

Professional Growth Plan:

Participants:

Projected Completion Date:

TOTAL $_____

Workshop/Conference/Site Visit:

Title/Sponsor	Date	Fee	Expenses
			Travel: Food: Hotel:
			Travel: Food: Hotel:

Total Workshop/Conference: $_____

Print Materials:

Title/Author	Amount

Total Print: $_____

Supplies:

Item	Amount

Total Supplies: $_____

Media/Software:

Title/Publisher	Amount

Total Software: $ _____

Substitutes:

# of Days	Projected Date(s)	Amount

Total Substitutes: $ _____

Miscellaneous:

Item	Amount

Total Miscellaneous: $_____

Grand Total*: $ _____

Comments:

*Please remember to include shipping and handling costs in your figures.

Blackline P-23 (Page 2 of 2)

Copyright © 2008 by Corwin Press. All rights reserved. Reprinted from *The Educator's Professional Growth Plan: A Process for Developing Staff and Improving Instruction, Second Edition,* by Jodi Peine. Thousand Oaks, CA: Corwin Press, www.corwinpress.com. Reproduction authorized only for the local school site or nonprofit organization that has purchased this book.

FORUMS AND FORMATS FOR SHARING WITH THE LEARNING COMMUNITY

- ◆ Staff Meetings

- ◆ Team Meetings

- ◆ Grade-Level Meetings

- ◆ Staff Exhibitions

- ◆ Presentations at Professional Conferences (local, state, regional, national)

- ◆ Multimedia Presentations

- ◆ Written Summaries Distributed to Staff

- ◆ Professional Newsletters

- ◆ Professional Journals

- ◆ Conducting a Workshop/Training for Staff

- ◆ Presentation to Board of Education

- ◆ Presentation to Parent Organization

Blackline P-24

Copyright © 2008 by Corwin Press. All rights reserved. Reprinted from *The Educator's Professional Growth Plan: A Process for Developing Staff and Improving Instruction, Second Edition,* by Jodi Peine. Thousand Oaks, CA: Corwin Press, www.corwinpress.com. Reproduction authorized only for the local school site or nonprofit organization that has purchased this book.

REQUEST FOR ASSISTANCE

Person(s) Requesting Assistance:

Date Submitted:

Date Needed:

Request:

Facilitator Response:

Date:

Blackline P-25

Copyright © 2008 by Corwin Press. All rights reserved. Reprinted from *The Educator's Professional Growth Plan: A Process for Developing Staff and Improving Instruction, Second Edition,* by Jodi Peine. Thousand Oaks, CA: Corwin Press, www.corwinpress.com. Reproduction authorized only for the local school site or nonprofit organization that has purchased this book.

WORK DAY PLAN

Please submit three days before workshop day.

Date of Work Day:

Work Site:

Participants:

Goals:

Planned Activities:

Resource Needs:

Miscellaneous/Comments:

Blackline P-26

Copyright © 2008 by Corwin Press. All rights reserved. Reprinted from *The Educator's Professional Growth Plan: A Process for Developing Staff and Improving Instruction, Second Edition,* by Jodi Peine. Thousand Oaks, CA: Corwin Press, www.corwinpress.com. Reproduction authorized only for the local school site or nonprofit organization that has purchased this book.

WORK DAY SUMMARY REFLECTION GUIDE

This form helps you document your work and reflect, as well as process your experiences. A summary is what happened. A summary documents effort. A reflection is an analysis of what happened, why it happened, and the significance of what happened. A reflection can document the acquisition of new knowledge and skills. It can also document the depth of reflective thinking. Remember complete sentences, perfect grammar, and neatness are not as important as your thoughts. Using the format below, provide the following information on a separate sheet of paper.

Date of Work Day: **Worksite:**

Participants:

Activities (briefly summarize what you did):

Answer the questions most appropriate to your experience.

Did you meet the goals you set for the day? Why or why not?

What new insights or surprises did you gain from your activities?

What problems/difficulties/frustrations did you experience? Could you resolve them? Why? How?

How will your activities impact your future work?

Will you make any changes or try something different as a result of what you learned? Briefly explain.

What do you need to do next as a result of these activities?

What help or assistance do you need that you had not anticipated?

Blackline P-27

Copyright © 2008 by Corwin Press. All rights reserved. Reprinted from *The Educator's Professional Growth Plan: A Process for Developing Staff and Improving Instruction, Second Edition,* by Jodi Peine. Thousand Oaks, CA: Corwin Press, www.corwinpress.com. Reproduction authorized only for the local school site or nonprofit organization that has purchased this book.

PROGRESS MEETING QUESTIONS

The following prompts can help facilitate discussion at the Progress Meeting. The purpose of these meetings is to ensure that you receive the necessary support and that you are making progress toward successful completion of the growth plan. You can write your answers before the meeting, or the questions can act as a conversation guide for the meeting. If problems or concerns have arisen, it may be beneficial to submit your responses to the school leader before the meeting to allow him or her some problem-solving time.

Where are you on your Action Plan? Are you on schedule? Explain.

What have you done to this point?

Do you feel you are making progress toward your established goals? Explain.

What insights or new information have you discovered?

Has anything you have done or read changed what you believed or understood? Explain.

Have you experienced any difficulties, frustrations, or obstacles? Explain what they are/were. Have you resolved them? How?

Has anything surprised you? What? Why?

Do you feel your goals are still appropriate? Do they need to be modified? If so, how? Why?

Do you feel your goals are still attainable? Do they need to be modified? Is so, how? Why?

Does your Action Plan still make sense? Do you need to make changes? What are they? Why?

Blackline P-28

Copyright © 2008 by Corwin Press. All rights reserved. Reprinted from *The Educator's Professional Growth Plan: A Process for Developing Staff and Improving Instruction, Second Edition,* by Jodi Peine. Thousand Oaks, CA: Corwin Press, www.corwinpress.com. Reproduction authorized only for the local school site or nonprofit organization that has purchased this book.

GROWTH PLAN SUMMARY ACTIVITIES

1. Summarize your plan in writing or on audiotape. Be sure to answer the following questions:

   - What new knowledge, skills, beliefs, or attitudes did you acquire?
   - How will this acquisition impact your practice?
   - What documentation shows evidence of your growth?
   - What did you learn about the way you learn?

2. Submit summary and portfolio to school leader.

3. Meet with school leader in summary conference.

4. Share completed growth plan with learning community.

Blackline P-29

Copyright © 2008 by Corwin Press. All rights reserved. Reprinted from *The Educator's Professional Growth Plan: A Process for Developing Staff and Improving Instruction, Second Edition,* by Jodi Peine. Thousand Oaks, CA: Corwin Press, www.corwinpress.com. Reproduction authorized only for the local school site or nonprofit organization that has purchased this book.

GROWTH PLAN SELF-EVALUATION

Please circle the number that correlates to your assessment of your Professional Growth Plan. A 1 represents the least amount of growth, and a 5 represents the greatest. Include any comments you feel are appropriate.

Acquisition of New Knowledge and Skills	1	2	3	4	5
Application of New Knowledge and Skills (changes in instructional practices)	1	2	3	4	5
Enhanced Reflective Practices	1	2	3	4	5
Contribution to Learning Community	1	2	3	4	5
Improved Student Achievement	1	2	3	4	5

Name: _____   Date: _____

Plan Topic:

Comments on back please.

Blackline P-30

Copyright © 2008 by Corwin Press. All rights reserved. Reprinted from *The Educator's Professional Growth Plan: A Process for Developing Staff and Improving Instruction, Second Edition,* by Jodi Peine. Thousand Oaks, CA: Corwin Press, www.corwinpress.com. Reproduction authorized only for the local school site or nonprofit organization that has purchased this book.

GROWTH PLAN SUMMARY
REFLECTION GUIDE

Use some or all of the following questions to help you prepare your Professional Growth Plan Summary. Your school leader may also use these questions during your summary conference.

What answer(s) did you find to your Essential Question?

Did you meet your Professional Goals? Explain.

What were the most important understandings you gained from your work?

What obstacles did you encounter? How did you overcome them?

What did you learn about your knowledge, beliefs, or practices as they relate to this topic?

What did you learn about your learning?

What evidence did you gather that helped you develop a deeper understanding of your topic?

What artifacts document your professional growth?

How do these document your professional growth?

How does what you have learned impact your teaching?

How will this inform and improve your teaching in the future?

GROWTH PLAN SUMMARY
REFLECTION GUIDE (Continued)

What evidence will exist two years from now that demonstrates you are using this new knowledge or skill?

Did you impact student achievement? How do you know? What evidence exists? If evidence does not exist currently, when do you expect to see improvement? What will be the evidence?

Did any of your beliefs or attitudes change as a result of your work? Explain.

What will you do differently because of your learning?

Who within our learning community could also benefit from this knowledge or skill?

How could the Professional Growth Plan Process meet your needs better?

Does what you have learned through your growth plan transfer to any other area of your teaching? Explain.

Have you incorporated any features of the Professional Growth Plan Process into your practice? What are they? Why have you chosen the features? How do you use them?

What other comments or insights would you like to share?

What topic would you like to explore next?

Blackline P-31 (Page 2 of 2)

Copyright © 2008 by Corwin Press. All rights reserved. Reprinted from *The Educator's Professional Growth Plan: A Process for Developing Staff and Improving Instruction, Second Edition,* by Jodi Peine. Thousand Oaks, CA: Corwin Press, www.corwinpress .com. Reproduction authorized only for the local school site or nonprofit organization that has purchased this book.

SHARING WITH THE
LEARNING COMMUNITY

Use the questions below to help you develop a plan to share your growth plan experience.

The questions should help you think about what you should share, how you should share, and with whom you should share your growth plan experience. Check with your plan administrator if you have questions or concerns.

What was your topic?

Why did you choose it?

What did you do?

What do you know and can do that you did not know and could not do before?

Why is that important?

How does it impact student achievement?

What do you think is the most important information and/or skills you gained from your growth plan experience?

Why should you share this information with the learning community?

SHARING WITH THE
LEARNING COMMUNITY (Continued)

What audience(s) could benefit most from this information?

___ Colleagues   ___ Grade level(s)   ___ Disciplines   ___ Everyone
___ Administration   ___ Board of education   ___ Students   ___ Parents

How can you best convey this information/skill?

___ Samples of student work   ___ Collected and interpreted data   ___ Demonstration
___ Discussion   ___ Exhibit of materials   ___ Panel discussion
___ Video/audiotape of experiences   ___ Photo journal   ___ Oral presentation
___ Summary

What did not work? Why do you think it did not work?

Of what significance is the failure? What did you learn from it?

What advice would you have for others?

What procedures, processes, or information were important to the success or failure of an individual activity or the growth plan itself?

Is this new information for the learning community?

Does this information validate beliefs the learning community already holds or practices?

Blackline P-32 (Page 2 of 2)

Copyright © 2008 by Corwin Press. All rights reserved. Reprinted from *The Educator's Professional Growth Plan: A Process for Developing Staff and Improving Instruction, Second Edition,* by Jodi Peine. Thousand Oaks, CA: Corwin Press, www.corwinpress .com. Reproduction authorized only for the local school site or nonprofit organization that has purchased this book.

References

Bereens, D. (2000). *Evaluating teachers for professional growth: Creating a culture of motivation and learning.* Thousand Oaks, CA: Corwin Press.

Brandt, R. (1998). *Powerful learning.* Alexandria, VA: Association for Supervision and Curriculum Development.

Brooks, J., & Brooks, M. (1999). *In search of understanding: The case for the constructivist classrooms* (2nd ed.). Alexandria, VA: Association for Supervision and Curriculum Development.

Burke, K. (1997). *Designing professional portfolios for change.* Thousand Oaks, CA: Corwin Press.

Caine, R., & Caine, G. (1997a). *Education on the edge of possibility.* Alexandria, VA: Association for Supervision and Curriculum Development.

Caine, R., & Caine, G. (1997b). *Unleashing the power of perceptual change: The potential of brain-based teaching.* Alexandria, VA: Association for Supervision and Curriculum Development.

Costa, A., & Garmston, R. (2006). *Cognitive coaching: A foundation for renaissance schools* (2nd ed.). Norwood, MA: Christopher-Gordon.

Danielson, C. (1996). *Enhancing professional practice: A framework for teaching.* Alexandria, VA: Association for Supervision and Curriculum Development.

Danielson, C. (2002). *Enhancing student achievement: A framework for school improvement.* Alexandria, VA: Association for Supervision and Curriculum Development.

Danielson, C., & McGreal, T. (2000). *Teacher evaluation to enhance professional practice.* Alexandria, VA: Association for Supervision and Curriculum Development.

DuFour, R., & Eaker, R. (1998). *Professional learning communities at work: Best practices for enhancing student achievement.* Bloomington, IN: National Educational Service.

DuFour, R., Eaker, R., & DuFour, R. (Eds.). (2005). *On common ground: The power of professional learning communities.* Bloomington, IN: Solution Tree.

Fullan, M. (1993). *Change forces: Probing the depths of educational reform.* Bristol, PA: Falmer Press.

Fullan, M. (1997). *What's worth fighting for in the principalship? Strategies for taking charge in the school principalship.* New York: Teachers College Press.

Fullan, M. (2005). *Leadership & sustainability.* Thousand Oaks, CA: Corwin Press.

Fullan, M., & Hargreaves, A. (1996). *What's worth fighting for in your school?* (2nd ed.). New York: Teachers College Press.

Fullan, M., & Hargreaves, A. (1998). *What's worth fighting for out there?* New York: Teachers College Press.

Fullan, M., Hill, P., & Crevola, C. (2006). *Breakthrough.* Thousand Oaks, CA: Corwin Press.

Glatthorn, A. (1997). *Differentiated supervision* (2nd ed.). Alexandria, VA: Association for Supervision and Curriculum Development.

Guskey, T. (2000). *Evaluating professional development.* Thousand Oaks, CA: Corwin Press.

Jensen, E. (1998). *Teaching with the brain in mind.* Alexandria, VA: Association for Supervision and Curriculum Development.

Mamchur, C. (1996). *A teacher's guide to cognitive type theory and learning style.* Alexandria, VA: Association for Supervision and Curriculum Development.

O'Neill, J., Conzemius, A., Commodore, C., & Pulsfus, C. (2006). *The power of smart goals: Using goals to improve student learning*. Bloomington, IN: Solution Tree.

Popham, W. J. (2001). *The truth about testing: An educator's call to action*. Alexandria, VA: Association for Supervision and Curriculum Development.

Reeves, D. (2006). *The learning leader: How to focus school improvement for better results*. Alexandria, VA: Association for Supervision and Curriculum Development.

Schlechty, P. (1990). *Schools for the 21st century: Leadership imperatives for educational reform*. San Francisco, CA: Jossey-Bass.

Schmoker, M. (1999). *Results: The key to continuous school improvement* (2nd ed.). Alexandria, VA: Association for Supervision and Curriculum Development.

Schmoker, M. (2006). *Results now: How we can achieve unprecedented improvements in teaching and learning*. Alexandria, VA: Association for Supervision and Curriculum Development.

Stronge, J. (2002). *Qualities of effective teachers*. Alexandria, VA: Association for Supervision and Curriculum Development.

Taggart, G., & Wilson, A. (2005). *Promoting reflective thinking in teachers: 44 action strategies*. Thousand Oaks, CA: Corwin Press.

Zemelman, S., Daniels, H., & Hyde, A. (2005). *Best practices: New standards for teaching and learning in America's schools* (3rd ed.). Portsmouth, NH: Heinemann.

Index

CORWIN PRESS

The Corwin Press logo—a raven striding across an open book—represents the union of courage and learning. Corwin Press is committed to improving education for all learners by publishing books and other professional development resources for those serving the field of PreK–12 education. By providing practical, hands-on materials, Corwin Press continues to carry out the promise of its motto: **"Helping Educators Do Their Work Better."**